JOHN DRYDEN

Modern Critical Views

These and other titles in preparation

Modern Critical Views

JOHN DRYDEN

Edited and with an introduction by
Harold Bloom
Sterling Professor of the Humanities
Yale University

CHELSEA HOUSE PUBLISHERS ◊ 1987
New York ◊ New Haven ◊ Philadelphia

© 1987 by Chelsea House Publishers, a division
of Chelsea House Educational Communications, Inc.,
  95 Madison Avenue, New York, NY 10016
  345 Whitney Avenue, New Haven, CT 06511
  5014 West Chester Pike, Edgemont, PA 19028

Introduction © 1987 by Harold Bloom

Printed and bound in the United States of America

∞The paper used in this publication meets the minimum requirements of the American National Standard for Permanence
of Paper for Printed Library Materials, Z39.48-1984.

Library of Congress Cataloging-in-Publication Data

John Dryden.

  (Modern critical views)
  Bibliography: p.
  Includes index.
  Summary: A collection of twelve critical essays on the work
of Dryden, arranged in chronological order of original
publication.
    1. Dryden, John, 1631–1700—Criticism and interpretation.
[1. Dryden, John, 1631–1700—Criticism and interpretation.
2. English literature—History and criticism] I. Bloom,
Harold. II. Series.
PR3424.J6 1987   821'.4   86-34306
ISBN 1-55546-277-4

Contents

Editor's Note

This book gathers together a representative selection of what I judge to be the most useful modern criticism of the writings of John Dryden. The critical essays are reprinted here in the chronological order of their original publication. I am grateful to John Rogers for his erudition and judgment as a researcher for this volume.

My introduction briefly considers Dryden's stance as a literary critic and then relates this position to the skeptical middle way taken up in his *Religio Laici*. John Hollander, poet and scholar of allusiveness, commences the chronological sequence with an analysis of ideas of music in the St. Cecilia Odes and "Alexander's Feast."

In a reading of Dryden's most celebrated drama, his revision of Shakespeare's *Antony and Cleopatra* as *All for Love,* Eugene M. Waith sets the work in the context of the poet's other plays. The same scholarly procedure informs Ruth Nevo's strong consideration of *Absalom and Achitophel,* which she studies in relation to other political and religious satires of the period.

Dryden's heroic plays (aside from *All for Love*) are dialectically investigated by Martin Price, after which George deForest Lord briefly discusses the political poems written by Dryden before *Absalom. Mac Flecknoe,* superb mock-heroic satire, is considered by Earl Miner as an instance of Dryden's heroic faith in the reality of experience.

Laura Brown, centering upon the contradictions and anxieties of the Restoration settlement, reads Dryden's poetic form as knowing more than it can say. This Marxist critique is supplemented by Michael McKeon's strenuous interlacing of Marxist critical theory and Dryden's fine comedy *Marriage à la Mode.* Paul Fry's brilliant Longinian defense of Dryden's critical stance provides a refreshing interval of a more aesthetic perspective in between these two instances of socially oriented analyses.

Religio Laici receives a more politically grounded discussion by Steven

Zwicker than that provided in my introduction, after which James Winn shrewdly reads the early elegy for Hastings as a prolepsis of Dryden's maturer poetry. In this book's final essay, Peter Sacks movingly studies Dryden's most accomplished short poem, the poignant elegy "To the Memory of Mr. Oldham."

Introduction

Bacon, Jonson, and Milton seem to me the principal critical consciousnesses of the later Renaissance, but none of them, not even Jonson, can be regarded as a literary critic in our sense. John Dryden, who leaps the gap between the later Renaissance and the Enlightenment, is surely a crucial literary critic in the Longinian tradition. He is also the resolution of the later Renaissance's debate between and about Ancients and Moderns, though the nature of that resolution is not entirely clear. Paul Fry, in his *The Reach of Criticism,* attempts to clarify Dryden's complex stance:

> Dryden is neither an Ancient nor a Modern, finally, because his belief in the priority of sense to language—of Homer's having exhausted invention, for example—is more or less evenly balanced by his unswerving faith in the progress or "refinement" of language, with the help of which he has "improved" Chaucer. It is too readily assumed that all Dryden's contemporaries shared his belief in the continued progress of language. Dryden himself admits that they did not: "Many are of a contrary opinion, that the English tongue [in Jonson's time] was in the height of its perfection" ("Defence of the Epilogue," 1, 171). It may well be asked, then, why it is so important for Dryden to insist that English is improving, that Denham and Waller are new benchmarks, and so on.
>
> These opinions constitute Dryden's last formalism and serve, like the formality with which the *Essay* was composed, to salvage the self-respect of the author and his contemporaries. The equilibrium between the vigor of the past and the refinement of the present is actually very precarious. Dryden reveals the weakness of his case in the difficulty he has maintaining it. He

insists, for example, that Chaucer will not scan (II, 281), despite
Speght's warning in the 1602 edition that probably Chaucer would
scan if only we understood his system. By expressing this conviction, Dryden commits himself to the lame idea that a person whom
he credits with the highest intelligence and with proficiency in all
the arts and sciences (II, 277, 287) is unable to count feet or to
invent a means of doing so. Dryden has no choice but to find
Chaucer wanting in this respect; otherwise there would be nothing
left to say for modernity, and in that case the reciprocity of benefit
between past and present souls, on the strength of which Dryden
justifies his own election to the symposium of his "Preface," could
no longer be demonstrated. Thus the assertion that "our numbers
were in their nonage" until Waller and Denham appeared (II, 281)
must be made by any handy means to seem stronger and more
conclusive than it is.

It is not only a matter of saving some few scraps of honor
for the Moderns, but of affirming what the Hobbesian Dryden
had always helplessly denied: the freedom of the will. Having
yielded priority in invention, characterization, and copiousness of
thought—all draughts of dead-coloring that can only be retouched
once they are laid down—Dryden then retrenches and maintains
that his own authority, his originative exercise of will, is directed
toward the refinement of the heroic couplet. But if this refinement is a worthwhile accomplishment, why not praise other sorts
of refinement as well? Dryden boasts of having improved a system
of versification, yet disparages Virgil for having *merely* improved
Homer's plot. In every respect—and there would be no harm in
this if the stakes were lower—the secondariness of the Moderns
is elaborative, interpretive in nature. It is an art of variation within
limits prescribed, not prescribed in this case by an Almighty Poet
but by the poetic tradition, a "thrid" of yet another kind that keeps
one from going astray even when one hopes to do so.

Fry catches an underlying sadness, perhaps even a creative desperation,
in the cheerful and hardworking Dryden. On this reading, the Moderns have
been defeated despite the positive program of Bacon and the Sublime example of Milton. Dryden stands midway between Jonson and the Swift of *The
Battle of the Books,* for whom precious few scraps of honor remain upon
the tattered ragamuffin Moderns. Whether Dryden's literary pessimism was
deeply informed by his uneasy belief in a cyclic view of history, we cannot
be certain. Skepticism was endemic in Dryden's era, but that also cannot

account for Dryden's curious sense of defeat. It was not so much that the faith in progress was waning, but that Milton, like Shakespeare before him, had closed out many of the apparent possibilities for the imagination.

It may be that the war between Ancients and Moderns throughout the seventeenth century was a mock epic only, since in such a literary war the precursors must always win unless the terms of the contest are changed once and for all. No poet ever could hope to usurp Homer, so long as invention was understood as an external struggle of gods and men. From Homer to Goethe, there is a continuous tradition, because the subject of literature had not changed and evidently could not change. What we have learned to call Romanticism, or a last stage of the Enlightenment, finally worked that change. Dr. Samuel Johnson, not only the greatest Enlightenment literary critic, but still the strongest critic in the Western tradition, yet allows himself to think of invention as being Homeric, with all subsequent figures falling away. But a great Romantic critic like Hazlitt knows that a giant older contemporary had begun anew, and had made of poetry a *tabula rasa*: Wordsworth. After Wordsworth, there are neither Ancients nor Moderns, but only strong or weak poets.

What the Western world calls literary criticism and literary theory has little to do now either with the ancient world or with the whole of the European Renaissance. By critical theory and *praxis* we mean Dr. Samuel Johnson and Samuel Taylor Coleridge, and those who came after, down to our present day. But in the long movement from Aristotle to the pragmatic Dryden, an inevitable prelude was enacted without which we could not be as we are. Are we Ancients? Are we Moderns? These questions, stimulated by Dryden's skepticism, are as darkly vital now as ever they were.

II

"The mind creates no order of its own," in Martin Price's reading of Dryden's view, "but the mind can give shape to whatsoever of the order of charity can be made the world's concern." Pascal's order of charity transcends the orders of body and of mind, and rebukes philosophers and poets who would substitute their own cleverness for sacred wisdom. Dryden, Ancient and Modern, quested for both orders, mind and charity, and longed always for the spiritual authority he found at last in the Roman Catholic Church. His religious poems, though not the equal of his masterpieces, the political satire *Absalom and Achitophel* and the mock-heroic satire *Mac Flecknoe*, haunt us with a singular intensity, partly because they suggest that there is no such genre as the religious poem. Dryden teaches us, implicitly, that literature is both secular and sacred, either all secular or all sacred, with the supposed distinction being founded only upon social or political dialectics.

The underlying sadness of Dryden's professedly religious poems is akin to his somewhat concealed literary pessimisms. What we hear in the celebrated opening of *Religio Laici* is an ultimate sense of spiritual loss:

> Dim as the borrowed beams of moon and stars
> To lonely, weary, wandering travelers,
> Is Reason to the soul; and, as on high
> Those rolling fires discover but the sky,
> Not light us here, so Reason's glimmering ray
> Was lent, not to assure our doubtful way,
> But guide us upward to a better day.
> And as those nightly tapers disappear
> When day's bright lord ascends our hemisphere;
> So pale grows Reason at Religion's sight;
> So dies, and so dissolves in supernatural light.
> Some few, whose lamp shone brighter, have been led
> From cause to cause, to nature's secret head;
> And found that one first principle must be:
> But what, or who, that universal He;
> Whether some soul incompassing this ball,
> Unmade, unmoved, yet making, moving all;
> Or various atoms' interfering dance
> Leapt into form (the noble work of chance);
> Or this great all was from eternity;
> Not even the Stagirite himself could see,
> And Epicurus guessed as well as he:
> As blindly groped they for a future state;
> As rashly judged of providence and fate:
> But least of all could their endeavours find
> What most concerned the good of humankind;
> For happiness was never to be found,
> But vanished from 'em like enchanted ground.
> One thought content the good to be enjoyed;
> This every little accident destroyed:
> The wiser madmen did for virtue toil,
> A thorny or at best a barren soil;
> In pleasure some their glutton souls would steep,
> But found their line too short, the well too deep,
> And leaky vessels which no bliss could keep.

Thus anxious thoughts in endless circles roll,
Without a centre where to fix the soul;
In this wild maze their vain endeavours end:
How can the less the greater comprehend?
Or finite reason reach Infinity?
For what could fathom God were more than He.

The poet Walter Savage Landor remarked to the diarist Crabb Robinson that "nothing was ever written in hymn equal to the beginning of Dryden's *Religio Laici*,—the first eleven lines." What Landor caught was the curiously hymn-like harmony of Dryden's opening, a harmony somewhat at variance with the *dianoia* or thought-content of those first eleven lines. Dryden's faith is movingly revealed as a yearning for revelation, rather than as the revelation itself. The burden of the opening is to mediate between the Deists, who discard revelation, and the Fideists, who reject reason. Metaphorically, Dryden's Reason dissolves into the supernatural sun whose beams it has borrowed, but the tonal affect of the passage suggests a darker skepticism. The hymn-like strain rises to lament "our doubtful way," and yet rises so strongly as to make equivocal Dryden's professed aim to keep to a middle way in religion.

How much, imagistically speaking, can Reason do for us, according to this passage? The moon and the planets together help little enough those "lonely, weary, wandering travelers," who do not seem to be traversing the best of all possible worlds. What reveals the sky does not illuminate us. "Dim," the poem's first word, sets the key for a cosmos where Aristotle himself cannot see the truths of creation, since here the philosophers are condemned to blind gropes and rash judgments. Reason perhaps stands in this passage like that proverbial glass we call half-full or half-empty depending upon our temperaments and circumstances.

Dryden will end his *Layman's Faith* with the dangerously bland assurances that "the things we must believe are few and plain," and that "points obscure are of small use to learn, / But common quiet is mankind's concern." Critically, we can acknowledge that the poem's opening was so mysteriously strong that no ending would have sufficed, but still no one ever has preferred the amiable close of *Religio Laici* to its illustrious opening. Something rich and strange in Dryden returns from repression in that immense beginning, and that something has one of its origins in Milton's *Paradise Lost,* particularly in the great invocation to book 3, where the blind prophet addresses the Holy Light:

So much the rather thou Celestial Light
Shine inward, and the mind through all her powers

> Irradiate, there plant eyes, all mist from thence
> Purge and disperse, that I may see and tell
> Of things invisible to mortal sight.

It is this inwardness that is deliberately lacking in Dryden, whose dim celestial light shines as an external image. What refreshes us in Dryden, the lack of prophetic election or an egotistical sublime, at last estranges him from us also. He appeals to all varieties of historicism—old and new—but perhaps not to the deepest reader in each of us. And yet his limitations were knowing ones, wisely maintained at every point. Consider his famous lines on Milton, printed under the prophetic engraved portrait of the greatest modern epic writer in Tonson's folio edition of *Paradise Lost* in 1688.

> Three poets, in three distant ages born,
> Greece, Italy, and England, did adorn.
> The first in loftiness of thought surpass'd,
> The next in majesty, in both the last:
> The force of Nature could no farther go;
> To make a third she join'd the former two.

The cognitive superiority of Homer, joined to the stylistic eminence of Virgil, compels Nature to drive beyond her limits in making Milton, who is a more-than-natural force. Dryden knows himself to be in the unenviable position of being the first major and representative post-Miltonic poet. Milton has usurped the kingdom of poetry, more powerfully because more permanently than Cromwell, his chief of men, usurped the kingdom of Britain. Greatest of Ancients *and* of Moderns, Milton leaves Dryden only the middle way, and the middle voice:

> All, all of a piece throughout:
> Thy chase had a beast in view;
> Thy wars brought nothing about;
> Thy lovers were all untrue.
> 'Tis well an old age is out,
> And time to begin a new.

JOHN HOLLANDER

The Sky Untuned: The Trivialization
of Universal Harmony in the Odes

It is primarily in the form of the musical ode . . . that the figure of the celestial harmony passes into the eighteenth century. The use of that figure was revivified particularly in the odes written over several decades for the musical St. Cecilia's Day celebrations in London, of which Dryden's two contributions remain the really impressive poems. In examining them, as well as the other musical odes that helped to establish the convention in which Dryden was working, we shall see how the schematic, almost programmatic structure of those odes allowed for a last gasp of renewed interest in the literary use of the universal harmony for concrete imagery, and how the problems of musical and encomiastic exposition could spark that interest which the changes in seventeenth-century rhetoric and poetic diction had caused to flag.

THE SONGS FOR ST. CECILIA'S DAY

The St. Cecilia's Day celebrations for which Dryden's "Ode" and "Alexander's Feast" were both commissioned seem to have originated on the Continent in the latter part of the sixteenth century. It was not until 1683, however, that annual "Musick Feasts" began to be held in London on the twenty-second of November by a group of musical professionals and amateurs calling themselves "The Musical Society." These occasions, which occurred more or less regularly until the middle of the next century, may have includ-

From *The Untuning of the Sky: Ideas of Music in English Poetry 1500–1700*. © 1961 by Princeton University Press, © 1970 by W. W. Norton & Co., Inc., © 1986 by John Hollander.

ed a specially composed anthem for a musical service and a sermon in defense
of music in churches. Their high point, however, was a formal offering in
praise of music, embodied in an ode, whose text and vocal and instrumental
setting by a poet and a composer of repute were commissioned in advance.

The festivities must have had a fraternal quality which, while not as
limited and parochial as that of the Catch-Societies, would appear to have
emanated from a group of celebrating, self-congratulating connoisseurs. The
text of "A Song, Sung at a Musick Feast," set by Pelham Humphrey some
time before 1674, was probably intoned on some smaller, less official occasion. It has the light-hearted tone of a catch or a later glee:

> How well doth this Harmonious Meeting prove
> A Feast of Musick is a Feast of Love,
> Where Kindness is our Tune, and we in parts
> Do but sing forth the consorts of our hearts.
> For friendship is nothing but concord of votes,
> And music is made by a friendship of notes.

From the tone of this solo, the chorus for three voices which follows hardly
seems to have been a necessary injunction:

> Come then to the God of our Art let us quaff
> For he once a year is reputed to laugh.

The stock metaphor of musico-social concord is trivialized here utterly, and
the "Feast of Love" is hardly a communion with the immutable order of the
universe.

For the odes written for St. Cecilia's Day, however, a mood of reverent
jubilation, rather than one of mere *camaraderie*, seems to have been requisite.
These were nevertheless public poems. The decidedly introspective exuberance
of Edward Benlowes's reflections on a musical evening might be cited to illustrate another extreme which the St. Cecilia's Day poems sought to avoid.
Probably written during the 1660s or 1670s, "A Poetic Descant Upon a
Private Music-Meeting" opens casually enough:

> Muse! Rise and plume thy feet, and let's converse
>   This morn together: let's rehearse
> Last evening's sweets; and run one heat in full-speed verse.
>
> Prank not thyself in metaphors; but pound
>   Thy ranging tropes, that they may sound
> Nothing but what our paradise did then surround.

(1–6)

Benlowes's muse betrays him shortly thereafter, though. After a description
of the ladies present in somewhat extravagant, abstract terms, a Pythagorean
conjunction of male and female numbers is implied at the appearance of the
musicians themselves:

> But, whist! The masculine sweet planets met,
>   Their instruments in tune have set,
> And now begin to ransack Music's cabinet.
>
> (19–21)

The various instrumentalists are then described as the various heavenly bodies,
after which

> Last Mercury with ravishing strains fell on,
>   Whose violin seemed the chymic-stone
> For every melting touch was pure projection.
>
> Chair'd midst the spheres of Music's Heaven, I hear,
>   I gaze; charm'd all to eye and ear;
> Both which, with objects too intense even martyred were.
>
> Th'excess of fairs, distill'd through sweets, did woo
>   My wav'ring soul, maz'd what to do,
> Or to quit eyes for ears, or ears for eyes forego.
>
> Giddy i' th' change which sex to crown with praise;
>   Time swore he never was with lays
> More sweetly spent; nor Beauty ever beam'd such rays.
>
> 'Twixt these extremes mine eyes and ears did stray,
>   And sure it was no time to pray;
> The Deities themselves then being all at play.
>
> The full-throng'd room its ruin quite defies:
>   Nor fairs, nor airs are pond'rous; skies
> Do scorn to shrink, though pil'd with stars and harmonies.
>
> Form, Beauty, Sweetness all did here conspire,
>   Combin'd in one Celestial Quire,
> To charm the enthusiastic soul with enthean fire.
>
> (49–69)

The rather forced ingenuity with which the two sexes are associated with
two senses represents the soggy lees of Metaphysical technique. It sorts ill
here with the programmatic promises of homeliness of diction in the first

two stanzas. Benlowes's piece is an essay, in a slightly more complex guise
than usual, into the convention examined earlier in [*The Untuning of the
Sky*]; it differs from the normal musical compliment only in that the range
of the praise is so expanded as to include the room as a whole. The universe
into which that room is urged, metaphorically, to merge is a polite one, and
one feels that it is a kind of formal *galanterie* alone that demands the presence
and equal status of the feminine counterpart of music, visual beauty. The
unconvincing unification of "fairs" and "airs" in "one Celestial Quire" leads
to a final apostrophe:

> Music! thy med'cines can our griefs allay
>   And re-inspire our lumpish clay:
> Muse! Thou transcend'st; Thou without instruments can play.
>
> (73–75)

This particular Muse would seem undeserving of such praise, were it not
for the fact that the commendation of music itself, in the two lines immediately
preceding, is so mechanical. Benlowes's attitudes toward formal musical doctrine, as well as those of his age, prevented him from merely versifying the
clichés relating *musica mundana* to actual performance. Unlike Marvell's,
his wit was inadequate to the task of figuratively encompassing earth and
heaven within the frame of human and cosmic music, and it was too ambitious to content itself with a smaller, well-turned but frankly hyperbolic
observation of the type of Lovelace's "To Gratiana Singing and Dancing,"
for example.

   A prototype of the musical ode may be found (as is so often the case
with seventeenth-century poetic forms) in the works of Ben Jonson. "An Ode,
or Song, by all the Muses. In Celebration of her Majesties birth-day" (1630)
is a strophic poem which assigns a stanza to each of the Muses in turn. Those
of Thalia and Euterpe are of interest here in that they combine the instrumental references with the encomiastic hyperbole in a way that anticipates the
later St. Cecilia's Day Odes and, specifically, those of Dryden:

> 3. Thal. Yet, let our Trumpets sound;
>   And cleave both ayre and ground,
>   With beating of our Drums:
>   Let every Lyre be strung,
>   Harpe, Lute, Theorbo sprung,
>   With touch of daintie thum's!
> 4. Evt.   That when the Quire is full,
>   The Harmony may pull
>   The Angels from their Spheares:

> And each intelligence
> May wish it selfe a sense,
>   Whilst it the Dittie heares.

These two stanzas, as we shall presently see, might be said to represent a canonical form that the musical ode was eventually to assume.

The earliest of the extant St. Cecilia's Day Odes are by no means overly ambitious. Two odes written for the initial celebration in 1683 and set by Henry Purcell are shorter by far than the later ones, and in their opening invocations make no extravagant claims to universality of subject. One of these, written by one Christopher Fishburn, openly addresses the assemblage itself:

> Welcome to the pleasures that delight
> Of ev'ry sense the grateful appetite!
> Hail, great assembly of Apollo's race!
> Hail to this happy place,
> This musical assembly, that seems to be
> The ark of universal harmony!

"Seems" in the penultimate line weakens the tone considerably, and narrows the range and the potency of any further images of *harmonia mundi*. The remaining twenty-five lines are primarily occupied with the joys that music can inspire. Passing acknowledgment is made to

> Beauty, thou source of love,
> And Virtue, thou innocent fire,
> Made by the Powers above
> To temper the heat of desire.

Only at the end is St. Cecilia mentioned at all. In another, anonymous ode, her name never appears. This poem begins with an injunction to the assembled instruments and voices to sound: "For this is sacred Music's holiday"; it ends anapestically on a note of good-hearted but undignified self-congratulation:

> Apollo's delighted with what we have done,
> And clapping his hands, cries, "Iô, go on";
> With a smile he does all our endeavours approve,
> And vows he ne'er heard such a concert above.

At the beginning of the ode, it is made clear that the god of music himself is expected to appear "Not to the eye, but to the ravish'd ear." Then follows a quatrain of tetrameters, quoting Apollo's command that "ev'ry gen'rous heart / In the chorus bear a part." The observation that, in response to this, "each pliant string / Prepares itself, and as an offering, / The tribute of some gentle sound does bring" leads to the conclusion with its reports of Apollo's delight. The metrical range of this simple piece is rather narrow; the odes that followed tended more and more to employ the elaborate resources of the Augustan "Pindaric" ode form. However, they shared its structure in that they remained narrative in the most primitive sense, their general order remaining roughly as follows: first came an exhortation to begin the music-making, then a description of the various instruments and observations of their respective powers to move the affections. These grew into separate strophes, each with a different metrical scheme. Appended to these was usually some exposition of the general value of harmony, often with a citation of the *harmonia mundi*. The final section of the odes returned to a hortatory diction, with some reference to St. Cecilia as the patroness of music, and a closing celebration of the heavenly singing.

To examine the odes for the next few annual celebrations is to see the growing elaboration of this basic theme. The 1684 poem, set by John Blow, was written by Dryden's friend John Oldham; that of the following year was by that Saint of Dullness, Nahum Tate. Both of these odes are longer than the earliest ones, and both reach into larger repositories of lore and doctrine for their observations on *musica speculativa*. Oldham, for example, remarks that

> When we are thus wound up to extacy,
> Methinks we mount, methinks we tow'r,
> And seem to antedate our future bliss on high.

This is a kind of specifically Christian allusion rare in any of the odes, with the exception of the mention of St. Cecilia herself. Nahum Tate's piece starts out with a flurry of instrumental reference; more usually, these were developed at length within the course of the ode.

> Tune the viol, touch the lute,
> Wake the harp, inspire the flute.

One cannot be sure here whether actual musicians are being enjoined to play, or whether some more abstract entity is being called up to infuse the instruments with song. At any rate, despite this apparent hurry to include most of what was becoming a traditional catalogue of instruments to be mentioned on such occasions, Tate finds the time later on to make a strange observation:

>In vain do wit and sense combine,
>Without this art to make our numbers shine;
>Words are the body: Music is the soul.

An older treatment of the metaphysics of music based on platonistic sources, such as Ficino's, for example, would have tended to reverse such an assertion on the grounds that words contribute an *ethos* to sounds, placing them in the relation of rational soul to body. Neoclassic thought might better tolerate such an image. "Musick and poetry have ever been acknowledged Sisters, which walking hand in hand, support each other: As poetry is the harmony of words, so musick is that of notes: and as poetry is a rise above prose and oratory, so is Musick the exaltation of poetry. Both of them may excell apart, but sure they are most excellent when they are joind, because nothing is then wanting to either of their perfections: for thus they appeare, like wit and beauty in the same person." So wrote Dryden, in a dedication to an edition of the music for Purcell's *The Prophetesse* in 1691. Tate's rather crude figure could thus, perhaps, be defended with reference to a notion that music animates a text and exalts it by giving life to its rhetorical power over the passions. What is most to the point here, though, is the arbitrary character of that figure in its argumentative context in the ode, where it cannot help but function as a shabbily supported, though perhaps "exalted" lyric gnome.

Tate's ode was bedecked with pastoral images of lambkins and frolicking kids, all protected by the beneficient power of St. Cecilia. It is not quite clear at exactly what point in history that Roman martyr became the patron saint of music. The legend that an angel, attracted by her beautiful musicianship, came down from heaven to visit her seems to have been current before the fifteenth century. It is this story which Dryden was to employ in both his odes. Before Dryden, the patroness of music tended to receive only passing mention, along with the various muses and the musical heroes of Antiquity. It was only in 1699, after the fame of Dryden's "Alexander's Feast" had become fairly secure, that Addison, in an ode set by Daniel Purcell, attempted any elaborate treatment of St. Cecilia. At the end of the celebrations of the several qualities of violins, flute, organ and trumpet, Echo too performs her part, who could surpass these others,

>And in a low expiring strain
>Play all the concert o'er again.

>Such were the tuneful notes that hung
>On bright Cecilia's charming tongue:
>Notes that sacred heats inspir'd
>And with religious ardour fired:

> The love sick youth, that long supprest
> His smother'd passion in his breast,
> No sooner heard the warbling dame
>   But by the secret influence turn'd,
> He felt a new diviner flame
>   And with devotion burn'd,
> With ravish'd soul and looks amaz'd
> Upon her beauteous face he gaz'd,
>   Nor made his amorous complaint:
> In vain her eyes his heart had charm'd,
> Her heavenly voice his eyes disarm'd,
>   And chang'd the lover to a Saint.

Here it is the main story of St. Cecilia's martyrdom that Addison employs for musical purposes. The "love sick youth" was her pagan suitor Valerianus, persuaded by her beauty and virtuous example to abjure his desires for her and to accept, along with his brother, conversion to Christianity. The power of St. Cecilia's persuasion is figured forth in terms of musical virtuosity, and the two stories of her evangelical and angel-charming successes are blended into one. This could be only logical in an age when music itself was valued most highly as an instrument of persuasiveness rather than as a concrete fact representing universal abstract order.

The handling of music's patron saint was only one of the many problems facing the authors of the St. Cecilia odes, however. If we examine the poems produced by Shadwell, Congreve, Nicholas Brady, D'Urfey, Theophilus Parsons, Christopher Smart, and Pope himself, we can see the conventional shape of the St. Cecilia ode maintaining itself, on the one hand, through such crude devices as simple tag lines either passed down quite deliberately or else successively "rediscovered" by subsequent authors. Dryden's line (in the "Song for St. Cecilia's Day"), "What Passion cannot MUSICK raise and quell!" is obviously some version of Tate's "What charms can Musick not impart" of three years earlier. On the other hand, we can see the later odes, especially those of the eighteenth century, reacting to critical pressures that were being clearly formalized by writers on poetry and music during the 1730s and 1740s. It came to be expected of odes to be set to music in general, were they sacred poems, cantata texts, occasional pieces, or the St. Cecilia songs themselves, that they be historical or narrative, rather than merely mythological; that they be smooth metrically and "lyric" in style, infused with a degree of passión, yet preserving simplicity; and that they utilize sentiment rather than imagery, on the grounds that composers were far too apt to paint *words* like "high" and "low" rather than *ideas*, as should have been proper. It is fairly clear that many of these criteria arose in some measure from the almost universal approval that "Alexander's Feast" continued to accumulate throughout the eighteenth century.

Our primary interest in all the St. Cecilia odes, however, remains confined to an understanding of a convention of formal and public *laus musicae* in which Dryden worked on two separate occasions, ten years apart, and which may be presumed to have solidified even during that interval. And although "Alexander's Feast" may be rightly judged, as indeed it has always been, superior to the earlier "Song for St. Cecilia's Day," the latter must remain of considerable interest to us as an example of Dryden's ability to hew extremely close to a convention while yet securing his finished work from the abyss of anonymity. It is only through a consideration of the varied problems that he faced in the composition of the first ode, and through a knowledge of the stylistic and ideological variables that governed the ideal model to which his poem must needs have conformed, that the elegance of his resulting effort may appear. Aside from some of the overall structural considerations which we have observed already, there remain such questions as the suitability of the text to the musical setting it was to receive, the concurrences of major climaxes in the setting, the formal Pindaric verse structure and the argued praise of music as well.

In examining Dryden's two St. Cecilia odes we shall watch for his avoidance of the clichés of speculative music employed, barely changed, by his precursors; but even more, for the ways in which, operating within the limits of what was becoming a canonical form, he managed to stamp the two odes with an impress of his own. And we shall see how, in very different ways, the "Song for St. Cecilia's Day" and "Alexander's Feast" contrive to overflow the boundaries of their openly occasional purpose, and to represent with unequalled success the attitudes toward music of the community that commissioned and praised them.

DRYDEN'S FIRST ODE: THE CANTATA OF MUSICAL GENESIS

Any critical reading of John Dryden's 1687 St. Cecilia's Day ode would do well to keep in mind both the literary convention of the musical ode in praise of music and the general fate of the poetic applications of *musica speculativa* after the Restoration. In general, one would want to conclude with Dr. Johnson that, although the first of the two odes seems "lost in the splendour of the second," it nevertheless contains "passages which would have dignified any other poet." But its particular success can perhaps be measured only against the resounding failure of Neoclassic poetry to versify musical doctrine in any but the most pedestrian fashion, on the one hand, and, on the other, against the relatively flabby way in which Dryden's predecessors had adapted the celebration of singing to the singing of that celebration, as it were, to the exigencies of a good cantata text.

On the first of these questions, we might turn for a moment to a prior case of Dryden's treatment of a theme of speculative music. Taken out of context, the opening of the third stanza of his great ode "To the Pious Memory of the Accomplisht Young Lady Mrs. Anne Killigrew, Excellent in the Two Sister-Arts of Poesie and Painting" (1686) might be thought to resemble some of the complimentary epigrams treated previously in this chapter:

> May we presume to say, that at thy *Birth*,
> New joy was sprung in HEAV'N as well as here on *Earth*?
> For sure the Milder Planets did combine
> On thy *Auspicious* Horoscope to shine,
> And ev'n the most malicious were in Trine.
> Thy *Brother-Angels* at thy *Birth*
>   Strung each his Lyre, and tun'd it high,
>   That all the People of the Skie
> Might know a Poetess was born on Earth.
>   And then if ever, Mortal Ears
>   Had heard the Music of the Spheres!
>
> (39–49)

But this superficial resemblance pales into insignificance before the poem's splendid elaboration of the theme of the angelic, the strict correspondence of poetry and music throughout, and the final commendation of earthly art itself toward which the whole elegiac structure moves. The "Musick of the Spheres" is no mere mechanical, intruded gesture of praise here, but has been prepared for in the first stanza's closing supplication:

> Hear then a Mortal Muse thy praise rehearse
>   In no ignoble Verse;
> But such as thy own voice did practise here,
> When thy first Fruits of Poesie were given,
> To make thyself a welcome Inmate there;
>   While yet a young Probationer,
>   And Candidate of Heav'n.
>
> (16–22)

The traditional relationship between *musica instrumentalis*, practical music at its most specific, and the *musica mundana* of celestial generality, is here applied to Anne Killigrew's life of art ("practise" seems to have the weight of both meanings here). The whole poem employs angels, earth, heaven, the traditional angelic activity of singing, etc., in substitution, in a way, for the conventions of pastoral elegy; and if the conceit of the "heavenly quire" is deemed overly conventional, it is because of its conventionality that it can be employed in such a way as it is here. Professor Tillyard has raised the issue of sincerity with respect to just this point about the angelic singing, but he sees quite rightly, I think, how if "there is no piety in his [Dryden's] references to heavenly music, yet through them he demonstrates how sincerely he prizes the practice of the arts on this earth." The point is that Dryden is able to make use of such references precisely because they are unbelieved, and precisely because music can function consistently as a surrogate for both painting and poetry, with none of the engagement of questions of belief that are occasioned by praising an actual singer by equating her music with that of the Universe.

Dryden is, of course, also capable, in his verses "On the Death of Mr. Purcell" (written one year before his "Alexander's Feast"), of employing the music of the spheres in a fairly traditional, complimentary way. The lines were set to music by Dr. John Blow ("Master to the famous Mr. H. Purcell" as his tomb in Westminster Abbey rightfully attests), and it is interesting to note that, at the end of the first stanza, Dryden was preparing some of his techniques for the "Alexander's Feast." We shall see shortly how the elaborate repetitions of phrase in the latter were contrived to meet the exigencies of the kind of setting that the text would receive; the line "And list'ning and silent, and silent and list'ning, and list'ning and silent obey" (9) prefigures this sort of repetition in a way in which nothing in the first ode does. The conventionalities of perfect musicianship enter at the middle of the second stanza, and although they are rather nicely tied to an Orphean conceit which operates through the comparison of Hell and Earth, rather than of Earth and Heaven, the old device of the practical musician outdoing the heavenly choir is unmistakably at work here:

> We beg not Hell our *Orpheus* to restore;
> Had He been there,
> Their Sovereigns fear
> Had sent Him back before.
> The pow'r of Harmony too well they knew;
> He long e'er this had Tun'd their jarring Sphere,
> And left no Hell below.

3.

The Heav'nly Quire, who heard his Notes from high,

> Let down the Scale of Musick from the Sky:
>   They handed him along,
> And all the way He taught, and all the way they Sung.

There is undoubtedly an increment of dramatic power produced by the use of the Underworld motif, and tuning "their jarring Sphere" has more literary plausibility, in a sense, than the customary silencing of the sweet, heavenly one would have. The image at the beginning of the final stanza suggests what Professor Tillyard characterizes as "the outrageous assertion that Anne Killigrew will lead the poetic throng to heaven." But the notion that the quasi-deified Purcell will ascend to heaven along a ladder of perfection that is so named as to suggest at once the musical gamut (in the Greek sense, the *harmonia*) and the *gradus ad Parnassum* of diligent practice and devoted effort, is extremely effective and moving.

The problems that Dryden faced in the composition of the 1687 "Song for St. Cecilia's Day" were virtually the same as those faced by Oldham and the other writers of the texts who had preceded him. But other impulses were at work in his case. There was his marvellous gift of exposition, particularly of summarizing, that triumphed in the dismissive conclusion of *The Secular Masque* (1700), wherein Diana, Mars and Venus, representing the three Stuart Courts, are appropriately and schematically rebuked:

> All, all of a piece throughout:
>   Thy Chase Had a Beast in View;
> Thy Wars brought nothing about;
>   Thy Lovers were all untrue.
> 'Tis well an Old Age is out,
>   And time to begin a New.

And there was that happy faculty of Dryden's which took so well to the irregular versification of the so-called "Pindarick ode," that faculty invoked by Mark Van Doren in his observation that Dryden "was constitutionally adapted to a form of exalted utterance which progressed by the alternate accumulation and discharge of metrical energy." In the first ode, these two talents combine to produce an admirable celebration of the power of music.

The ode falls into three main sections, commencing with an introductory narrative of the role played by music, treated as abstract Harmony at the beginning, in the Creation (1–15). A second section, comprising the next five strophes (16–47), poses the question "What Passion cannot MUSICK raise and quell?" (16); and after a celebration of some original performance by Jubal upon "the chorded Shell," the original *testudo* or tortoise-shell thought to have been the first lyre, successive strophes go on to celebrate the particular affective and passion-eliciting qualities of trumpet, drum, flute, lute, violin, and organ. The last section (final strophe and added "Grand Chorus") introduces St. Cecilia, in comparison with whom Orpheus comes off unfavorably, and proceeds to complete the cycle whose commencement is invoked in the opening lines. Music, this time treated as the sounds of the ultimate trumpet, blown by the archangel to announce the end of that second of eternity containing all of human history, is seen as playing an equally effective role in the Destruction as it played in the Creation.

From the very beginning of the piece, the exposition is activated by a kind of narrative excitement:

> From Harmony, from heav'nly Harmony
> This universal Frame began;
> When Nature underneath a heap
> Of jarring Atomes lay,
> And cou'd not heave her Head,
> The tuneful Voice was heard from high,
> Arise, ye more than dead.
> Then cold and hot and moist and dry
> In order to their Stations leap,
> And MUSICK's pow'r obey.
>
> (1–10)

What jars here is not "disproportion'd sin," as in "At a Solemn Musick," but rather the atoms of chaos, which associate themselves with their proper elemental status "in order to their Stations" under the organizing influence of Harmony. While this seems only barely reminiscent of Marvell's recounting of music's creation of a world along specifically political lines, it suggests much more his treatment of Cromwell as Amphion in "The First Anniversary of the Government under O.C.," where the creative, wall-building music accomplishes its ends by ordering what had been chaotic previously. The conclusion of the opening strophe turns a connective "from" into a "to," and changes the meaning of "Harmony" slightly; what is meant now is a melody, an interval, or more probably a chord, instead of the abstract sense of harmony as order in the original and repeated lines:

> From Harmony, from heavenly Harmony
> This universal Frame began:
> From Harmony to Harmony
> Through all the Compass of the Notes it ran,
> The Diapason closing full in Man.
>
> (11–15)

The octave, that is, the perfect consonance (next to the unison, of course), is the proper "close" (or, in modern terminology, "cadence") for the actual musical composition of Creation, moving along, as Dryden probably meant specifically, over a thoroughbass, "From Harmony to Harmony." Man is that octave cadence, and his shaping crowned the whole act of Creation, and was followed only by the silences of the first Sabbath.

The central portion of the ode, employing separate sections for the celebration of the virtues of each instrument, holds more to the pattern of some of the earlier cantata-texts. Obbligatos on the appropriate instruments would seem to have been the order of the day (although Handel's setting, first performed in 1739, makes much more elaborate use of these than Draghi's original one appears to have done). Dryden does not seem to have kept in mind, in composing his text, that clear distinctions would be drawn, in the setting, between passages of recitative, aria, duet, chorus, etc.; his "Grand Chorus" is the only indication of a textual division that was obviously planned to correspond to a musical one. The vivid metrical variation in strophe 3 ("The TRUMPETS loud Clangor / Excites us to Arms," etc.) is much more effective (with its abrupt switch out of its quasi-dactylic scheme, into "The double double double beat / Of the thund'ring DRUM," and back again) on paper, than when set; although any late Baroque musical setting would set up rhythms of its own to correspond to the effects that Dryden's verse achieved. The second stanza does have the enrichment of the delicate second reference to the "Shell"-lyre:

> Less than a God they thought there could not dwell
>   Within the hollow of that Shell,
>   That spoke so sweetly, and so well
>
>   (21–23)

where the overtones of the roaring sea-shell seem implicit, somehow, beneath the conventional epithet.

But it is the concluding strophes, along with the first, that are of most interest here. The last one before the chorus compliments St. Cecilia in some of the same terms in which countless "Fair Singers" during the preceding fifty years had been complimented:

> *Orpheus* cou'd lead the savage race,
> And trees unrooted left their Place,
>   Sequacious of the Lyre;
> But bright CECILIA rais'd the Wonder High'r:
> When to her Organ vocal Breath was given,

> An Angel heard, and straight appear'd
> Mistaking Earth for Heav'n.
>
> (48–54)

Dryden has here combined the two elements of the St. Cecilia legend into his little dramatic climax: the angel that the historical saint's *praying* summoned is here treated as having appeared at the sound of the organ, her visible attribute. One cannot be sure whether Dryden was consciously suggesting that it was the "music," the affective beauty of her prayer, which "drew an Angel down," or whether this is merely a rather effective bit of wit. Dryden may also very well have appropriated Ben Jonson's line from "The Musical Strife," but there is certainly sufficient tradition for the figure in the complimentary convention to have allowed him to come upon it himself, quite naturally.

The final chorus, which together with the opening brackets the whole ode, is of a more original stuff:

Grand CHORUS

> *As from the Pow'r of Sacred Lays*
> *The Spheres began to move,*
> *And sung the great Creator's Praise*
> *To all the bless'd above;*
> *So, when the last and dreadful Hour*
> *This crumbling Pageant shall devour,*
> *The TRUMPET shall be heard on high,*
> *The dead shall live, the living die,*
> *And MUSICK shall untune the Sky.*
>
> (55–63)

Just as the trumpet of Gabriel and of the Koran's Israfel is completely separate from the purely martial trumpet celebrated earlier in the ode, the music that untunes the sky must be referred back to the opening lines: it is only as the dissolvent counterpart of the original ordering that we can make more than the most extravagant sense of the final line. Dr. Johnson wished that "the antithesis of *music untuning* had found some other place"; and he evidently found the penultimate line so "awful in itself" that he could not bring himself precisely to designate it. But I think that the music untuning the sky is more than merely a figure representing the transcendence of music, even across the dissolution of the universe. "This crumbling Pageant" is the cosmos, of course; but Professor Van Doren may be hinting at something else, in his remark that Dryden's "finale is the blare of a trumpet, and his last glimpse is of painted scenery crashing down on a darkened stage." The conclusion of the ode seems quite close to some of the conventions of the masque at this point. We have observed the self-congratulatory tone and import of some of the earlier St. Cecilia's Day odes. Here, the "Pageant" is the musical meeting itself, in much the same way as, in a masque, the allegorical texture of plot, dramaturgy, and theater come to equate the world of the masque's imagery with the parochial, but momentarily universal, world of the court in which it is presented. The London music meetings had none of the masque conventions, of course, such as the identity of the masquers, the closing measures in which spectacle and audience unite, etc. But the marvellous finale quality of the chorus here is considerably enhanced by the fact that the whole cantata, starting up with the literal tuning of strings, should end with an "untuning"; by the fact that the text draws upon the conventional notion of psychic *tonus* (although rather for praise, than for *prayer*, here) in a kind of reversal, implying that, now that the praise of music has been completed, the souls of the singers and hearers will "untune," or "slacken," as have the strings of the actual instruments.

But whatever the force of the ultimate line, it cannot be denied that it is the first and last sections of the ode that are truly distinguished. They are devoted to the eternal subsistence of music, seen as both abstract *harmonia mundi* and final trump; but like the outraged angels and humbled spheres of the epigrams, that "music," a sophisticatedly wrought construction from the stock of *musica speculativa*, is employed in praise of a practical music that is *mundane* rather than *mundana*, worldly rather than universal. The second member of this pair has become merely a term with which to exalt the other.

"ALEXANDER'S FEAST": THE DRAMA OF MUSICAL POWER

If the "opening" and "finale" of the first St. Cecilia's Day ode give evidence of a sense on Dryden's part of a kind of musical programmatic dramaturgy, however, it is to the "Alexander's Feast; Or, the Power of Musique" of ten years later that we must turn for the fulfillment of that promise. Questions ranging from that of overall theme to those of more minute details of arrangement of line and repetition of word, raised by the musical setting of the first ode, were settled quite definitively in the execution of the second one. Draghi's setting of the closing line, for example, actually involved the singing of "And Musick shall untune the sky, untune, untune, and Musick shall, and Musick shall," etc. Then there was the problem of adapting the vigorous and flexible strophic structure to the exigencies of the setting's alternation of chorus, solo, duet, etc., and the final crucial matter of theme, and of a move from the expository to the dramatic. As a solution of all these problems, "Alexander's Feast" must be considered as a true libretto, rather than merely as another in the series of commendatory odes. It is almost proverbial now how Dryden found the prospect of writing another ode "troublesome, & no way beneficiall," and how its actual composition was accompanied with great concern and some nervousness. The original setting by Jeremiah Clarke (? 1673–1707) was never published and no trace of it remains, so that we cannot know precisely the degree to which Dryden's efforts were successful in the case of some of the more technical matters which he faced as librettist. But the authority with which the ode celebrates its epoch's dominant myth of music is unimpeachable, and its brilliance as a poetic text completely apart from its musical setting has always been dazzling.

His search for a subject could not have taken him far. His dramatic libretto called for one of the old stories of affective music: Orpheus, Arion (rather than the more strictly political Amphion), the Sirens, and Ulysses. Less likely candidates were the stories of the musical martyrs of one sort or another: Orpheus' dismemberment, Herakles' murder of his teacher Linus with the man's own lyre, the punishment of Terpander for adding an extra string to the lyre, the ridicule of the historical Timotheus of Miletus for his innovations along similar lines, Marsyas and his unfortunate espousal of the hateful *aulos*, Midas and his grossly ridiculed lack of taste. All of these must have seemed either overly grotesque or patently ridiculous. Even the story of St. Cecilia herself was too bare of canonical and familiar musical incident. The *philomelamachia* ending in death was not only unsuitable because of its tragic conclusion, but because such a subject would seem better adapted to a chamber dialogue than to the expansion of a cantata. But another Timotheus, a purely fictional Alexandrian *aulos*-player who became confused with the historical composer of *nomoi* mentioned above, had served from the very beginning as part of the Orpheus-figure, as a Baroque poet-musician-rhetorician-hero. Writers in English for the hundred years previous had used as an instance of the power of music the story of how Alexander the Great, in the version of John Case from *The Praise of Musicke* (1586), "sitting at a banquet amongst his friends, was nevertheles by the excelent skil of Timotheus a famous musician so inflamed with the fury of *Modus Orthius*, or as some say of *Dorius*, that he called for his spear & target as if he would presently have addressed himself to war." But immediately thereafter, Case remarks, "the same Timotheus seeing Alexander thus incensed, only with the changing of a note, pacified this moode of his, & as it were with a more mild sound mollified & asswaged his former violence." Aside from the fact that Case has his "modes" mixed up here (Dorian, as well as Phrygian, might be considered a "warlike" mode, but "*Modus Orthius*" is a purely rhythmic

term having nothing to do with melody), his account remains pretty much
the standard one in English. It has been observed how Cowley, Burton,
Playford, and Jeremy Collier, among others, all have versions, of differing
degrees of detail, of the Timotheus story; as a probable source, Collier's recounting of the story has its date of appearance (1697) and the liveliness of
the scene it sketches on its side: "One time when *Alexander* was at Dinner,
this man play'd him a *Phrygian* Air: The Prince immediately rises, snatches
up his Lance, and puts himself in a Posture of Fighting. And the Retreat was
no sooner Sounded by the Change of the Harmony, but his Arms were
Grounded, and his Fire extinct, and he sat down as orderly as if he had come
from one of *Aristotle's Lectures*. I warrant you *Demosthenes* would have been
Flourishing about such a Business a long Hour, and may not have done it
neither, But *Timotheus* had a nearer Cut to the Soul: He could Neck a Passion at a Stroke, and lay it Asleep." Here, as throughout this essay, inciden-
tally, Collier seems to have been motivated by common sense as much as
by his traditional modal *ethos*. "By altering the *Notes*, and the *Time*," he
carefully remarks, he could sweeten a hearer's "Humour at a trice." Any late
seventeenth-century audience would comprehend such a notion that made
no appeal to what had become the purely literary schemata of the music of
Antiquity.

But however it came to him, the story of Timotheus was Dryden's program, as the ultimately persuasive powers of music were his theme. The ode's
unity keeps to the story, and it is only in the seventh strophe that St. Cecilia
is allowed to appear in a cadential, climactic way. As far as the overall structure of the ode is concerned, Dryden has not only repeated the closing lines
of each strophe as a chorus, but he has so arranged each stanza that the truncated section, brilliant and summary in itself, is no mere caudal appendage,
but bound to the rest by rhyme or metrical phrase. The end of the third
strophe, for example, starts out with the announcement of the arrival of
Bacchus:

> Now give the Hautboys breath; He comes, He comes.
> > *Bacchus* ever Fair and Young
> > > Drinking Joys did first ordain;
> > *Bacchus* Blessings are a Treasure;
> > Drinking is the Soldiers Pleasure;
> > > Rich the Treasure;
> > > Sweet the Pleasure;
> > Sweet is Pleasure after Pain.
>
> > > > > > (53–60)

The last five lines are repeated as a chorus, and the repetitions and echoing of short phrases attest here, as elsewhere throughout the poem, to Dryden's concern for the safety of his text during the process of setting. But the overall scheme allows the various stanzas to contain, each within itself, a separate episode; a feeling appropriate to the action of each episode is exemplified throughout each strophe, and particularly in the chorus. Thus, in the first one, the scene is laid, and Alexander, "the lovely *Thais*" and "his valiant Peers" are shown feasting after the victory over Xerxes: "Their Brows with Roses and with Myrtles bound. / (So should Desert in Arms be Crown'd:)" (7–8). The atmosphere is one of love following victory, the myrtle of Venus and the sensual rose, it is pointed out, are the proper guerdon of warlike prowess. Alexander and Thais, "In Flow'r of Youth and Beauty's Pride," are invoked in the chorus:

> *Happy, happy, happy Pair!*
> *None but the Brave,*
> *None but the Brave,*
> *None but the Brave deserves the Fair.*
> (16–19)

And here is the first of many cases of that brilliant shift from iambic to trochaic measures to the catalectic dactyls such as those of "*None but the Brave*," etc., which marks in particular the prosodical artistry of the whole poem.

The next section introduces "Timotheus plac'd on high / Amid the tuneful Quire," surely not complimented in these lines (although the cliché of praise seems to be in evidence here), but rather depicted as in the high choir-loft or musicians' gallery, under "the Vaulted Roofs" of a sumptuous palace. In contrast to this, however, his playing is elaborately praised, as we are told how he

> With flying Fingers touch'd the Lyre:
> The trembling Notes ascend the Sky,
> And Heav'nly Joys inspire.
> (22–24)

And while "Heav'nly Joys" commends rather more than describes, the remainder of the second section is devoted to the treatment of the theme of the empyrean. The muse governing this stanza, and Timotheus's first song, is Clio:

> The Song began from *Jove*;
> Who left his blissful Seats above,
> (Such is the Pow'r of mighty Love.)
> A Dragon's fiery Form bely'd the God:

Sublime on Radiant Spires He rode,
When He to fair *Olympia* press'd:
And while He sought her snowy Breast:
Then, round her slender Waist he curl'd,
And stamp'd an Image of himself, a Sov'raign of the World.

(25–33)

But the muse has become the patroness of fiction, rather than of history.
The story, recorded in Plutarch, of how Alexander's mother Olympias claimed
to have been impregnated by some divine dragon, was one which Dryden
had elsewhere condemned in no uncertain terms: "Ye Princes, rais'd by Poets
to the Gods, / And Alexander'd up in lying Odes, / Believe not ev'ry flatt'ring
Knave's report," he warns the readers of his rewriting of Chaucer's "Nun's
Priest's Tale." But here the fiction is identified with the magic of the music,
and is praised at the end when we are told that Timotheus "rais'd a Mortal
to the Skies," almost as if the greatest triumph of his musicianship had been
the creation of the noble fiction of Alexander's divine paternity. But it is as
a God that Alexander is acclaimed by the crowd at the end of the strophe:

A present Deity, they shout around:
A present Deity, the vaulted Roofs rebound.
    With ravish'd Ears
    The Monarch hears,
    Assumes the God,
    Affects to nod,
And seems to shake the Spheres.

(35–41)

If the Spheres are disturbed as a result of Timotheus's transcendent musicianship, it is only through the almost rabble-rousing effects of his music and
his fictions that create a din, on the one hand, and half-convince all that the
Monarch "Assumes the God," on the other. Only here, in the entire poem,
is the heavenly apparatus in evidence. The myth of music throughout is the
affective one in terms of which music activates feeling through the medium
of sense, and from this point on, Timotheus's playing is to move by persuasion, rather than to affect through "lying."

    The third stanza celebrates Bacchus, starting out with the report of what
subject it was that "the sweet Musician" actually sang, and then moving
almost imperceptibly into the invocation, itself, of Bacchus: "Now give the
Hautboys breath; He comes, He comes," etc. We are not told here, as we
are in the fifth section, which *harmonia* it actually was that Timotheus played;
we may presume that it was the Ionian, which, with the Lydian that in sec-

tion five becomes the erotic mode, was designated by Plato as one of the
"soft or drinking harmonies." Dryden has carefully allowed only wind instruments to occur in this section. The fourth section recounts Alexander's
hallucinatory, perhaps drunken (but whether on wine, or music, or both is
left deliberately vague) revelry ("Fought all his Battails o'er again; / And thrice
He routed all his Foes, and thrice he slew the slain"). But then, we are told,

> The Master saw the Madness rise,
> His glowing Cheeks, his ardent Eyes;
> And while He Heav'n and Earth defy'd,
> Chang'd his Hand, and check'd his Pride.
>> He chose a Mournful Muse,
>> Soft pity to infuse.
>
> (69–74)

This would have been a Mixolydian mode that Timotheus employed to
chasten his King's exuberance by using it to accompany the remainder of
the death of Darius, which had, according to Plutarch, moved Alexander
deeply. His song of Darius, "Fallen, fallen, fallen, fallen, / Fallen from his
high Estate," causes tears to come to the eyes of Alexander. But in the next
strophe, we are told that the Musician sang in "*Lydian* measures" (97), to
soothe the king and turn him to amorous feelings. (It is interesting that Dryden
should have called the Lydian melodic mode a metrical one, but the additional meanings of "dance" and "means," as well as the rhyme with "Pleasures"
operate to enforce the equivalence, rather than the identity, of the two.)

> War, he sung, is Toil and Trouble;
> Honour but an empty Bubble.
>> Never ending, still beginning,
> Fighting still, and still destroying,
>> If the World be worth thy Winning,
> Think, O think, it worth Enjoying.
>> Lovely *Thais* sits beside thee,
>> Take the Good the Gods provide thee.
> The Many rend the Skies, with loud applause;
> So Love was Crown'd, but Musique won the Cause.
>
> (99–108)

Here again, the strophe moves into Timotheus's song itself. This time,
it is as much moral argument as pure emotional exhortation; it is a little like
a Cavalier lyric about Love and Arms inserted into the ode at this point. The
theme of Mars and Venus, at any rate, served to introduce the whole scene,
and the sixth strophe, the concluding one of the Timotheus story, ends itself

with a comparison of Thais to the greatest heroine of war fought all for love. After the king had sunk in sleep upon the breast of his courtesan, Timotheus struck "the Golden Lyre" again, this time, we should guess, with Phrygian strains. Certainly the prosody of this stanza is the most varied and elaborate. "Revenge, revenge" is the musician's text, and a full complement of Furies, Snakes, "a ghastly Band, / Each a Torch in his Hand!" conjured up in the minds of all by the ecstatic mode, incite the king to wreak that revenge upon the very palace in which he has been revelling:

> Behold how they toss their Torches on high,
>> How they point to the *Persian* Abodes,
> And glitt'ring Temples of their Hostile Gods.
> The Princes applaud with a furious Joy;
> And the King seized a Flambeau with Zeal to destroy;
>> *Thais* led the Way,
>> To light him to his Prey,
> And, like another *Hellen*, fir'd another *Troy*.
>
> (142–50)

It is Love, then, which concludes the story, as it opened it. In the final strophe, we are given the climactic mention of Timotheus:

> Thus long ago,
> 'Ere heaving Bellows learn'd to blow,
>> While Organs yet were mute,
>> *Timotheus*, to his breathing Flute
>> And sounding Lyre,
> Cou'd swell the Soul to rage, or kindle soft Desire.
>
> (155–60)

The flute and lyre mentioned together may, of course, stem from the traditional confusion of the two Timotheus figures, the historical lyricist and the fictional *auletes*; but it also harks back to the opening theme of Love consummating the warrior's victory, with perhaps an overtone of Horace's second epode with its "*bibam, / sonante mixtum tibiis carmen lyra, / hac Dorium, illis barbarum?*" wherein the battle of Actium was to be celebrated with mingled musics of a gravely victorious and frenziedly celebratory nature.

But Timotheus is, finally, outdone, in a sudden intrusion of St. Cecilia that, on the surface, seems rather unconvincing. She is complimented as having "Enlarg'd the former narrow Bounds, / And added Length to solemn Sounds," that is, as combining the virtues of classical measures and of the benefits of the music of Christian worship. It cannot be for this only that Dryden demands,

> Let old Timotheus yield the Prize,
>   Or both divide the Crown:
> He raised a mortal to the Skies;
>   She drew an Angel down.
> (167–70)

Dr. Johnson remarked that this "conclusion is vicious; the music of Timotheus, which *raised a mortal to the skies*, had only a metaphorical power; that of Cecilia, which *drew an angel down*, had a real effect: the crown therefore could not reasonably be divided." To debate this conclusion might not necessarily entail an excursion into ontology to show that for Dryden the power was metaphorical in both cases, but such a debate should be avoided in any event. The final appearance of St. Cecilia as a peculiar sort of *deus ex machina* must be understood as operating within the convention of the St. Cecilia's Day music meetings, with which Dryden was of course familiar. She triumphs over Timotheus (or only meets his accomplishment; Dryden is significantly noncommittal) only through the antithesis of the final conceit, but the intention of this seems quite clear. The reference to her attraction of the angel is casually tossed off, as if to indicate that this story was an accepted part of what was almost a liturgy of these music meetings. The close of the ode is a conventional one, a ritual in itself, and the final piece of wit serves to tie the whole ode and its subject into its proper occasional function. But, in another sense, it is indeed St. Cecilia who has been unthroned.

For all of "Alexander's Feast" has gone to praise not only the power and glory of earthly, affective music, but it has gone to praise poetry as well. It is Timotheus the myth-maker, the forger of fictions, who is commended at the beginning of the poem and at the end; and throughout its course the ode seems to depend upon almost bootlegged poetic references, such as the "Measures" of line 97, and the argument about War and Love in the lines following. It is at any rate the "goddess PERSUASION," who, as Shaftesbury put it, "must have been in a manner the mother of poetry, rhetoric, music, and other kindred arts," that triumphs at the conclusion of the celebration of music.

Both as a libretto and as a poem, "Alexander's Feast" commends the power of that goddess. The brilliant musical dramaturgy of the cantata text gives way, on reading, to the marvellous metrical effects, which not only serve themselves to excite, calm, chasten, etc., but to imitate in some way the actual musical setting that they would receive, and in which they would be immolated. The poem is a "musical ode" in many of the senses suggested by that compound: an ode set to, about, purporting to resemble, and even substituting for music. More than that, it implicitly stipulates for its own age and for successive ones as well what music is, and how it should be considered. It is to be *made* rather than, as in the first ode, to be expounded like doctrine, even if that doctrine puts down all the cosmological orthodoxies about the music of universe. In a very real sense, the 1687 ode contains a program for the later one, just as it sums up so succinctly not the history of music in the lives of Western men, but the history of what those men have thought and felt and imagined that very music to be. Music itself, practical music, the music of opera and public concert, the music of the highly-trained, status-seeking professional, is the hero (or, in its variousness, a hero-heroine) of "A Song for St. Cecilia's Day." It has untuned the sky in the sense that it has already rendered the notion of heavenly music, whether as an actuality or in any one of the many, active metaphorical versions which we have studied above, as trivial as it rendered silent the singing spheres. The untuned sky is the abandoned monochord of *musica speculativa,* and "Alexander's Feast" is no mere strand of *exemplum* from that ancient instrument, but a brilliant performance whose only lesson is its own worth.

EUGENE M. WAITH

The Herculean Hero
in All for Love

The comparison of *All for Love* with Shakespeare's *Antony and Cleopatra* has been an exercise for innumerable students, the subject of at least one German dissertation, and of a few sentences in every history of the drama. Here, aside from an occasional reference to Shakespeare, the context will be Dryden's other plays. It is easy to exaggerate the differences between *All for Love* and [*The Conquest of Granada* and *Aureng-Zebe*]. Dryden himself led the way towards putting it in a category apart not only by abandoning couplets to "imitate the divine Shakespeare," but by his comment in the late essay "A Parallel of Poetry and Painting" that he never wrote anything (presumably meaning any of his plays) for himself but *Antony and Cleopatra*. Since Dryden's time critics have considered it exceptional in having an artistic merit which they deny to *The Conquest of Granada* or *Aureng-Zebe,* and one of the most astute of the recent critics has seen it as an exception in Dryden's thematic development. There can be no doubt that there are differences, but the resemblances which bind *All for Love* to its predecessors, if less obvious, are very strong. The verse is certainly much freer; yet it retains often the antithetical balance common to heroic couplets, as when Cleopatra says of Caesar:

> He first possess'd my person; you, my love:
> Caesar lov'd me; but I lov'd Antony.
>
> (2.353–54)

From *The Herculean Hero in Marlowe, Chapman, Shakespeare and Dryden.* © 1962 by Eugene M. Waith. Columbia University Press, 1962.

Though emotion is presented with more immediacy in this play than in *The Conquest of Granada,* the basic concerns from which the emotions arise remain very similar, and the entire framework of feeling and thought within which the characters discuss their problems is the same. If the characters of *All for Love* are less stylized in presentation, they are still of the same family as the characters in Dryden's other heroic plays.

One of the family connections is seen in the traits of the Herculean hero which reappear in Antony. Though the title of the play leaves no doubt about the primacy of the theme of love, the hero, like his prototype in Shakespeare's play, is a warrior whose nobility and generosity are combined with strong passion and a contemptuous disregard for the mores of his society. Dryden's Antony manifests these characteristics in ways which relate him even more closely to Almanzor and Morat than to Shakespeare's hero. And Cleopatra is much more closely related to other Dryden heroines than to Shakespeare's Cleopatra. These relationships must now be examined in more detail.

The first extended description of Antony is given by his general, Ventidius, who is known to the Egyptians as one who does not share in Antony's debauches, "but presides / O'er all his cooler hours" (1.103–4):

> Virtue's his path; but sometimes 'tis too narrow
> For his vast soul; and then he starts out wide,
> And bounds into a vice, that bears him far
> From his first course, and plunges him in ills:
> But, when his danger makes him find his fault,
> Quick to observe, and full of sharp remorse,
> He censures eagerly his own misdeeds,
> Judging himself with malice to himself,
> And not forgiving what as man he did,
> Because his other parts are more than man.
>
> (1.124–33)

Here again is an "irregular greatness" which cannot be quite contained within the bounds of virtue. Antony is farther than Almanzor from being a "pattern of perfect virtue," much farther than Aureng-Zebe, and not so far as Morat. The admiration of Ventidius is apparent, but equally so is his Roman attempt to distinguish neatly between what is to be praised and blamed in Antony. As Aureng-Zebe tries to dissect the paradox of Morat into man and brute, Ventidius divides Antony into erring man and "more than man," but in spite of this logical division the implication of the speech is that virtue and vice are distinctions of secondary importance when discussing so vast a soul. Later in the play, echoing the "taints and honours" speech of Shakespeare's Maecenas, he says:

And sure the gods, like me, are fond of him:
His virtues lie so mingled with his crimes,
As would confound their choice to punish one,
And not reward the other.

(3.48–51)

The impossibility of confining Antony's spirit is the essence of his heroic
individuality. When his fortune has ebbed to its lowest point, he compares
his fortitude to a "native spring" which again fills the dried river-bed to
overflowing:

I've still a heart that swells, in scorn of fate,
And lifts me to its banks.

(3.133–34)

The image recalls Shakespeare's Antony, but echoes Almanzor more closely:

I cannot breathe within this narrow space;
My heart's too big, and swells beyond the place.

(1 *Conquest*, 5.3.23–24)

In Ventidius's initial description Antony's love is sharply differentiated
from his virtue. It is obviously the vice into which the great man has "bounded" — an unruly, excessive infatuation. It may be compared with the "wild
deluge" of the opening lines of the play, where Serapion is talking of "portents
and prodigies." To stem this disastrous flow is the task which Ventidius has
set himself, regardless of the admiration he has for Antony's largeness of spirit.

It is a commonplace of criticism that the first act of Dryden's play is
dominated by Ventidius. Never again are we so completely in the warriors'
world. From a dramatic point of view the showpiece of this act, and indeed
one of the best scenes of the entire play, is the quarrel and reconciliation
of Antony and his general. It has always been thought to derive from the
famous quarrel and reconciliation of Brutus and Cassius, and Hart and
Mohun, who took these parts in Shakespeare's play, distinguished themselves
as Antony and Ventidius. Dryden preferred the scene, as he states in the
preface, to anything he had written "in this kind." It bears a certain
resemblance to the reconciliation of Aureng-Zebe with his father and more
to the quarrel and reconciliation of Dorax and Don Sebastian, written many
years later. In all of these scenes the generosity of the heroic mind triumphs
over *amour propre*.

The significance of Antony's scene with Ventidius, however, is totally
different from that of Aureng-Zebe's scene with the Emperor. Not only is
the hero in this instance more sinning than sinned against, but the result of

the dialogue is to arouse, not to pacify, the party at fault. The Emperor had
to be induced to give up the senseless persecution of his son; Antony has
to be roused from the torpor of remorse. Antony's change is presented in
a highly dramatic contrast. At the beginning of the scene he throws himself
on the ground, calling himself the "shadow of an emperor" and thinking of
the time when he will be "shrunk to a few cold ashes." At the end, standing
with Ventidius, he says:

> O, thou has fir'd me; my soul's up in arms,
> And mans each part about me.
>
> (1.438–39)

The vital spark which makes him great has been restored.

In *All for Love* appears again the contrast between the fiery spirit and
the cold one, analogous, as I have suggested, to Dryden's familiar contrast
between wit and dullness. Though Antony is cold and torpid at the beginning, he is by nature fiery, and is brought to himself by the force of friendship. Caesar, his opposite, is the "coldest youth," who gives "so tame" an
answer to Antony's challenge, has not even warmth enough to die by a fever,
and rather than risk death will "crawl upon the utmost verge of life."
(2.113–30).

> O Hercules! Why should a man like this,
> Who dares not trust his fate for one great action,
> Be all the care of heav'n?
>
> (2.131–33)

The task that Ventidius accomplishes in the first act may be looked at
in two ways. It is in one sense a curbing and controlling of Antony. This
aspect is suggested early by Ventidius's stern disapproval of Cleopatra's lavish
plans for celebrating Antony's birthday. But it is also the firing of Antony's
soul, and this is the aspect which is emphasized. To Ventidius the enemy
is, of course, Cleopatra, but the worst of her effect on Antony is to have
made him a "mute sacrifice" and "the blank of what he was." The state of
mind which Ventidius has to combat directly is a paralysing remorse:

> You are too sensible already
> Of what y'have done, too conscious of your failings;
>
> (1.312–13)

> you sleep away your hours
> In desperate sloth, miscall'd philosophy.
>
> (1.336–37)

In fact, Antony is at this time in a state very similar to Samson's when Manoa comes, in the second episode of *Samson Agonistes*, to warn him against being "over-just" with himself. The maintaining of the inner fire is so important a part of Dryden's concept of the heroic that it is stressed even in the depiction of Cleomenes, the nearly perfect hero of Dryden's last tragedy. The words of Cleomenes' mother might be almost as well applied to Antony:

> This melancholy flatters, but unmans you.
> What is it else, but penury of soul,
> A lazy frost, a numbness of the mind,
> That locks up all the vigour to attempt,
> By barely crying,—'tis impossible!

Only when Cleomenes assures her that his is a grief of fury, not despair, is his mother satisfied. "Desperate sloth," "penury of soul," "a lazy frost"—by the heroic code these are the true sins, beside which other forms of moral deviation pale.

Cleopatra is first seen as the cause of Antony's unmanning. The theatrical strategy of this first unfavourable impression, established only to be radically altered later on, is almost the only similarity between Dryden's teatment of his heroine and Shakespeare's. After exposure to the charms of Shakespeare's Cleopatra, who manages to remain marvellously attractive even at her most hoydenish and deceitful ("holy priests bless her when she is riggish") one is apt to find the Cleopatra of Dryden shockingly tame and stiff. While it is easy to picture Shakespeare's Cleopatra in anything from Egyptian dress to the bodice and farthingale she probably wore on the Elizabethan stage, Dryden's Cleopatra belongs in late seventeenth-century court dress, complete with train. Passion never quite robs her of dignity. There is no haling of messengers by the hair, no riggishness. To understand this Cleopatra is an essential preliminary to understanding the play.

She dominates the second act as Ventidius does the first. In her initial appearance with Iras and her eunuch, Alexas, she proclaims her love a "noble madness" and a "transcendent passion" which has carried her "quite out of reason's view" till she is "lost above it" (2.17–22). Force and excessiveness combine here with nobility as they do in Ventidius's first description of Antony. The heroine is no mere temptress to lure the hero from the path of virtue. She is herself carried away by a passion of heroic proportions like his. Serapion's description of the flood, already suggested as an analogue for Antony's love, may be associated even more properly with Cleopatra's:

> Our fruitful Nile
> Flow'd ere the wonted season, with a torrent

> So unexpected, and so wondrous fierce,
> That the wild deluge overtook the haste
> Ev'n of the hinds that watch'd it.
>
> (1.2–6)

Dryden has taken over Shakespeare's insistence on the resemblances between the lovers and added another in giving Cleopatra a heroic stature like Antony's. Grandeur and largeness of mind are hers as much as they are his. In fact it is her high-mindedness rather than her sensual attraction which persuades Antony not to leave her. The telling blow is her announcement that she refused a kingdom from Caesar because of her loyalty to Antony (in her noble contempt for wealth she resembles the Cleopatra of Fletcher and Massinger's *The False One*). By the end of the act these similar lovers have been brought together to the dismay of Ventidius, but it is to be noticed that Antony's conviction that Cleopatra is worth more than all the world does not alter his heroic determination to fight with Caesar. There is now the additional motive of revenge for Caesar's attempt to corrupt Cleopatra. Love for her is not entirely the effeminizing passion Ventidius thinks it to be, and despite her dignified bearing she is far from tame.

One sentence of self-description has exposed Cleopatra to a great deal of unfriendly laughter:

> Nature meant me
> A wife; a silly, harmless, household dove,
> Fond without art, and kind without deceit.
>
> (4.91–93)

The comparison is not apt, and it is particularly unfortunate that the incongruity blocks the understanding of a crucial point—Cleopatra's attitude towards being a wife. In Shakespeare's play "Husband I come" owes its brilliance as much to its unexpectedness as to its rightness. It signals a transformation in Cleopatra matching the re-emergence of the heroic Antony. In Dryden's play the change is a much smaller one, and so thoroughly prepared that it is no shock to hear:

> I have not lov'd a Roman, not to know
> What should become his wife; his wife, my Charmion!
> For 'tis to that high title I aspire.
>
> (5.412–14)

Her first reference to marriage is contemptuous, as one might expect. Charmion has brought a message that, though Antony is leaving, he will always respect Cleopatra, and she picks up the word with obvious irritation:

> Is that a word
> For Antony to use to Cleopatra?
> O that faint word, *respect*! how I disdain it!
> Disdain myself, for loving after it!
> He should have kept that word for cold Octavia.
> Respect is for a wife: am I that thing,
> That dull, insipid lump, without desires,
> And without pow'r to give 'em?
>
> (2.77–84)

The speech not only expresses Cleopatra's pique but establishes an attitude towards the cold and the dull exactly like that of Antony (the speech precedes Antony's comments on Caesar by only thirty lines). Though Cleopatra in other moods and other circumstances speaks more favourably of being a wife, she retains to the end her scorn of a "dull, insipid lump." Immediately after vowing to follow the dead Antony as a dutiful wife, she adds:

> Let dull Octavia
> Survive, to mourn him dead: my nobler fate
> Shall knit our spousals with a tie too strong
> For Roman laws to break.
>
> (5.415–18)

The opposition between "spousals" and "Roman laws" provides the necessary clue here. Cleopatra considers her love above and beyond law as it is above and beyond reason, yet she borrows from marriage law the terms which distinguish this love from an infatuation of the senses. Her unfortunate self-comparison to a household dove (the context of which will have to be examined later) is part of this process of distinguishing her feelings both from the dullness of the routine and everyday and from the purely sensual and transient.

A glance back at *The Conquest of Granada* will make the distinction clear. Cleopatra's love (and Antony's too) is the sort that Queen Isabella defines:

> Love's a heroic passion which can find
> No room in any base degenerate mind:
> It kindles all the soul with honor's fire,
> To make the lover worthy his desire.
>
> (2 *Conquest*, 1.1.145–48)

The fire and honour of such a love distinguish it from the "lethargy" to which Abdalla succumbs under Lyndaraxa's spell and also from the mere legality of Almahide's relationship to Boabdelin, "When all I knew of love, was to obey!" Almanzor at first takes love for a "lethargy," but by the time of his debate with Lyndaraxa he has learned that though it is not controlled by reason it is both constant and strong:

> 'Tis an enchantment where the reason's bound;
> But Paradise is in th'enchanted ground.
>
> .   .   .   .
>
> My love's my soul; and that from fate is free;
> 'Tis that unchang'd and deathless part of me.

(2 Conquest, 3.3.146–47, 179–80)

Similarly, Antony is lethargic at the opening of the play, seemingly unmanned by love. He is "fired" first by Ventidius, though still half unwilling to leave Cleopatra. When she has persuaded him of the nobility of her love, he identifies his passion with his heroism, much as Almanzor does, and prepares with a whole heart for his battle with Caesar. The spectacle of triumph with which the third act opens presents the momentarily successful fusion of warrior and lover.

When Cleopatra compares herself to a household dove she is explaining to Alexas why she does not want to adopt his plan of flirting with Dolabella to arouse Antony's jealousy: she is opposed to all deceit. Repeatedly during the play her plainness is brought out. Though she finally takes the advice of Alexas, she is unable to maintain the counterfeit. Later, when the false news of her death is carried to Antony, she, unlike Shakespeare's heroine, is unaware of the ruse. Antony, too, has a transparent nature, and both of them in this respect resemble Almanzor, who compares his heart to a crystal brook. Antony complains of his "plain, honest heart," and compares himself to "a shallow-forded stream" (4.432–40). Plainness is another heroic trait which Dryden has given to Cleopatra; his desire to emphasize it in the scene with Dolabella leads him to force the comparison of his heroine to a wife, who is further compared to a fond and artless dove. If Cleopatra lacks the dullness of a wife, she hopes to prove that she lacks the meretriciousness of a mistress.

The comparison of two kinds of love is best seen in Cleopatra's interview with Antony's legal wife, who is hardly more like a household dove than Cleopatra. Dryden was well aware that the unhistorical introduction of Octavia in act 3 was his most daring innovation. I doubt whether it has the effect which Dryden most feared, of dividing the audience's sympathies (and he notes that no critic made this objection), but it has other consequences, very likely unintentional, though by no means damaging to the total effect of the play. Briefly stated, they are the shift from the contrast between

Cleopatra and Caesar to the contrast between Cleopatra and Octavia and the resulting transfer of heroic values to the realm of love.

In Shakespeare's play Caesar remains throughout the chief embodiment of the Roman point of view as Cleopatra of the Egyptian. Caesar's ideal of heroic man is a Stoic concept of the warrior, whereas Cleopatra's includes both warrior and lover. The same might be said of the ideals of these two characters in *All for Love*, but from the moment that Octavia appears, she usurps her brother's antipodal position. The confrontation with Cleopatra establishes her firmly as Antony's alternative choice. Even Ventidius, who represents Roman values though qualified by his admiration for Antony, relies on Octavia to make the Roman ideal compelling. Thus, though the issue remains Antony's choice of love or his responsibilities in the world, the stage presents as the dramatic symbols of these alternatives two women, Cleopatra and Octavia, and the choice at the centre of the play becomes one between love and marriage. The turn of the third act which determines Antony for the second time to leave Cleopatra is not, as it was in the first act, the responsibility to fight Caesar in order to show the world who is master, but duty to a wife, through whom he may reach a peaceful understanding with Caesar. Octavia's weapons are her unrequited love and her children. Cleopatra, who was portrayed in the first act as a deterrent to heroic action, now appears as an alternative to domestic love. When the two women meet, they naturally quarrel over which one of them loves Antony more, and Cleopatra stakes her claim on the very extravagance of her love, which has made her give up her good name in order to become Antony's mistress. The fourth act in effect tests the truth of this love in the episode of Dolabella, showing that it is too great to be concealed. Octavia's love, in this same act, is overwhelmed by outrage. When she leaves in the midst of angry (though justifiable) accusations, it is reduced to duty, its basic component all along.

In the fifth act Antony is separated from both women. Octavia has left and he has quarrelled with Cleopatra over her supposed liking for Dolabella. The problems of empire are raised again but only to be reabsorbed in the problems of love. Though the Egyptian fleet has deserted and Caesar is at the gates, Antony is primarily concerned with Cleopatra's feelings towards him. When he thinks that she has fled, his first thought is that she has "fled to her Dolabella"; the accusation that she has turned to Caesar comes second. The idea of a heroic last stand is banished in an instant by the false news of Cleopatra's death, which seems to prove her innocence. The only possible heroic action now is suicide, since

> I was but great for her; my pow'r, my empire,
> Were but my merchandise to buy her love.
>   (5.270–71)

The structure of the play has been called episodic. Noyes says [in his edition of the play] that "like that of *The Conquest of Granada*, it deals with successive adventures in the life of one man, not with one central crisis." Jean Hagstrum says the play "is not a closely concatenated action that unfolds moral justice. It is a gallery of related heroic poses intended to arouse our sympathy . . . and our admiration" (*The Sister Arts*). The second judgment is much the more acceptable, and surely the relatedness which Hagstrum recognizes is provided by the crisis in the love-relationship of Antony and Cleopatra, the concern of each act in the play. It is strange to complain of looseness of structure in a play whose strength resides in concentration upon one problem. In this respect the structure is a refinement upon that of *The Conquest of Granada* and *Aureng-Zebe*. The three plays constitute a series in progressive tightness and simplification.

In *All for Love* the Herculean hero's quest for unbounded power is replaced by a quest for unbounded love. In *The Conquest of Granada* a noble love modifies the masculine drive for power, redirecting it towards a goal acceptable to society. In *Aureng-Zebe* Indamora tries to exert a similar modifying and redirecting influence, but without achieving the same results as Almahide. Aureng-Zebe's love for her is his one unruly passion, and Morat gives up his ambition for "unjust dominion" only to replace it by a love which ignores marital bonds. We never see Antony, as we do Almanzor and Morat, at a time when military conquest is his chief aim. In spite of the efforts of Ventidius, the problems of empire rapidly sink to a position of secondary importance, hardly competing in Antony's mind with his desire for Cleopatra. At the end of the play, instead of the heroic image of him conjured up by Shakespeare's Cleopatra, we are presented with a stage picture of the bodies of the two lovers, regally attired and seated next to each other in thronelike chairs. When Serapion finds them he says:

> See, see how the lovers sit in state together,
> As they were giving laws to half mankind!
>
> (5.507–9)

Only in this paradoxical image is the idea of world-conquest restated, and even here it is subordinated to the triumph of love.

It is a curious fact that this play, which is so thoroughly a love-tragedy, is in one important respect closer to the pattern of Herculean plays than either *The Conquest of Granada* or *Aureng-Zebe*. In both of these plays the final emphasis is on a reconciliation of heroic energies with the laws of society. Almanzor remains an invincible hero but in the service of Ferdinand and Isabella. Morat's case is more ambiguous, but at the end death has removed his irregular greatness, and the compelling image of the hero lying at Indamora's feet gives way to tableaux of orderly family relationships. Aureng-Zebe, after a quarrel, is reconciled to Indamora. Melesinda marches in a religious procession to her husband's funeral pyre, where she will commit suttee. Nourmahal, the spirit of restless disorder, dies on the stage. Aureng-Zebe, having succeeded in restoring his father to power, receives the crown from his hands. In *All for Love* the effort to tame or redirect the hero's energies is totally unsuccessful. The love which the play celebrates soars beyond reason and legality, leading the lovers to defiance of the world and a final self-assertion in suicide. In his unrepentant commitment to a highly individualistic ideal Antony is a logical successor to Morat, but far more Herculean than Almanzor or Aureng-Zebe.

For different reasons, the play as a whole is more like the other Herculean plays than is Shakespeare's *Antony and Cleopatra*. There Antony's love is more clearly an alternative to heroic action, however attractively that alternative is presented. In *All for Love* it is not merely that the world is well lost for such a love, but that Dryden, largely through his treatment of Cleopatra, has elevated the love and made its truth and strength unquestionable, though to attain it the world must be defied. Thus presented, it becomes a suitable enterprise for a hero.

In the preface Dryden makes it clear that the lovers are to be blamed for not controlling their passions and finds the attraction of the story in the "excellency of the moral," but he also states that he has drawn the characters of the hero and the heroine as favourably as his sources would permit him. His emphasis on the greatness and nobility of their love is obviously part of this process. The result is a powerful claim on the sympathy of the audience and perhaps less moral instruction than Dryden liked to think. In fact, the love of Antony and Cleopatra, elevated to the level of a "heroic passion," contains the very sort of contradictions which make a moral judgment of Tamburlaine or Bussy so difficult. The love itself is an extravagant, fiery force, knowing no obligations, and yet ennobling in spite of its extralegality. It is a pattern of loyal commitment. One might say that the moral is not (as Dryden implies) the punishment of lovers who fail to control their passions, but the tragic limitations imposed by human existence on the infinite aspirations of heroic passion.

RUTH NEVO

Absalom and Achitophel

That kingly power, thus ebbing out, might be Drawn to the dregs of a Democracy.

THE USE OF DRAMA AND THE USE OF SCRIPTURE

Dryden's triumph, in *Absalom and Achitophel*, lies in his having found a way to take his opponents with perfect seriousness. He has perfected a complex literary instrument which can at once place and present in the most compromising light the rascally lowness of his opponent's pretensions to power, while at the same time giving that lowness itself an epic quality. The poem is densely packed with reference and allusion, operating in different, if complementary, directions and at different levels of response; for this reason the task of analyzing the separate strands which go to its making is a difficult one. There are, however, certain cardinal points crucial to an understanding of the way in which Butler's similar idea is here bettered.

The latest and fullest attempt to account for the excellence of *Absalom* is Ian Jack's valuable *Augustan Satire*. He there joins issue with Weldon Williams, who had said that while both Oldham and Dryden were searching for a dignified vehicle for satire, "Oldham's poems are in a falsely inflated style. . . . Dryden's stayed much closer to the idiom and atmosphere of the lampoon or libel, even while reacting against it as a form." Jack finds this misleading. "Oldham," he says, "used an unsuccessful heroic style, while Dryden scored a signal success with an original blending of the heroic with the witty." It would seem that while there is little disagreement as to the quality of Absalom, the peculiar source of its effectiveness has yet to be fully accounted for. Jack sums up his view of the poem thus: "It was because Charles

From *The Dial of Virtue: A Study of Poems on Affairs of State in the Seventeenth Century.* © 1963 by Princeton University Press.

43

was a witty man that Dryden was free to use for his poem a new alloy—a skilful blend of heroic panegyric, satire, 'discourse' and witty commentary."

But this "alloy" as such was not new. It had existed in Marvell's *Last Instructions*, and before Marvell in Cowley's *Poem on the Civil War*, a piece which Dryden evidently admired and which was included in the *Third Miscellany*, the *Examen Poeticum*, published by Tonson in 1693. Both those poems, however, had lacked (as well as the elegant turn of the couplet) a form, an action into which the alloy could be cast. Dryden's poem produces the effect of a self-contained whole in which the structure is organic, growing from within, and not a mere formal pattern imposed from without. Indeed the weakness of Cowley, Marvell, and Butler is that they lack even the latter. The *Civil War*, the *Last Instructions*, and *Hudibras* have no inevitable beginning, middle, and end, let alone an inner curve of climax, crisis, and resolution, or an organized variation of tension and tempo.

Yet it was Butler and Oldham, each in his own way, who set political satire moving in the direction of dramatization. Each provides an at least rudimentary dramatic action through which the satire can be exhibited. Dryden admired both poets greatly, with certain reservations, and it is probable that it was their work, coupled, of course, with his own experience in the theater subsequent upon the exercise in heroic narrative which had been his last long poem, that opened his eyes to the possibility of dramatic character, as opposed to the formal "character," as a medium for both the satiric and the panegyric content he had in mind. What had been held in suspension, as it were, by Cowley, Marvell, Oldham, and Butler, Dryden was exactly equipped to condense, through his command of dramatic oratory and through the agency of his allegorical fable, into the hard gem that is *Absalom and Achitophel*.

The fable is all-important. Without it he could not have exercised his forensic art of ironic sophistry, not lifted the witty analytic lampoon to the level of dramatic significance. It is through the fable that the conflict is projected in terms of opposing characters and the forces represented by them, to produce the dialectical suspense and the dynamic forward-moving impetus of drama. Even more important than the casting of his satire into the form of a fable is the stereoscopic effect of the allegory in the fable. This generates the intellectual interest of reading on two distinct but parallel planes at once, each well known but novel in the stimulating juxtaposition, so that each becomes charged with the emotional associations and energies of the other.

The significance, moreover, of this particular choice of allegory is far from fully accounted for, or fully interpreted by a check-list of forerunners from whom he might have taken the hint.

Jack has drawn attention to the use in John Caryl's *Naboth's Vineyard*,

1679, on the "Popish" side, and in D'Urfey's *The Progress of Honesty*, 1680, of biblical allegory in the treatment of the Popish Plot. R. F. Jones, in "The Originality of Absalom and Achitophel," has shown that sermons written as early as 1627 present Achitophel as the idea of a Wicked Politician, with contemporary reference, and has gathered numerous instances during the Restoration (when the analogy of Charles' exile and return with David's had become a commonplace) of the allegorical use, in a contemporary context concerning disloyal advisors, of Absalom, David and Achitophel. As we have seen in the satires reviewed [elsewhere], biblical analogy becomes more and more prevalent, especially, of course, in the hands of republicans, dissenters and Whigs, as the shadow of the accession crisis darkens and the consequent sense of a crisis in world history—a moment when Providence is present and manifest—returns. Scriptural ammunition however was no monopoly and in 1680 Monmouth was finally identified as Absalom and Shaftesbury specifically as Achitophel in *Absalom's Conspiracy*, or *The Tragedy of Treason*. Several months before Dryden's poem appeared, a tract called *The Badger in the Fox-Trap* announced in doggerel but unambiguous terms:

> Some call me Tony, some Achitophel,
> Some Jack-a-Dandy, some old Machiavel.

Thus biblical allegorizing at the time of the Popish Plot was frequent, but sporadic and not consistently pursued. And no one had seized with such brilliant aptness and generality the biblical types in the present situation. *Naboth's Vineyard* is a case in point. It comes nearer than any previous poem to Dryden's treatment (even the phrasing is echoed by Dryden at times). It contains the "character" projected in a dynamic situation, and dramatically exposing himself in what is in effect a development of satiric parody:

> *Malchus*, a puny Levite, void of sence,
> And Grace, but stuft with Noise and Impudence,
> Was his prime Tool; so *venomous a Brute*,
> That every place he liv'd in, spued him out;
> Lyes in his Mouth, and Malice in his Heart,
> By Nature grew, and were improv'd by Art.

> "In great Designs it is the greatest Art,
> To make the Common People take your part:
> Some words there are, which have a Special Charm
> To wind their *Fancies* up to an *Alarm*.
> *Treason, Religion, Liberty*, are such;
> Like *Clocks* they strike, when on those points you touch."

Caryl turns the couplet neatly to the uses of acid comment:

> Ahab distrest, bow'd to his Lord, and pray'd;
> Ahab victorious, proudly disobey'd.

Yet the choice of the poor man's vineyard as emblem does not offer the same scope for political generality, complexity, and penetration as the story of Absalom and Achitophel, even taking into consideration the fact that Caryl is not dealing with the Monmouth aspect of the Plot, but only with the plight of the unjustly treated Catholics.

It is, in fine, not so much the choice of this or that biblical character or circumstance for the allegory, as the unwavering and detailed consistency of the total allegory Israel-England that is the very root and heart of *Absalom's* success. Unlike Butler, who had placed his unheroic hero against a standard of the heroic not only outdated but by definition inimical to middle-class pretensions, Dryden has chosen to pay the enemy in his very own coin. It was his genius to exploit the perception that scripture, while no monopoly of a single class or party, is nevertheless the fundamental well-spring of the epic view of life as it existed in his day in Puritan myth and republican ethos, as opposed to the classicizing, strongly Epicurean tendencies of the court culture. The mock-heroic element in the poem is in the exercise of that ironic duplicity whereby, while speaking to an entire (literate) nation in a language available to all, he is enabled subtly to undermine his opponent's position by evoking the latter's own sacred and incontrovertible text. Thus the triumphantly conclusive effect of such passages as

> True, they petition me t'approve their choice:
> But Esau's hands suit ill with Jacob's voice.
> (l. 981)
> The Jews, a headstrong, moody, murm'ring race,
> As ever tried th'extent and stretch of grace;
> God's pamper'd people, whom, debauch'd with ease,
> No king could govern, nor no God could please;
>
> . . . .
>
> Those very Jews, who, at their very best,
> Their humor more than loyalty express'd,
> Now wonder'd why so long they had obey'd
> An idol monarch, which their hands had made;
> Thought they might ruin him they could create,
> Or melt him to that golden calf, a State.
> (l. 45)

In the *Discourse concerning Satire*, Dryden, as we have seen [elsewhere], while insisting upon the virtue of Horace's "delicate touches of fine raillery," bases his preference for Juvenal upon the serious vehemence of his morality—the condition for the "pleasure of concernment in all he says." In the significant passage which has already been noticed he says: "His thoughts are sharper; his indignation against vice is more vehement; his spirit has more of the commonwealth genius; he treats tyranny, and all the vices attending it, as they deserve, with the utmost rigor: and consequently, a noble soul is better pleas'd with a zealous vindicator of Roman liberty, than with a temporising poet, a well-manner'd court slave, and a man who is often afraid of laughing in the right place; who is ever decent, because he is naturally servile . . . it was no longer time to turn into ridicule the false opinions of philosophers, when the Roman liberty was to be asserted."

It is possible that this nostalgia for the sturdy Roman "commonwealthsman" was rooted in Dryden's perception that the truly heroic view of life had indeed passed from court to city in his day. His own increasing Toryism, his conversion to Rome—the extreme reaction from wayfaring Christianity—and the mood of disillusionment expressed finally in *The Secular Masque* may all be interpreted as confirmatory of such a view of his emotional progress: the growing feeling, that is, that his party had fallen behind in the historical race for predominance and leadership in the nation and its culture. It is at all events sufficiently established that his constant aspiration was towards the writing of epic. And it therefore seems not improbable that in his own deepest insight into the contemporary situation lay the origin of his idea—the turning of the tables upon those who held the key to epic in his day by the appropriation to his scheme of their authoritative myth, and the triumphant vindication, on his terms, of the great biblical hero as Charles, and of his "small but faithful band of worthies." Nor is it improbable that it is his own emotional though perhaps scarcely recognized "concernment" in the matter which lends such zest to the performance.

Ostensibly Dryden had ample and adequate motive (apart from royal command) for his enterprise in *Absalom and Achitophel*. He would bring to bear upon the "Hot distempered State" the sovereign remedy of cool reason. He will be in the long and honorable line of gentlemen wits serving the cause of a well-conducted rationalism. Spectator's qualifications for the writing of Horatian epistles seem exactly to fit this side of Dryden's achievement: "He that would excell in this kind must have a good Fund of strong Masculine Sense: To this there must be joined a thorough Knowledge of Mankind, together with an Insight into the Business, and the prevailing Humours of the Age. Our Author must have his Mind well seasoned with the finest Precepts of Morality, and be filled with nice Reflections upon the bright and dark sides of human Life; He must be a master of refined Raillery, and understand the Delicacies, as well as the Absurdities of Conversation. He must have a lively turn of Wit, with an easie and concise manner of Expression; Everything he says, must be in a free and disengaged manner. He must be guilty of nothing that betrays the air of a Recluse, but appear a Man of the World throughout." This is an admirable description of the style, and yet not quite enough, one feels, to account for the inimitable, calculated, nonchalant insolence of such passages as the opening:

> In pious times, ere priestcraft did begin,
> Before polygamy was made a sin;
> When man on many multiplied his kind,
> Ere one to one was cursedly confin'd;
>
> . . . .
>
> Then Israel's monarch after Heaven's own heart,
> His vigorous warmth did variously impart
> To wives and slaves; and, wide as his command,
> Scatter'd his Maker's image thro' the land.

or

> (Gods they had tried of every shape and size,
> That god-smiths could produce, or priests devise.)
>
> (l. 49)

No description of Horatian raillery, however perspicacious, can quite cover this unless the ironic element outlined above—the sense of the opponent being hoist with his own petard—is taken into account. Of all Dryden's critics, Reuben Brower has perhaps done the greatest justice to what he calls the "imaginative union of tones and levels," the "blend of manners" which is the essence of Dryden's witty heroic or mixed style. It is the exact stance or poise of the sophisticated court spokesman, supremely aware of the social nuance of language, supremely aware of the reactions and assumptions of his heterogeneous audience, and confident, at least then, in the heat of the battle in which his poem played no insignificant a part, of an alternative structure of values to stand against those he deflates with such consummate and impudent irony.

A comparison with *The Medall*, on the one hand, and the satirical passage in *The Hind and the Panther*, on the other, will make clear the great gain in ironic deflation which the scriptural mechanism allows.

In *The Medall*, for instance, Shaftesbury,

> A vermin wriggling in th'usurper's ear
> Bart'ring his venal wit for sums of gold,
>
> . . . .

cast himself into the saintlike mold;
Groan'd, sigh'd and pray'd, while godliness was gain,
The loudest bagpipe of the squeaking train.

(l. 31)

In *The Hind and the Panther* the "*wolfish* race"

Appear with belly gaunt, and famish'd face:
Never was so deform'd a beast of grace.
His ragged tail betwixt his legs he wears,
Close clapp'd for shame; but his rough crest he rears,
And pricks up his predestinating ears.

. . . .

With teeth untried, and rudiments of claws,
Your first essay was on your native laws;
Those having torn with ease, and trampled down,
Your fangs you fasten'd on the miter'd crown,
And freed from God and monarchy your town.
What tho' your native kennel still be small,
Bounded betwixt a puddle and a wall;
Yet your victorious colonies are sent
Where the north ocean girds the continent.
Quickn'd with fire below, your monsters breed
In fenny Holland, and in fruitful Tweed:
And like the first, the last effects to be
Drawn to the dregs of a democracy.
As, where in fields the fairy rounds are seen,
A rank sour herbage rises on the green;
So, springing where these midnight elves advance,
Rebellion prints the footsteps of the dance.

(l. 160)

The perfect articulation of the verse, the variety, copiousness, and distinction of the language does not alter the fact that this is a variety of the direct vilification and abuse with which royalists had been belaboring their presumptuous inferiors on the republican or Presbyterian or Puritan side since the early 1630s. The traditional approach is once more directly stated in the *Epilogue to Amboyna:*

Well may they boast themselves an ancient nation,
For they were bred ere manners were in fashion;
And their new commonwealth has set 'em free
Only from honour and civility.

In *Absalom and Achitophel*, on the other hand, the obliquity made possible by the biblical characterization allows a far greater keenness and density of irony, and, paradoxically perhaps, a greater realism of treatment. The "if the cap fits" effect of Dryden's keen analysis of the "malcontents of all the Israelites" is due both to the apparent objectivity and to the witty aptness of the applications:

> The best, (and of the princes some were such,)
> Who thought the pow'r of monarchy too much;
> Mistaken men, and patriots in their hearts;
> Not wicked, but seduc'd by impious arts.
> By these the springs of property were bent,
> And wound so high, they crack'd the government.
> The next for interest sought t'embroil the State,
> To sell their duty at a dearer rate;
> And make their Jewish markets of the throne,
> Pretending public good, to serve their own.
> Others thought kings an useless heavy load,
> Who cost too much, and did too little good.
> These were for laying honest David by,
> On principles of pure good husbandry.
>
> . . . .
>
> Who follow next, a double danger bring,
> Not only hating David, but the king:
> The Solymaean rout, well-vers'd of old
> In godly faction, and in treason bold;
> Cow'ring and quaking at a conqu'ror's sword;
> But lofty to a lawful prince restor'd;
>
> . . . .
>
> Hot Levites headed these; who, pull'd before
> From th'ark, which in the Judges' days they bore,
> Resum'd their cant, and with a zealous cry
> Pursued their old belov'd Theocracy:
> Where Sanhedrin and priest enslav'd the nation,
> And justified their spoils by inspiration.
>
> (l. 495)

In the individual portraits the biblical mask enables Dryden to exhibit the qualities the royalists constantly satirized—meanness of birth or behavior, hypocrisy or pharisaism, mercenary motivation, not, as Butler had done, through burlesque logic and burlesque action, but by sly reference to the scripture-reader's own consecrated tenets of behavior. It is as if Dryden is not criticizing his victims as falling short of his standards; on the contrary, he is ironically commending them for maintaining their own standards, or, at least, their version of those standards. Shimei, for instance

> Did wisely from expensive sins refrain,
> And never broke the Sabbath, but for gain;
> Nor ever was he known an oath to vent,
> Or curse, unless against the government.
> Thus heaping wealth, by the most ready way
> Among the Jews, which was to cheat and pray,
> The city, to reward his pious hate
> Against his master, chose him magistrate.
>
> .   .   .   .
>
> During his office, treason was no crime;
> The sons of Belial had a glorious time;
> For Shimei, tho'not prodigal of pelf,
> Yet lov'd his wicked neighbor as himself.
>
> .   .   .   .
>
> If any leisure time he had from pow'r,
> (Because 'tis sin to misemploy an hour,)
> His bus'ness was, by writing, to persuade
> That kings were useless, and a clog to trade;
>
> .   .   .   .
>
> Cool was his kitchen, tho' his brains were hot.
> Such frugal virtue malice may accuse,
> But sure 'twas necessary to the Jews;
> For towns once burnt such magistrates require
> As dare not tempt God's providence by fire,
> With spiritual food he fed his servants well,
> But free from flesh that made the Jews rebel;
> And Moses' laws he held in more account,
> For forty days of fasting in the mount.
>
> (l. 587)

Thus aristocratic disdain for the "rascal rabble . . . whom kings no titles gave, and God no grace" is both objectified and sanctioned by such travesty of Holy Writ.

THE TWO ANCIENT WORLDS

The values against which these ironies are set can in general be labelled Augustan and divided under the heads Church, King, and classical culture.

It is, however, the latter, with its aspirations towards neoclassical sublimity and nobility, which is most clearly and closely woven into the texture of the verse. In the panegyric passages, though these are kept within the framework of biblical reference, the Virgilian allusions are most marked, and the values evoked are significantly the familiar attributes of the life of the man of honor—magnanimity and the liberal profession of arts and arms. Barzillai, for instance, "practic'd the court,"

> not the courtier's art:
> Large was his wealth, but larger was his heart,
> Which well the noblest objects knew to choose,
> The fighting warrior, and recording Muse.
>
> (l. 825)

The elegy upon his son is closely Virgilian and diametrically opposed to any mood of biblical elegiac in such a way as to place the maximum distance between the two ancient worlds so subtly employed by Dryden to focus and evaluate contemporary affairs:

> His eldest hope, with every grace adorn'd,
> By me (so Heav'n will have it) always mourn'd,
> And always honor'd, snatch'd in manhood's prime
> B' unequal fates, and Providence's crime;
> Yet not before the goal of honor won,
> All parts fulfill'd of subject and of son:
> Swift was the race, but short the time to run.
>
> . . . .
>
> O ancient honor! O unconquer'd hand,
> Whom foes unpunish'd never could withstand!
> But Israel was unworthy of thy name;
> Short is the date of all immoderate fame.
>
> (l. 831)

Indeed, all the panegyrics to the small but faithful band are thus dexterously touched and flavored with classical echo, myth, image, or concept. The tour de force is the greater for the ostensible consistency with the biblical frame of reference. Thus Amiel, chief of the Sanhedrin, and enjoying at the end "the sabbath of his toils," emerges unmistakably as an antique rhetor:

> Of ancient race by birth, but nobler yet
> In his own worth, and without title great:
> The Sanhedrin long time as chief he rul'd,
> Their reason guided, and their passion cool'd:

So dext'rous was he in the crown's defense,
So form'd to speak a loyal nation's sense,
That, as their band was Israel's tribes in small,
So fit was he to represent them all.
Now rasher charioteers the seat ascend,
Whose loose careers his steady skill command:
They, like th'unequal ruler of the day,
Misguide the seasons, and mistake the way.

(l. 900)

It is in the light of these perceptions that the crowning achievement of the poem—the character of Corah—can best be appreciated. For it is in this character that the two great rival systems of evaluation, which, through subtle repetition throughout the poem have attained a wide symbolic significance, are simultaneously brought to bear, in a kind of double battery, upon the exposure of the arch-hypocrite, the arch-pretender to importance. Classical monumental fame, Mosaic redemption, perjury and prophecy all combine to articulate the inimitable, densely packed scorn of the following lines:

Yet, Corah, thou shalt from oblivion pass:
Erect thyself, thou monumental brass,
High as the serpent of thy metal made,
While nations stand secure beneath thy shade.
What tho' his birth were base, yet comets rise
From earthy vapors, ere they shine in skies.
Prodigious actions may as well be done
By weaver's issue, as by prince's son.
This arch-attestor for the public good
By that one deed ennobles all his blood.
Who ever ask'd the witnesses' high race,
Whose oath with martyrdom did Stephen grace?
Ours was a Levite, and as times went then,
His tribe were God Almighty's gentlemen.

.   .   .   .

His long chin prov'd his wit; his saintlike grace
A church vermilion, and a Moses' face.

.   .   .   .

Some future truths are mingled in his book;
But where the witness fail'd, the prophet spoke:

.   .   .   .

Let Israel's foes suspect his heav'nly call,
And rashly judge his writ apocryphal;

> Our laws for such affronts have forfeits made;
> He takes his life, who takes away his trade.
>
> (l. 632)

The utter rascality and presumption of this counterfeit are themselves raised to epic proportions; given a sheer magnitude of audacity by words charged with the dignity of classical association. Oblivion, monument, brass, prodigious actions, shining comets, and ennobled blood, are responsible for inflating the dimensions of the arch-attestor. On the other hand, the sarcastic biblical reference to Mosaic serpents, prophecies, calls, apocrypha, with the additional echoes of Deuteronomy and Shylock in the last line, are responsible for the deflating effect which punctuates the whole passage. Dryden is as it were constantly setting up his ninepins only to knock them down immediately. Any possible comic sympathy for the sheer size of the audacity (such as Jack claims is aroused for Mac Flecknoe in somewhat the same manner as for Falstaf) is instantly neutralized here. For, in addition to the clashing associations indicated above, Corah's irredeemable social inferiority is constantly kept in mind—by the nonchalant contempt of the colloquialisms ("the Lord knows where," "as times went then"), the lip-curled scorn of "God Almighty's gentlemen"—which are given for the particular delectation of the cultivated élite among whom this weaver's issue will never *rise* to belong.

THE STRUGGLE FOR POWER

The subtly denigrating purpose of the satire is thus achieved, but it does not exhaust the full intention with which Dryden went to work. There remains to be considered the way in which he places his contemptibly vulgar opponents in the context of the struggle for power in the state. For this is no less the object of his enterprise than that manipulation of anger, laughter, and scorn which is the aim of satire. These successors of Hudibras are to appear as pretenders, not to an outworn code of chivalry, but to real political power. Dryden's view of this aspect of the political disturbances he dealt with is very clear and decisive. In *The Medall* he defines the succession issue as the conflict between "Property and Soveriegn Sway." It is Harrington's perception of the politics of property, but Dryden, of course, unlike the republican author of *Oceana*, interprets the sway of property as anarchic, and sees behind the Whig "princes," themselves misled, leading and using others, that bugbear of the conservative mind, the "Almighty crowd."

> Almighty crowd, thou shorten'st all dispute;
> Pow'r is thy essence; wit thy attribute!

Nor faith nor reason make thee at a stay,
Thou leaps't o'er all eternal truths in thy Pindaric way!
(l. 91)

Dryden's satire constantly reiterates the connection between property, money interest, the merchant classes, and sedition. These are presented as proliferating varieties of self-interest—low, grasping, mercenary, and hypocritical—in opposition to faith, reason, and the eternal verities. It is the linking of these motifs which characterizes the livelier parts of *The Medall*, and it is worth noticing that it is to be found, in *Absalom* part 2, only in Dryden's section—the part dealing with the "troop of busy spirits." There is none of it in Tate's, which is largely devoted to generalized argument upon the rights and wrongs of the situation. In *Absalom and Achitophel* the problem of power in the state is the essential significance of the last and inmost sphere of allusion—the Miltonic—with which we have now to deal.

Miltonic echoes in the poem have frequently been noticed. Shaftesbury as Tempter is deliberately reminiscent of Milton's arch-tempter. In *The Medall* he becomes "a vermin wriggling in the'usurper's ear" (l. 31). Here

Him he attempts with studied arts to please,
And sheds his venom in such words as these.
(l. 228)

and, conclusively, in the characteristic Miltonic inversion which follows the susceptible Absalom's fatal rationalization "Desire of greatness is a godlike sin":

Him staggering so when hell's dire agent found,
While fainting Virtue scarce maintain'd her ground,
He pours fresh forces in, and thus replies.
(l. 373)

If, as Dryden well knew, and as he points out in the preface to *Religio Laici*, the Bible is a magazine for Papist and Sectary alike to furnish themselves with the weapon of authority for whatever disobedience and rebellion their interests dictate, Milton was a source nearer home both of epic sublimity and of republican argument. "And 't is to be noted by the way," Dryden continues in the same preface, "that the doctrines of king-killing and deposing, which have been taken up only by the worst party of the Papists, the most frontless flatterers of the Pope's authority, have been espous'd, defended, and are still maintain'd by the whole body of Non-conformists and Republicans. 'Tis but dubbing themselves the people of God, which 'tis the interest of their preachers to tell them they are, and their own interest to believe; and after that, they cannot dip into the Bible, but one text or another will turn up for their purpose; if they are under persecution, (as they call it,) then that is a mark of their election; if they flourish, then God works miracles for their deliverance, and the saints are to possess the earth."

The allusion to *Paradise Lost* puts a further double edge upon Dryden's rapier. Through the identification of Achitophel with Satan, the historical struggle between "Property and Sovereign Sway" can be seen as the epic and eternal struggle between the forces of good and evil. At the same time, through the subtle sophistry of the temptation itself, he is enabled to dramatize the very characteristics of argument which he attributes in the preface to *Religio Laici* to "the whole body of Non-conformists and Republicans" when they rationalize the scriptures in the light of Calvinist theology. The equation is: sophistical prevarications based on the sanctimonious forcing of texts to ulterior purposes equals the republicans' lust for power equals the ultimate evil that menaces the ordered state, and threatens to set up in its stead the Golden Calf of Commonwealth.

Thus Achitophel's first attempt upon Absalom consists of the classic Machiavellian appeal to *virtu,* diametrically opposed, in its assertion of the preeminence of Fortune and heroic will, to the idea of supreme Providence.

> How long wilt thou the general joy detain,
> Starve and defraud the people of thy reign?
> Content ingloriously to pass thy days
> Like one of Virtue's fools that feeds on praise;
> Till thy fresh glories, which now shine so bright,
> Grow stale and tarnish with our daily sight.
> Believe me, royal youth, thy fruit must be
> Or gather'd ripe, or rot upon the tree.
> Heav'n has to all allotted, soon or late,
> Some lucky revolution of their fate;
> Whose motions if we watch and guide with skill,
> (For human good depends on human will,)
> Our Fortune rolls as from a smooth descent,
> And from the first impression takes the bent:
> But, if unseiz'd, she glides away like wind,
> And leaves repenting Folly far behind.
>
> . . . .
>
> Had thus old David, from whose loins you spring,
> Not dar'd, when Fortune call'd him, to be king,
> At Gath an exile he might still remain,
> And Heaven's anointing oil had been in vain.

(l. 244)

The seed planted, and duly taking root, Achitophel then, in his second encounter, parries the wavering Absalom's pangs of conscience with a neat shift
of premise. His fresh forces consist of an argument from Providence, not
against it:

> Th' eternal God, supremely good and wise,
> Imparts not these prodigious gifts in vain:
> What wonders are reserv'd to bless your reign!
> Against your will, your arguments have shown,
> Such virtue's only giv'n to guide a throne.
>
> (l. 376)

One is reminded of Butler's Hypocritical Non-Conformist, who "does
not care to have any thing founded in Right, but left at large to *Dispensations* and *Outgoings* of Providence, as he shall find Occasion to expound
them to the best advantage of his own Will and Interest." But this is far from
the only source of prevarication in the tempter's onslaught. The speech is,
of course, a tissue of sophistry, a shining example of the art of having one's
cake and eating it. Thus Absalom is told not to let his father's love for him
enchant his generous mind, since that love is merely

> Nature's trick to propagate her kind.
>
> (l. 424)

In the subsequent breath, however, he is urged to put that love to the proof.

> God said he lov'd your father; could he bring
> A better proof, than to anoint him king?
>
> (l. 429)

From the Dispensations and Outgoings of Providence to "women's lechery"—
all is grist to Achitophel's sophisticated mill—as all, indeed, is grist to Dryden's
sophisticated audience.

> If so, by force he wishes to be gain'd;
> Like women's lechery, to seem constrain'd.
> Doubt not: but when he most affects the frown,
> Commit a pleasing rape upon the crown.
>
> (l. 471)

It was perhaps less "because Charles was a witty man" that Dryden was
able to write his masterpiece than because Dryden belonged to Charles' party, and thus could share the supreme self-assurance that is the prerogative
of the privileged class.

Whether it was the lack of this self-confidence or simply the lack of

requisite ability which made effective reply to *Absalom and Achitophel* or
The Medall so difficult, it would be hard to say—most likely the latter, since
the Tory satire of the time is no more distinguished than the Whig efforts
at defence. These fall into two chief kinds. One group, the most numerous,
casts indignant, at times positively hysterical, abuse at the author, denigrating
his wit, reminding him, with ample reference to Judas Iscariot, of his
panegyric to Cromwell, and flatly denying, though with pathetically
transparent literal-mindedness, the relevance of his matter. Too many instances would be tedious; one or two will serve to show the state of impotent fury to which Dryden's ironic effectiveness reduced his adversaries:

> Near to the King he falls on Monmouth next,
> Makes the Story of proud Absalom his Text.
> This Noble Duke he makes his Absalom,
> As if a Traitor to the King and Crown;
> Oh thou Incongruous Fool, what parallel
> Thats congruous twixt these two canst thou tell?
> (Absalom was . . .)
> A compleat Rogue, Ambitious, Arrogant,
> Ungrateful, Lying, a Dissembling Wretch, . . .
> And must brave Monmouth be his parallel,
> By renegado Wits of Old Cromwell.
> Five hundred Guinnies makes him sell his sense,
> His King and Country, and his Conscience.
> (*A Key* (*with a Whip*) to open the Mystery, and
> Iniquity of the Poem called Absalom and Achitophel)

"He has an easiness in Rime, and a knack at versifying, and can make
a slight thing seem pretty and clinquant; and his Fort is, that he is a indifferent good Versificator. If at any time he has wit of his own, tis in Rayling,
when the venome of his malice provokes his fancy. His Panegyricks are full
of such nauseous flattery, that they are Libels; and he is now become so in-
famous, that his Libels will be thought Panegyricks" (Shadwell, *The Medal
of John Bayes*: A Satyr against Folly and Knavery).

> Thou stil'st it Satyr, to call Names, Rogue, Whore,
> Traytor, and Rebel, and a thousand more.
> An Oyster-wench is sure thy Muse of late,
> And all thy Helicons at Billingsgate.
> Good humour thou so awkwardly put'st on,
> It fits like Modish Clothes upon a Clown.
> (*The Medal of John Bayes*)

Clearly Dryden had nothing to fear from his colleagues. And the one adversary [Shadwell] who apparently went too far on the subject of "wretched mercenary Bayes . . . Pied thing! half Wit! half Fool!" and coward and slave to boot, received his proper punishment in due time.

The second type of reply borrows the apparatus of *Absalom* and applies it to the Papists, to the tyranny, lust, and pride of Rome, or to the desire for arbitrary power of the Tories, who "have tryed all ways imaginable, to push on the people to a Rebellion that (they) might have a pretence to cut their throats" (S. Pordage, *The Medal Revers'd:* A Satyre against Persecution). *Azaria and Hushai* may stand as an example:

> In impious Times, when Priest-craft was at height,
> And all the Deadly Sins esteemed light;
> When that Religion only was a Stale,
> And some bow'd down to God, and some to Baal;
>
> .   .   .   .
>
> These subtil Priests, in Habit black and grave;
> Each man a Saint in shew, in Heart a Knave,
> Did in Judea swarm, grew great withall,
> And like th'Egyptian Frogs to Court they crawl:
> Where, like them, too, they never are at rest;
> But Bed and Board of Kings with Filth infest.

Even Dryden himself could not repeat the achievement of *Absalom and Achitophel.* By 1688 the tide had turned. The alliance between landed wealth and city wealth which changed the nature of the monarchy in England made its repetition impossible. The revolution changed completely, or signalized the change in, the alignment of social forces from which Dryden's satire had drawn its strength. Since the long battle between court and city was now virtually over, the state poem which reflected it largely disappears. The characteristic political poetry of the eighteenth century—Whig panegyric and Tory satire—are works of quite another color.

Though perhaps no eighteenth century satire or panegyric, Whig or Tory, can be fully appreciated without a knowledge of the works dealt with in [*The Dial of Virtue*], nevertheless, in respect to poems on affairs of state, *Absalom and Achitophel* is the last of its kind. For the division between Whig and Tory was never again as momentous, radical, or fateful as the struggle between republican and royalist for the future of the nation. The literature of affairs of state in the seventeenth century, of whatever quality or tendency, had been nourished upon that sense of destiny, and upon the inflamed passions, and passionately held ideologies, which had sprung from it.

Thenceforth the tendency would be towards a generalized didacticism; in Tory satire, for instance, on the vanity of human wishes, or the baseness of man; or towards the excoriation of an individual personality robbed of his significance as representative in a struggle between great opposing forces, upon the issue of which the destiny of the entire nation depends. Or, in Whig panegyric, a similar tendency would take the form of the heroic hypostasized as Britannia, or Empire, or Commerce.

After a brief continuation of the older epic and historic presentation of great personality in the shape of the Benevolent Monarch, William of Orange, and Marlborough, none of the Georges seemed able to fill the role of hero; the court yielded its powers to a managed parliament, manipulated by a small circle of political oligarchs, and the glorification of mercantilism and trade came more and more to take the place both of the princely heroic of a court culture, and the redemptive, or messianic, heroic of a Puritanism newly aware of itself, newly surging up from the once inarticulate depths of the nation. It is not by chance that the Augustan peak of literary achievement is a mock-heroic satire, in which the heroic standard has receded from the contemporary scene to the remote Imperia of Rome, and the content, though splendidly and seriously general, is nevertheless the characteristic concern of a social, literary, and cultural establishment.

MARTIN PRICE

Dryden and Dialectic:
The Heroic Plays

Ev'n mighty monarchs oft are meanly born,
And kings by birth, to lowest rank return;
All subject to the pow'r of giddy chance,
For fortune can depress, or can advance:
But true nobility is of the mind,
Not giv'n by chance, and not to chance resign'd
— Translation of Boccaccio's
Sigismonda and Guiscardo

The world of the heroic play is a world of chance. Events are never predictable. Victories are abruptly overturned; power shifts between one faction and another; the populace is swayed by the latest voice. For the central characters love descends suddenly and irresistibly, and where it remains constant, its claims conflict with other loyalties, to parent or king; it is likely at any moment to become half of an impossible moral choice. Those who are indifferent to the claims of love are driven by harsh compulsions of ambition; they fix their desire upon an object that is always precarious. There is no clear indication that their intention will succeed or their sacrifice be rewarded; no one can foresee how his life or even his day will end.

In such a world the common specter is meaninglessness. The gods are ineffectual; they do nothing to confirm the values of men. To the lazy sensualist they seem gods at their ease, untroubled by the "little emmets" below; to the fiery egotist they seem criminal gods who have won their own power by ruthlessness and condone cruelty in men. It remains, then, for man to create his own meaning and his own values by self-assertion. The traditional

From *To the Palace of Wisdom: Studies in Order and Energy from Dryden to Blake.* © 1964 by Martin Price. Southern Illinois University Press, 1964.

codes by which he lives have often become a travesty of true Order: the Emperor who demands reverence may be a debauched and guilt-ridden old man, as in *Aureng-Zebe*. In a world where the representatives of Order are too often self-centered, power-seeking men, the debased traditions seem more vicious than a state of nature. Men manipulate, disregard, reject these traditions rather than surrender their will, and they must do this whether they are slaves of appetite or defenders of their own integrity.

In this world the hero stands out by the fullness and firmness of his commitment. Only he can be fully tested, for he will not bend to expediency and cannot live in a confusion of orders; he must remain intransigently the lover, the patriot, whatever he has chosen to be. He may have no basis for this choice but will, the mere act of having chosen; the appeal to honor or other sanctions is hard to maintain in a world of impossible choices and of overriding chance. He may exult in his strength of will; it is not the calm or serenity of the passionless Stoic he will attain, but the posture of defiance and a passion of self-fulfillment. The utmost self-assertion is achieved when every reward is withheld from virtue, when the defiance must be carried to the point of furious battle or scornful self-sacrifice. This extreme becomes a spectacle of heroic obduracy, its gestures large and formal, its language preposterously orotund. Yet, even as it risks self-parody (and indeed courts it and accepts it in its defiance) it provides us with an image—stylized and purified—of a common situation most men will recognize and find true to the center of their own moral experience.

These works are an artful playing with postures that, in less pure form, are imposed upon all of us by skeptical minds or a precarious world. The playing—which allows us to see with comparative detachment what so often immerses us, to set at a distance by style what more often we face all about us as predicament—may both account for the extravagance of heroic drama and help to explain its appeal to a worldly and sophisticated audience. A comparably sophisticated audience today might expect a tragicomic extravagance that moves closer to the farcical; our present-day stage is filled with tragical farces—by Anouilh, Ionesco, Dürrenmatt, Genet, who accommodate the stylized gestures but confront them with the ludicrous. Ionesco professes to turn away from Molière because all of Molière's problems can be resolved. "There is no solution to the intolerable," Ionesco writes, "and only that which is intolerable is truly theatrical." He wants a "hard comedy, without finesse, excessive. No dramatic comedies either. But a return to the intolerable. Push everything to a state of paroxysm, there where the sources of tragedy lie. Create a theatre of violence: violently comic, violently dramatic. . . . Avoid psychology, or rather give it a metaphysical dimension."

What Ionesco has pushed to the extreme of the farcically intolerable, the heroic play—at least in Dryden's hands—holds closer to traditional tragic form. But it is obvious, not simply from the tragicomic endings, but also from the argumentativeness of its heroes, the absurd effrontery of their heroism, the dance-like symmetries of their predicament, that the heroic play is trying for an experience different from the tragic. In making fate so obvious, oppressive, and busy an agent, Dryden prevents the action from moving inexorably to its central tragic reversal; instead, we are given a succession of reversals. The solution of any one problem only introduces the next. The forfuitous world makes these characters almost comically impotent. Only their intransigence gives them stability. These characters are not immovable, they are inextinguishable; and their movement, the constant reforming and redirection of their will and self, is the only form of constancy available to them. Dryden's heroic plays are closer to the comic than he himself ever admitted, or than most readers have been ready to see. But they also accommodate a near-tragic awareness of the instability of human assertion, even at its most splendid. As with Donne's lovers, of whom we are reminded so often, the heroic is carried to the point where its magnificence derives from its precariousness. Dryden's heroes are statements of the problematic nature of heroism, and as such they thrive on excess. They are themselves, as are so many of their speeches, conceived with the levity of brilliant overstatement, the dialectical excess of an extreme position.

Within the fortuitous world of the heroic play there are several attitudes taken toward experience, or, in Pascal's terms, several orders of experience. The naturalistic view, which is commonly taken by villains, has its coloring of Hobbesian thought and Machiavellian application. The naturalistic character seeks power for the sake of satisfying his desires or pursues it as an end in itself. Such a character may be the slave of a ruthless mistress who demands an act of treason before he can enjoy her; or it may be a cold, reptilian seductress like Lyndaraxa, whose only passion is for domination:

> Yes! I avow th' ambition of my soul,
> To be that one to live without control!
> And that's another happiness to me,
> To be so happy as but one can be.
>   (1 *Conquest of Granada*, 2.148–51)

Lyndaraxa is the quintessential Hobbesian woman: her life is a restless pursuit of power, and she can be content with nothing less than supremacy. In fact, Lyndaraxa is a grotesque heightening of what Hobbes saw in all men, and her death—like Nourmahal's in *Aureng-Zebe*—is the final reduction of all her self-assertion to the phantasy of madness. Her disenchanted lover dies after giving her a fatal blow, and Lyndaraxa exclaims:

> Die for us both; I have not leisure now;
> A crown is come, and will not fate allow:
> And yet I feel something like death is near.
> My guards, my guards,—
> Let not that ugly skeleton appear!
> Sure Destiny mistakes; this death's not mine;
> She dotes, and meant to cut another line.
> Tell her I am a queen—but 'tis too late;
> Dying, I charge rebellion on my fate.
> Bow down, ye slaves:—   [*To the Moors.*]
> Bow quickly down, and your submission show.—
>   [*They bow.*]
> I'm pleased to taste an empire ere I go.
>   [*Dies.*]
>   (2 *Conquest,* 5.4.125–36)

Dryden departs from Hobbes in showing Lyndaraxa's anxiety about fate, her need—in a delusive moment of triumph—to domineer over fate itself and to taste, if only for an instant, what her appetite has taken as its only object. There is a magnificent consistency in her nature, and Dryden can realize its frightening power. He does something even more outrageous at the close of *Aureng-Zebe* with the death of Nourmahal, who rushes in feverish with the poison she has drunk:

> I burn, I more than burn; I am all fire.
> See how my mouth and nostrils flames expire!
> I'll not come near myself—
> Now I'm a burning lake, it rolls and flows;
> I'll rush, and pour it all upon my foes.

And as she sees her husband, the old Emperor:

> Pull, pull that reverend piece of timber near:
> Throw't on—'tis dry—'twill burn—
> Ha, ha! how my old husband crackles there!

It is all ludicrous, extravagant in the manner of Ovid; yet its tortured wit has a curious force in catching the explosion of a mind that can no longer contain the pressure of its will. These death scenes are the culmination, in each case, of the natural energy of passion. It breaks through the limits of reality into the regions of madness where it can still sustain itself.

The cases of Lyndaraxa and Nourmahal are only the extremes of the naturalistic view of life conceived according to Pascal's order of the flesh.

Tellingly, in both *The Conquest of Granada* (1670) and *Aureng-Zebe* (1675) the ruler is an old man who has outlived the active energy of conquest and declined into a debased sensuality. Of the Emperor in *Aureng-Zebe* a courtier remarks:

> So he, who in his youth for glory strove,
> Would recompence his age with ease and love.
>
> (2.1)

Still the Emperor, however sad his decline, is capable of total arrogance when he learns that a subject has been pursuing the woman he hopes to make his mistress:

> Did he, my slave, presume to look so high?
> That crawling insect, who from mud began,
> Warmed by my beams, and kindled into man?
> Durst he, who does but for my pleasure live,
> Intrench on love, my great prerogative.
>
> (2.1)

The arrogance is painfully threadbare; the Emperor's image of the sun breeding life out of slime no longer carries the traditional force of the King as vice-regent of God. This Sun King is a petulant and impotent old man, and his despotic dream that all exists for his sole pleasure only confirms the barrenness of his self-assertion. As in Pascal's disenchanting view of the order of the flesh, power has ceased to have function except for the sake of failing pleasure; the impositions of the ruler are all imposition, without a trace of sanction or dedication.

Again, in lesser figures, we find the simple rule of appetite. Abdalla sees the futility of his love for Lyndaraxa, but he cannot resist:

> This enchanted place
> Like Circe's isle, is peopled with a race
> Of dogs and swine; yet though their fate I know,
> I look with pleasure, and am turning too.
>
> (1 *Conquest*, 3.93–96)

The very clarity of utterance emphasizes the breakdown of rational control. It is, in this case, the language of the knowing victim, and it can parody the idiom of religion:

> Your love I will believe with hoodwink'd eyes—
> In faith, much merit in much blindness lies.
>
> (2 *Conquest*, 2.2.138–39)

Or, at the last:

> O that you still could cheat, and I believe!
>
> (2 *Conquest,* 4.2.121)

Beside these naturalistic characters Dryden places another group. These are characters of principle as well as passion, figures who have the energy of the naturalistic characters without their limiting egoism. Almanzor bursts into *The Conquest of Granada* an invincible hero, a natural man. He has no known ancestry. He is free of the obligations imposed upon man in general by a social contract or upon particular men by their birth into an ordered society. He can say to the king, Boabdelin:

> Obey'd as sovereign by thy subjects be,
> But know that I alone am king of me.
> I am as free as nature first made man,
> Ere the base laws of servitude began,
> When wild in woods the noble savage ran.
>
> (1 *Conquest,* 1.205–9)

When Boabdelin hears this, his immediate response is that of a Hobbesian theorist; man in the state of nature is a wolf to man, and therefore the natural man who survives in society "should be hunted like a beast of prey" (212). But Almanzor's role as natural man implies a fuller conception of nature. He rejects Boabdelin's sovereignty, but he invokes the old Stoic law of nature as the rule of justice, the social dimension of universal Order. Almanzor's first words upon encountering the war of factions had been:

> I cannot stay to ask what cause is best;
> But this is so to me, because opprest.
>
> (1 *Conquest,* 1.128–29)

So, now, he can reproach Boabdelin for failure to be a just king:

> I saw th' oppress'd, and thought it did belong
> To a king's office to redress the wrong;
> I brought that succor which thou ought'st to bring,
> And so, in nature, am thy subjects' king.
>
> (1 *Conquest,* 1.218–21)

Almanzor, then, is not the Hobbesian image of the natural man. He is not self-seeking; rather he is immediately moved to impose justice, as if by a natural instinct. He is a rebel against the existing social order, but he rebels in the cause of an authentic order. His rebelliousness is the necessary criticism of a mock-order, and his energy is the very pulse of life that should animate a true order:

> Vast is his courage, boundless is his mind,
> Rough as a storm, and humorous as wind:
> Honor's the only idol of his eyes.
>
> (1 *Conquest,* 1.253–55)

He has the true authority of the "one great soul" who can command and order the restive populace; he is, in fact, the seventeenth-century superman.

Rough and wild, Almanzor provides a splendid contrast to the decadent Boabdelin, whose own legitimacy of rule is highly questionable in any case. But Almanzor is suspicious of all kings and believes none worthy of respect; he imputes to the Christian Ferdinand's true kindness and legitimacy of rule the same base, mercenary power-quest that he finds in Boabdelin and others. Like the satirist—whose name is derived from that rough beast, the satyr, in the folk etymology of the Renaissance—he is uncontrolled in his vehemence and indiscriminate in his suspicions. To that extent he resembles the naturalistic characters who explain away all legitimacy as the pretension of power; yet, unlike them, Almanzor holds to a principle of honor and legitimacy he finds embodied in no one but himself. He is not without a vision of a moral order, but he questions every actual claimant to that title. Nor does he rely upon any divine force beyond fallible men. When the Christian Duke of Arcos says of Ferdinand, "My king his hope from heaven's assistance draws," Almanzor mockingly replies, "The Moors have heaven, and me, to assist their cause." Almanzor is the loneliest character of all: he trusts no human order, he relies on no divine order, he creates his own.

Friendship—the personal, chosen relationship—outweighs in his mind all the impositions of sovereignty. He is a transparent man, without a mask:

> My heart's so plain,
> That men on every passing thought may look,
> Like fishes gliding in a crystal brook.
>
> (1 *Conquest,* 4.1.43–45)

He is also a man whose self-assertion is his only form of stability:

> The word, which I have giv'n, shall stand like fate.
>
> (1 *Conquest,* 3.9)

He becomes in fact, not only his own king but his own god. When he scorns Abdalla and withdraws his friendship, he professes to doom him:

> Like heav'n, I need but only to stand still,
> And, not concurring to thy life, I kill.

And godlike he commands fate:

> Thou know'st this place,
> And like a clock wound up, strik'st here for me;
> Now Chance, assert thy own inconstancy,
> And Fortune, fight that thou may'st Fortune be!
>   (2 *Conquest,* 3.1.193–96)

When Almanzor finds himself suddenly numbed by "the lethargy of love," he fights the chains of Almahide's beauty and struggles against her fettering of his will. When he finally accepts love, he accepts it heroically. Just as Nourmahal in her death throes cries, "I am all fire," so Almanzor embraces his love completely, "I am all o'er love, / Nay, I am love." This fury of identification is the heroic response, a full acceptance in contrast to the overpowering consumption by passion of Nourmahal. It is only the restraint of Almahide that prevents Almanzor from dismissing her vows to Boabdelin; her own integrity meets his and masters it with a rigorous observance of the scruples of honor. Yet, even as she restrains him, Almahide recognizes the value of his love. Until she knew Almanzor she "with a vulgar good [was] dully blest."

> 'Twas life becalmed, without a gentle breath;
> Though not too cold, yet motionless as death.
> A heavy quiet state; but love, all strife,
> All rapid, is the hurricane of life.
>   (1 *Conquest,* 5.3.200–3)

"Rough as a storm, and humorous as wind," Almanzor becomes the animating power that awakens her to life, but it is a power she must govern for fear it destroy the life it creates:

> You, like some greedy cormorant, devour
> All my whole life can give you, in an hour.
>   (1 *Conquest,* 5.3.288–89)

She must impose upon both of them the sacrifice of their fulfillment for the sake of honor, the acceptance of a course that denies them every reward.

Throughout the play, we have, in contrast to Almahide's integrity, Lyndaraxa's artful teasing of her would-be lovers, alternately fanning their passion and dismissing them as their usefulness ebbs. She loves the king, whoever he happens finally to be. Almahide, in contrast, suffers the torture of conflict but sustains her self-command: "My heart's not mine but all my actions are." When Almanzor tempts Almahide most severely with a vision of ecstatic consummation, she can scorn his "mercenary" demands, "for whatever may be bought, is low." He has saved the husband she does not love; she loves him passionately; yet she is ready to stab herself rather than allow herself to surrender to him. When Almanzor, "half-converted," respects her virtue, she sets forth the discipline he must master: he must "mount above [his] wish, and lose it higher." When, for all her scruples, the Emperor falsely accuses them of adultery, Almahide once more asks Almanzor to save her husband's life and his kingdom. His exclamation as he accedes outdoes even Donne's canonized lovers in its brilliant ascent beyond this world:

> Listen, sweet heaven, and all ye blest above,
> Take rules of virtue from a mortal love!
> (2 *Conquest*, 5.3.123–24)

The natural man has become the courtly lover *par excellence*, capable of extravagant sacrifice just as he has been capable of heroic self-assertion. The self-assertion is still there, in Almanzor's defiance of heaven; this sacrifice of all hope of winning Almahide in order to save her husband's life is the highest pitch of refinement the world can achieve, and it is offered as a model rather than a tribute to heaven. But the play crowns this with the descent of Christian hope; Almahide's slave, a convert, teaches her mistress to transcend mere virtue:

> Virtue's no god, nor has she power divine:
> But He protects it, who did first enjoin.
> Trust then in Him; and from His grace implore
> Faith to believe what rightly we adore.
> (2 *Conquest*, 5.2.11–14)

At the close, Almanzor finds his better self in the Christian Ferdinand:

> Something so kingly, that my haughty mind
> Is drawn to yours, because 'tis of a kind.
> (2 *Conquest*, 5.4.155–56)

He turns out to be the son of Ferdinand's general, a foundling like Tom Jones, whose natural goodness now seems to have its source in his concealed origins. We may think of Dryden's words to the deists in *Religio Laici*: " 'Tis revelation what thou think'st discourse." The natural wisdom of which men boast is ultimately divine revelation in disguise; it is given to man, not created by him. Yet, for all the Christian wedlock of Almanzor and Almahide and their absorption into the court of Spain, the stress of the play has been upon the puzzling world that must be endured without revelation.

We are, consequently, left with unresolved questions. The natural man is capable of true greatness, and he can ascend to the highest level of neo-Stoic moral discipline. But is he truly natural, or does he seem natural only because he carries within him a higher order of being? We see him from the first showing a sense of justice and a capacity for friendship; we find him capable of more intense love than any other man. Is this the order of the flesh outdoing the order of mind? Are free and generous passions more to be trusted than those that, sacrificed to principle, will subvert the principle and use it as a disguise? Is the vigor of Almanzor the proper embodiment of an order of charity in contrast to the crassly self-seeking or the coldly righteous? These puzzles recur throughout the century to follow. Clarissa Harlowe and Tom Jones, in their quite different ways, are distinguished from their fellow creatures by dangerously passionate natures and a capacity for goodness. And the celebration in Shaftesbury of nature's varied order gives an authenticity to wilds and deserts not to be found in princely gardens.

Dryden's own treatment of the state of nature is always marked by ambiguity. In his great political satire, *Absalom and Achitophel*, he opens with that ironic picture of "pious times, ere priestcraft did begin," times of liberty

> When nature prompted, and no law denied
> Promiscuous use of concubine and bride.

David, "Israel's monarch after Heaven's own heart," imparts his "vigorous warmth" indiscriminately and scatters "his Maker's image through the land." Absalom's beauty and bravery may be due to the "diviner lust" and "greater gust" with which his father begot him. Again, in his version of the opening of Juvenal's Sixth Satire, Dryden presents a mocking image of "hard primitivism" and the chastity it produced:

> When in a narrow cave, their common shade,
> The sheep, the shepherds, and their gods were laid:
> When reeds, and leaves, and hides of beasts were spread
> By mountain huswifes for their homely bed,
> And mossy pillows rais'd, for the rude husband's head.
>
> . . . .
>
> Those first unpolisht matrons, big and bold,
> Gave suck to infants of gigantic mold;
> Rough as their savage lords who rang'd the wood,
> And fat with acorns belch'd their windy food.
> For when the world was buxom, fresh, and young,
> Her sons were undebauch'd and therefore strong;
> And whether born in kindly beds of earth,

> Or struggling from the teeming oaks to birth,
> Or from what other atoms they begun,
> No sires they had, or, if a sire, the sun.
>
> (11.3–7, 12–21)

And in his epistle *To Sir Godfrey Kneller* (1694) we find this passage written by poet to painter:

> Our arts are sisters, though not twins in birth;
> For hymns were sung in Eden's happy earth
> By the first pair, while Eve was yet a saint,
> Before she fell with pride, and learn'd to paint.
> Forgive th' allusion; 'twas not meant to bite,
> But satire will have room, wheree'er I write.
>
> (11.89–94)

The last line recalls the play of Dryden's mind, the skeptical turning of the mind back upon itself which qualifies any unguarded statement and introduces a note of levity into an extreme position. The play upon the word *paint* is the very stuff of Augustan ambiguity. We see it again in that famous passage of Pope's *The Rape of the Lock* where Belinda at her dressing table paints like the fallen Eve and "bids a purer blush arise" from her cheeks. We know that Belinda is applying rouge (unless she is striking her cheek with the back of her hairbrush), but, as Cleanth Brooks has said, she is not simply disguising nature. She is bringing it to its full realization; her cosmetic art is making the color more complete ("purer" in one sense), but it is also making it what Nature would have wished to achieve (*The Well Wrought Urn*, New York, 1947). Eve's painting, in Dryden's lines, is the bedizening of the fallen woman who can no longer enjoy naked innocence; but it is the beginning of art, which repairs the Fall and gives us, in Sir Philip Sidney's words, "a golden world."

A skeptical play of mind does not imply that Dryden seriously adopted naturalistic views or that he found a strict alliance between natural appetite and moral goodness, but rather, that he was capable of breaking down categories that were too pat. If Almanzor is nobler than all the Moorish court, this can be accounted for by the generosity of his large nature, or by his Christian origins and descent from a court that espoused heroic passion in the cause of piety. The architecture of *The Conquest of Granada* is designed to show, in the first play, the emergence of Almanzor into the moral rigor or neo-Stoic self-denial and then to include this, in the second play, within the Christian framework that transcends mere human virtue. Such lesser characters as Ozmyn and Benzayda play out comparable roles on a smaller scale; they do not have the fine excess of Almanzor, and their happy solution is more easily achieved. Closer to Almanzor's transfiguration is that of Morat, the villain of *Aureng-Zebe*, whose fiery nature is finally absorbed at death into a moral order. The resolution Dryden provides cannot be underestimated, for it supplies a link with his major satires and religious poems. But the intensity with which he poses problems is equally important, and this can be seen throughout the heroic plays and tragedies. I will consider three of them here and defer *All for Love* to a later chapter.

In *The Indian Emperor* (1665) Cortez becomes a prototype of the troubled proconsul. He descends upon Mexico only to find it an earthly paradise, ruled by a benevolent rational monarch. Cortez falls in love with Montezuma's daughter; but the dignity and generosity of Montezuma are a rebuke to the conquistador who comes to despoil in the name of Pope and Emperor. Montezuma has his own cruel and superstitious rites, but Dryden makes these the blandly conventional ceremonies of an established church that serves a free-thinking monarch's power. Montezuma accepts a traditional Aztec faith, but the personal role he assumes is that of the rationalistic critic of the temporal claims of Christianity. Cortez offers little in reply. Pressed by his Aztec critics, he can only assert his honor and his need to carry out his imperial task, which he undertakes joylessly. When later in the play Montezuma is put to the rack by the Christian priest who wants the Aztec sacred ritual objects for their gold, Cortez is outraged at the priest's presumption and saddened by the curse of gold which, once it has entered Europe, will induce countless crimes of this sort.

In his fight against Cortez Montezuma's aggression arises only from his slavish devotion to his haughty empress; she disdains the claims of honor when they thwart her own appetites and assumes the typical naturalistic view of insatiate willfulness:

> For mean remorse no room the valiant finds,
> Repentance is the virtue of weak minds.
>
> · · · · · · · · · · · · · ·
> . . . daring courage makes ill actions good.
>
> (3.1)

The closest that Montezuma himself can approach to this view is in his acceptance of greatness; in this he resembles Almanzor or Morat (in *Aureng-Zebe*) as he addresses his gods:

> Great souls are sparks of your own heavenly pride:
> That lust of power we from your god-heads have,
> You're bound to please those appetites you gave.
>
> (2.4)

Montezuma accepts the fate of kings to the end: "Power is their life; when that expires, they die." But as an individual, Montezuma is the high-minded rationalist. Like the people of Voltaire's Eldorado in *Candide*, he mocks the mighty European emperor who "poorly begs" for the gold the Aztecs despise. He questions the Church that "nourishes debate, not preaches love," that confuses temporal power over new lands with spiritual power in men's souls, that subverts morality by setting a low price upon sin, and that threatens the undivided sovereignty of monarchs by its own temporal claims. Later, when he is suffering on the rack, Montezuma rejects the Christian priest's arrogant dogmatism; man cannot go beyond natural reason without risking the self-deceptions of pride. He cannot accept the authority of an "unerring head" of the Christian church:

> MONT: Man, and not err! What reason can you give.
> PRIEST: Renounce that carnal reason, and believe.
> MONT: The light of nature should I thus betray,
>   'Twere to wink hard, that I might see the day.
>
> (5.2)

Montezuma's tolerant acceptance of a "middle way" between disbelief and dogmatism is met by the Christian priest's use of force and torture. In contrast to this conflict is the bond of honor that joins Montezuma and Cortez. If he must endure defeat, Montezuma generously exclaims, he will be happy to have a man like Cortez succeed him.

Both Cortez and Montezuma have a sense of the difficult and confusing plight of man. In despair Cortez can cry:

> We toss and turn about our feverish will,
> When all our ease must come from lying still:
> For all the happiness mankind can gain
> Is not in pleasure, but in rest from pain.
>
> (4.1)

Montezuma stabs himself when life has become intolerable; like Othello, he can reassert his original self in this one act: "He wants no subject, who can death command" (sc. 7). Again we have the image of confused values and contradictions, of guilt and doubt; and meeting it is the assertion of self-command.

In *Tyrannic Love* (1669) Dryden created his first sketch of unruly greatness. Maximin is a "Thracian shepherd" become tyrant. He scorns his wife's high Antonine birth as well as her piety; where she sees divine Order acting in their son's death, Maximin sees only the spite and jealousy of gods threatened by human greatness.

As we first see Maximin, his restless valor seems the nobler for the slothful ease of Rome, which has chosen two "tame gowned princes" to rule. Maximin disdains a mixed state of checks and balances:

> Two equal pow'rs, two different ways will draw,
> While each may check, and give the other law.
> True, they secure propriety and peace;
> But are not fit an empire to increase.

Constitutional ideas are met by the force of conquest and the Hobbesian logic of absolute power; the concern with property ("propriety") is reduced to the caution of a "thrifty state" that would "rather lose a fight than over-buy."

Saint Catherine of Alexandria challenges the force of Maximin. She outdoes fifty Roman philosophers in a combat of reason, and although a captive she enters Maximin's presence with a "high air and mien" that show "the greatness of a queen." Maximin scornfully sets his philosopher-priest against her ("You gain by heaven," he tells him, "and, therefore, should dispute"), but the defense of Stoic virtue cannot withstand her ampler view. The Stoic virtues are accepted by the Christian but transformed and extended: "Yours but reach the action, ours the mind." When she converts his advocate, she arouses Maximin's love.

Catherine conquers the conqueror by her utter transcendence of his order; she scorns his gifts and promises, for she enjoys "the humble quiet of possessing naught." She rejects the view that sees the greatness of the gods in their indifference to the "little business of the world":

> This doctrine well befitted him who thought
> A casual world was from wild atoms wrought:
> But such an order in each chance we see
> (Chain'd to its cause, as that to its decree)
> That none can think a workmanship so rare
> Was built, or kept, without a workman's care.
>
>   (3.1)

This grand vision of Order is incidental to Catherine's assertion of an order of charity. But Maximin cannot begin to comprehend such transcendence:

> For what a greater happiness can be
> Than to be courted and be lov'd by me?

Catherine's scorn for his offer must take the only terms he can grasp, the language of power:

> Such pow'r in bonds true piety can have,
> That I command, and thou art but a slave.

The conflict between orders is given a masquelike presentation when a sorcerer calls up an "earthly fiend" to tempt Catherine. The fiend's power is overwhelmed by a guardian angel, before whom he can only bow:

> Thou, prince of day, from elements art free;
> And I all body when compared to thee.
>
> . . . .
>
> Gross-heavy-fed, next man in ignorance and sin,
> And spotted all without, and dusky all within.
>
> . . . .
>
> I reel, I stagger, and am drunk with light.
>
> (4.1)

As Catherine's spiritual power is magnified, Maximin is revealed more and more as a maddened tyrant who thinks he is a god:

> I'll find that pow'r o'er wills, which heav'n ne'er found.
> Free-will's a cheat in any one but me;
> In all but kings, 'tis willing slavery;
> An unseen fate which forces the desire,
> The will of puppets danc'd upon a wire.
>
> . . . .
>
> Mine is the business of your little fates.
>
> (4.1)

Catherine is quick to point out the weakness and febrility of his self-assertion:

> Qualmish and loathing all you had before,
> Yet with a sickly appetite to more,
> As in a fev'rish dream you still drink on,
> And wonder why your thirst is never gone.
>
> (4.1)

As Catherine converts others around him, the court becomes invulnerable to Maximin's power; his victims welcome death and martyrdom. His exasperation with his converted empress is eminently understandable: "Behead her, while she's in so good a mind." But the frustration of Maximin makes him the more assertive. "I love not for her sake but my own," he exclaims as he sends Catherine to death. "Our gods are gods 'cause they have power and will"; and so, "if this be sin, I do myself forgive." When his world crumbles, he defies the gods with magnificent bravura that recalls his disdain for mercantile Rome:

> Look to it, Gods, for you th' aggressors are.
> Keep you your rain and sunshine in your skies,
> And I'll keep back my flame and sacrifice.
> Your trade of heav'n shall soon be at a stand,
> And all your goods lie dead upon your hand.
>
> (5.1)

As his body gives way to death, his assertion persists:

> I'll shake this carcass off, and be obey'd,
> Reign an imperial ghost without its aid.

And his last words are the highest pitch of titanlike defiance:

> I'll mount, and scatter all the Gods I hit.

Maximin looks back to Marlowe's Tamburlaine, and ahead to Camus's *Caligula*. Caligula is oppressed by the meaninglessness and absurdity of a world that has undone his rational and humane order. He seizes upon every whim of arbitrary power to create his own meaning by sheer fiat and to induce in others the same collapse of belief that he has undergone. He must absorb all control of his world into himself by one means or another, and he dies in the impossibility of his increasingly savage quest.

Maximin's plight does not have the same origins as Caligula's; he is no disenchanted man of reason, although he has lost a son to the jealous gods, as Caligula has lost a sister. It is his desire for Catherine as much as metaphysical anguish that leads him to commit his infamies. Nor does he become a sardonic teacher. Yet he does resist a force that seems meaningless to him, if not to us; he tries to impose meaning through force, to make the order of the flesh the order of his world even as something incomprehensible irrupts into it. *Tyrannic Love* is awkward in many ways, but its strength lies in Dryden's play of mind. He can entertain Maximin's own view of his situation sufficiently to make his plight far more compelling than Saint Catherine's. If Maximin's tyranny submits easily to moral diagnosis, his titanism still carries force and wins a sympathy it does not ask.

Don Sebastian (1689) is late enough in Dryden's career to show the survival of the heroic forms beyond the Revolution of 1688. The play has two heroes. The arrogance is given to Dorax, the Spanish renegade turned Moor; he is a man of disenchanted idealism whose speeches recall the Juvenalian satires Dryden was in the process of translating. The heroic will and mastery of fate are given to Don Sebastian and to Almeyda, whom he loves but at the last discovers to be his sister. There is, moreover (as in *Marriage à la Mode* and *The Spanish Friar*) a comic underplot concerned with profiteering and seduction: its motivation is consistently low, cunning, and fleshly.

The division of the heroic role allows Dryden to make Dorax a mordant railer: "all mankind," he says, "is cause enough for satire." He keeps looking for a true man, one that is "his maker's image" and he scorns the "glut" of the battlefield: "A hundred of 'em to a single soul."

The language of Dorax is echoed at moments by the Moorish despot, Muley-Moloch ("These are but garbage, not a sacrifice"); but the Moor's scorn is all complacent arrogance. He does not yearn, as Dorax does, to pay reverence to a true hero; nor does he know Dorax's bitterness at being dreadfully wronged by the one apparent hero he has known. Muley-Moloch can exclaim, "What's royalty, but power to please myself?" Don Sebastian (the true hero in whose motives Dorax is mistaken) takes a different view: "Kings, who are fathers, live but in their people." It becomes clear that Dorax, although he is a renegade and a rebel, is one only in the cause of righteousness. He can savagely attack the temporal ambitions of the Church, but he asserts a vision of Order and refuses to be drawn into treason:

> Why then, no bond is left on humankind!
> Distrusts, debates, immortal strifes ensue;
> Children may murder parents, wives their husbands;
> All must be rapine, wars, and desolation,
> When trust and gratitude no longer bind.
>
> (2.1)

Dorax insists upon a distinction between rebellion and treacherous betrayal; and when his Christian faith revives within him, it too is called rebellion: "Down, thou rebelling Christian in my heart!"

Don Sebastian is a man who "seems ashamed / He's not all spirit," who can reject his captivity and fate:

> I beg no pity for this mould'ring clay;
> For, if you give it burial, there it takes
> Possession of your earth;
> If burnt and scatter'd in the air, the winds,
> That strow my dust, diffuse my royalty,
> And spread me o'er your clime; for when one atom
> Of mine shall light, know, there Sebastian reigns.
>
> (1.1)

He cannot be conquered: "Souls know no conquerors." His love for Almeyda is as exalted as the Moorish Emperor's is brutish, and Sebastian can look down upon the raging Emperor with scorn from another order of awareness:

> Barbarian, thou canst part us but a moment!
> We shall be one again in thy despite.
> Life is but air,
> That yields a passage to the whistling sword,
> And closes when 'tis gone.
>
> (3.1)

When the Emperor condemns Sebastian to death, Almeyda also can rise to the sense of rebellious outrage we have seen in Dorax. She turns upon the gods who have allowed the Emperor his power:

> O Pow'rs, if Kings be your peculiar care,
> Why plays this wretch with your prerogative?
> Now flash him dead, now crumble him to ashes,
> Or henceforth live confin'd in your own palace;
> And look not idly out upon a world
> That is no longer yours.
>
> (3.1)

Her grandeur of spirit and rebellious defiance of unjust authority fuse the assertion of Sebastian and the moral indignation of Dorax. As Camus has pointed out, "The most elementary form of rebellion, paradoxically, expresses an aspiration to order." The metaphysical rebel "blasphemes primarily in the name of order, denouncing God as the father of death and as the supreme outrage" (*The Rebel*, revised trans. by Anthony Bower, Vintage Books, New York, 1956).

Dryden reconciles rebel and hero in an impressive scene between Dorax and Sebastian. Dorax has been envious and unfair; Sebastian is just and kind. Their relationship is defined by an undercurrent of references to Satan and God. Sebastian knew

> as Heaven
> Foreknew, among the shining angel host,
> Who would stand firm, who fall.
>
> (4.3)

When it turns out that the favorite Sebastian had preferred—a man Dorax had taken to be an effeminate sycophant—died in battle at Sebastian's side, all of Dorax's jealous reading of events breaks down. Unlike Satan, he can recognize the authentic goodness of his preferred rival and acknowledge his superiority. In having become a vengeful renegade, in turning from his life as Spanish and Christian Alonzo to the satirical Dorax, he has "lost, like

Lucifer, [his] name above." "Have I," he asks, "been cursing heaven, while heaven blest me?"

Dryden has explored the pattern of rebellion and allowed for the power of Dorax's vision. Sebastian can attest to that in forgiving Dorax's vengefulness: "Thou meant'st to kill a tyrant, not a king." Dorax's outraged sense of justice has been born of error and confirmed by envy, but it has been a consistent vision with its own morality. If it buckles finally before true goodness, it does not lose its dignity. Satan reconciled is, up to a point, Satan justified; his rebellion has been against "the supreme outrage," and his pride proves less significant than his sense of justice. Dorax looks ahead, however dimly, to the romantic view of Satan, and it is the dialectical nature of Dryden's plays that allows him this force.

Once Dorax is reconciled, he thinks he has regained heaven:

> Joy is in every face, without a cloud;
> As, in the scene of opening paradise,
> The whole creation danc'd at their new being,
> Pleas'd to be what they were, pleas'd with each other.
>
>   (5.1)

It is a transitory joy, for Don Sebastian and Almeyda soon learn that their marriage is incestuous. Before he departs for his hermit's cell (as Almeyda for a convent) Sebastian voices the "impious" thoughts he must learn to subdue:

>   one moment longer,
> And I should break through laws divine and human,
> And think them cobwebs spread for little man,
> Which all the bulky herd of nature breaks.
> The vigorous young world was ignorant
> Of these restrictions; 'tis decrepit now;
> Not more devout, but more decay'd, and cold.
>
>   (5.1)

We are close once more to the heroic primitivism of Almanzor.

Sebastian rejects these thoughts just as Almanzor eventually submits his to the discipline of the Christian court. Yet the assertions are memorable, and Sebastian's primitivism has had its support in Dorax's scourging satire of courts and priestcraft. The play imposes a moral order upon its events and looks to an order of the spirit in the religious exercise of its ill-fated hero and heroine; but it has given heroic feeling both strength and clarity of vision. The worlds of Dorax's satiric rage and of Sebastian's sinful love are worlds that have their own consistency and their own expression of the idea of justice. The vigor of their deep feelings and proud demands is a necessary part of the order Dryden creates, an order that risks anarchy and division so that it may include energy and greatness.

GEORGE deF. LORD

The Restoration Myth
from Astraea Redux
to Absalom and Achitophel

THE RESTORATION MYTH
FROM *ASTRAEA REDUX* TO "THE SECULAR MASQUE"

In Dryden's political poems from *Astraea Redux* (1660) to *Absalom and Achitophel* (1681) we find a central myth of renewal and restoration following a crisis of civil war, defeat, destruction, or exile. The contemporary event is always presented *sub specie aeternitatis* by means of analogues usually drawn from classical mythology, Roman history, or the Old Testament. Thus no contemporary event or issue is seen as unique, and the participants in these national dramas are generally reduced to types. Each contemporary event or issue has its counterpart in Augustan Rome, or in the book of Samuel, or in the *Aeneid*. Dryden's good characters in the political poems are especially lacking in individuality. The public-spirited and self-effacing qualities of virtue as Dryden here conceives of it—in striking contrast to the egotism of his dramatic heroes—helps to define the admired monarchs and statesmen and warriors in terms of functions and relationships rather than in terms of extraordinary gifts or *virtù*. This is plainly seen in the case of Barzillai's heroic son (in real life the Earl of Ossory) and of the handful of faithful followers David relies on in the crisis of *Absalom and Achitophel*.

> Now more than half a Father's Name is lost.
> His Eldest Hope, with every Grace adorn'd,
> By me (so Heav'n will have it) always Mourn'd,

From *Writers and Their Background: John Dryden*, edited by Earl Miner. © 1972 by G. Bell & Sons Ltd. Ohio State University Press, 1972.

> And always honour'd, snatcht in Manhoods prime
> By' unequal Fates, and Providences crime:
> Yet not before the Goal of Honour won,
> All parts fulfill'd of Subject and of Son;
> Swift was the Race, but short the Time to run.
> Oh Narrow Circle, but of Pow'r Divine,
> Scanted in Space, but perfect in thy Line!
>
> (831–39)

Individuality entered the picture with Dryden's villains. The catalogue of rebels, dreamers, informers, and plotters includes more eccentric characters than any other English poem except, perhaps, for *The Canterbury Tales*. Wickedness is conceived of as eccentric and egocentric. Each villain is wicked in a special way, while the good are all good in the same way. Because they are incapable of the reciprocal loyalties that link king and subject, master and servant, god and man, or father and son, these villains are very much cut off from others. Their eccentricity is further emphasized by idiosyncrasies of appearance and manner. It is significant that none of the good characters in *Absalom and Achitophel* is given a physical description, while all the evil ones are marked by unforgettable physical features.

It follows that with Dryden's aversion to the idiosyncratic there should be a corresponding aversion to novelty. The central conspirators of the exclusion Crisis are the slaves of the New. Achitophel is "Restless, unfixed in principles and place, / In power unpleased, impatient of disgrace," and Zimri is hailed as "Blest madman, who could every hour employ, / with something new to wish or to enjoy." Dazzled by ambition or bemused by mad schemes for innovation the rebel leaders are seen as prisoners of the moment. The essence of Dryden's profound mistrust of political alteration is conveyed in one of the most powerful couplets in *Absalom and Achitophel:*

> All other Errors but disturb a State;
> But Innovation is the Blow of Fate.
>
> (799–800)

With his aversion to innovation Dryden also seems to feel a certain anti-intellectualism. Among David's supporters the only one to whom intellectual brilliance is attributed is "Jotham of piercing wit and pregnant thought," and even here the emphasis on perspicuousness rather than originality is significant. All the other virtuous characters, including the King, are recognized for their sense of duty and loyalty, not for their brilliance. Dryden's implicit anti-intellectualism is expressed in the much-quoted couplet:

> Great Wits are sure to Madness near ally'd;
> And thin Partitions do their Bounds divide.
>
> > (163–64)

Intellectual brilliance is as dangerous in its own way as the inner light of the spirit, that fallible guide of the sects:

> Plain *Truths* enough for needfull *use* they found;
> But men wou'd still be itching to *expound:*
> Each was ambitious of th' obscurest place,
> No measure ta'n from *Knowledge*, all from GRACE.
> *Study* and *Pains* were now no more their Care;
> *Texts* were explain'd by *Fasting*, and by *Prayer:*
> This was the Fruit the *private Spirit* brought;
> Occasion'd by *great Zeal*, and *little Thought.*
>
> > (*Religio Laici*, 409–16)

The devotees of the novel, whether in religion or politics, are doomed to an ephemeral existence:

> A Thousand daily Sects rise up, and dye;
> A Thousand more the perish'd Race supply.
>
> > (*Religio Laici*, 421–22)

Thus *Religio Laici* indicts the Dissenters whose shifting political allegiances *Absalom and Achitophel* had arrainged in these lines:

> For, govern'd by the *Moon,* the giddy *Jews*
> Tread the same track when she the Prime renews:
> And once in twenty Years, their Scribes Record,
> By natural Instinct they change their Lord.
>
> > (216–19)

Dryden's innovative Jews seem to illustrate Santayana's remark that "those who do not remember the past are condemned to repeat it."

Perhaps the most striking aspect of Dryden's conservatism is that it permeates every part of his political verse: it is explicitly stated and argued; it is illustrated by a wide variety of examples; and it is represented in the very structure and style of the poems. All these aspects of Dryden's conservatism have been extensively treated by others, and so I would like to concentrate on what seems to me to be an important but rather neglected subject, Dryden's concept of history in the political poems. This, I think, points to a radical issue which divided Conformist and Dissenter, Whig and Tory,

Puritan and Anglican throughout the great religious and political crises of
the seventeenth century.

To begin with I would like to point out that in *Absalom and Achitophel,*
his most important political poem, Dryden showed very clearly his central
concern with the relationship of the present to the past. Because the story
of David had already been widely used by various pamphleteers to figure
forth the story of Charles II, it has often been assumed that Dryden's contribution to the use of myth was mainly a question of greater dexterity and
wit. While there is no doubt about the technical superiority of his poem over
its models and predecessors, this should not be allowed to blind us to Dryden's
real innovation in the use of Old Testament myth—that is in the *amalgama-
tion* of present and past. We do not see the present through an allegory from
or an analogy with the past; we see past and present simultaneously. David
does not simply stand for Charles II; he does not merely resemble him; David
is Charles. Dryden is not saying that we can learn lessons from the past. He
is everywhere affirming that we can *only* understand the present when it is
amalgamated with the past.

At the heart of Dryden's conservatism is the feeling that past, present,
and future coexist. We can see in Dryden those aspects of the Anglican temper
defined by James Sutherland:

> To some extent it is possible to see the division between Anglicans
> and Nonconformists as another aspect of the battle between the
> Ancients and the Moderns. The Anglican priest naturally felt
> himself to be the trustee of a venerable ecclesiastical tradition,
> performing the unvarying offices of the Church and celebrating
> its time-hallowed ritual.
>
> (*English Literature of the Late Seventeenth Century*)

While Dryden's anticlericalism would have rejected such an assumption of
an ecclesiastical role, he undoubtedly regarded himself as the trustee of
venerable political and religious traditions and the celebrator of time-hallowed
rituals. At the centre of his thought throughout his career was something
like what Mircea Eliade has called "the myth of the eternal return," in which
the chief feature is a recurrent restoration and resanctification of the community after losses and violations. This "primitive" ontological conception
Eliade describes thus:

> An object or an act becomes real only insofar as it imitates or
> repeats an archetype. Thus, reality is acquired solely through
> repetition or participation; everything which lacks an exemplary
> model is "meaningless," i.e., it lacks reality. Men would thus have
> a tendency to become archetypal and paradigmatic. This tenden-

cy may well appear paradoxical, in the sense that the man of a traditional culture sees himself as real only to the extent that he ceases to be himself (for a modern observer) and is satisfied with imitating and repeating the gestures of another. In other words, he sees himself as real, i.e., as "truly himself," only, and precisely, insofar as he ceases to be so.

(Cosmos and History)

A quick survey of the recurrent rituals of restoration in Dryden's political verse will demonstrate this point. *Astraea Redux,* which proclaims the theme in its title, carries as its epigraph the well-known lines from the most famous of Virgil's *Eclogues* (the fourth), in which the restoration of Justice is hailed:

Iam Redit & Virgo, Redeunt Saturnia Regna.

The restoration of Charles II after a long exile is thus identified with the restored Saturnian Age in which the departed Astraea (Divine Justice) returns to earth. Since Virgil was celebrating the birth of a prophecied redeemer in the fourth Eclogue, and since this eclogue was often regarded as an anticipation of the birth of Christ, the cosmogonic implications of this identification of Charles with the newborn son of the Consul Pollio could scarcely be more powerful. But Dryden extends them even further by including an identification with an Old Testament type as well:

Thus banish'd *David* spent abroad his time,
When to be God's Anointed was his Crime.
(79–80)

Toward its close the poem hails the inception of the new age under this new Augustus (yet another powerful identification):

And now times whiter Series is begun
Which in soft Centuries shall smoothly run.
(292–93)

In the next forty years Dryden's poetry is imbued with this theme of restoration, renewal, and return, culminating in the haunting chorus of *The Secular Masque:*

All, all, of a piece throughout;
Thy Chase had a Beast in View;
Thy Wars brought nothing about;
Thy Lovers were all untrue.
'Tis well an Old Age is out,
And time to begin a New.
(92–97)

The restoration of Charles II with its archetypes of David's return from exile and the investiture of Augustus as emperor, becomes Dryden's central pattern for a long series of restorations. *To His Sacred Majesty, a Panegyrick on His Coronation* celebrates that crown "Preserv'd from ruine and restor'd by you." This motif of restoration is combined with Aeneas's escape from Troy and founding of Rome in a passage from *To My Lord Chancellor Presented on New-years-day* (1662):

> When our great Monarch into Exile went
> Wit and Religion suffer'd banishment:
> Thus once when *Troy* was wrapt in fire and smoak
> The helpless Gods their burning shrines forsook;
> They with the vanquisht Prince and party go,
> And leave their Temples empty to the fo:
> At length the Muses stand restor'd again
> To that great charge which Nature did ordain;
> And their lov'd Druyds seem reviv'd by Fate
> While you dispence the laws and guide the State.
>
> (17–26)

Of course the conclusion of *Absalom and Achitophel* is the most prominent instance of the restoration theme—in fact here Dryden is emphasizing a *re*-restoration:

> Henceforth a Series of new time began;
> The mighty Years in long Procession ran:
> Once more the Godlike *David* was Restor'd,
> And willing Nations knew their lawful Lord.

As a recent critic remarked, the Godlike David is more Godlike than God, whose only function in this poem is to nod affirmatively in response to David's reassertion of his power. These lines combine in an exemplary fashion all the main ingredients of Dryden's restoration myth: divine sanction, inauguration of a new age, the identification of the Kind as David with undertones of Aeneas, and the re-establishment of the nations' obedience to their lawful lord. In fact, Dryden's attachment to these themes verges on the tedious, and one soon becomes adept at anticipating the exact point at which these plangent heroic notes will come in. One forsees the climax of *Threnodia Augustalis*: Dryden's strategy is already dictated by past practice, and so the death of Charles is inevitably subordinated in the conclusion of the poem to the succession of his brother:

> with a distant view I see
> Th' amended Vows of *English* Loyalty.

And all beyond that Object, there appears
The long Retinue of a Prosperous Reign.

While starting from his Oozy Bed
Th' asserted Ocean rears his reverend Head;
To View and Recognize his ancient Lord again:
And with a willing hand, restores
The *Fasces* of the Main.
(504–7, 513–17)

Although the myth is most centrally expressed in those numerous poems that deal with the restoration and succession of the Stuart line, Dryden extends it to include a variety of subjects, from Charleton's discoveries at Stonehenge to the Duchess of York's return from a trip to Scotland. Sometimes its use seems perfunctory, as it does in the flattering condescension to the Duchess, but it is more discriminating in the Charleton poem. Dryden wittily combines Dr Walter Charleton's theory that Stonehenge was built by the Danes as a temple for the coronation of their kings with an allusion to Charles's alleged asylum there after the Battle of Worcester and an implied reference to the founding of Rome:

These Ruines sheltred once *His* Sacred Head
Then when from *Wor'sters* fatal Field *He* fled;
Watch'd by the Genius of this Royal place,
And mighty Visions of the *Danish* Race.
His *Refuge* then was for a *Temple* shown:
But, *He* Restor'd, 'tis now become a *Throne*.
(53–58)

Stonehenge is implicitly identified with the temple of Apollo at Cumae where Aeneas descended into the underworld and saw mighty visions of the *Roman* race. Thus Dryden constantly juxtaposes recent or contemporary events with mythic or historical counterparts in a distinctively Virgilian way. In an equally Virgilian way he establishes a relation between losses and gains in the fate of the royal line and the nation: defeat and flight, exile and wandering, become the swelling prologue to the imperial theme. *Il faut reculer pour mieux sauter.*

Dryden employs the same principle in treating the devastation of London by the Great Fire of 1666. Since the remarkable rebuilding of the city had scarcely begun, there was as yet little tangible reason for hailing London's renewal as he does in *Annus Mirabilis* (1667). Here is no actual equivalent to the Restoration of Charles, and so Dryden's implicit argument seems to be, *because* the city was burned, it will be renewed like the Phoenix:

294

Already, Labouring with a mighty fate,
  She shakes the rubbish from her mounting brow,
And seems to have renew'd her Charters date,
  Which Heav'n will to the death of time allow.

295

More great then humane, now, and more *August,*
  New deifi'd she from her fires does rise:
Her widening streets on new foundations trust,
  And, opening, into larger parts she flies.

At the height of the Exclusion crisis Dryden again used the legend of Noah and the Flood (another version of the basic theme) which he first alluded to in these opening lines of *To His Sacred Majesty*:

In that wild Deluge where the World was drownd,
When life and sin one common tombe had found,
The first small prospect of a rising hill
With various notes of Joy the Ark did fill.

The Epilogue to the King . . . at Oxford . . . 19 March 1681 treats the turbulence of the times and the desperate hope for a peaceful solution to the crisis in terms of the same myth:

Our Ark that has in Tempests long been tost,
Cou'd never land on so secure a Coast.
From hence you may look back on Civil Rage,
And view the ruines of the former Age.
Here a New World its glories may unfold,
And here be sav'd the remnants of the Old.

(17–22)

Here Dryden employs one of their favourite weapons against the predominantly Dissenting and Whiggish champions of Exclusion by appropriating to the King's side their customary designation of themselves as the saving remnant.

In an interesting anticipation of Pope's treatment of the *translatio studii* in the *Essay on Criticism* and the *Dunciad,* Dryden in 1684 hails the restoration to England of Greek and Roman learning in Roscommon's *Essay on Translated Verse:*

The Wit of *Greece,* the Gravity of *Rome*
Appear exalted in the *Brittish* Loome;

> The Muses Empire is restor'd agen,
> In *Charles* his Reign and by *Roscomon's* Pen.
> (26–29)

One concluding example will show how pervasive the theme of restoration is in Dryden's poetry. In a poem of pure compliment welcoming the Duchess of York after one of her sojourns abroad Dryden turns the following dainty conceit:

> The Muse resumes her long-forgotten Lays,
> And Love, restor'd, his Ancient Realm surveys;
> Recalls our Beauties, and revives our Plays.
> (Prologue to the Dutchess on Her Return
> from Scotland, 1682, 2.30–32)

THE REJECTION OF INNOVATION

Whenever Dryden celebrates a public event, then, he combines it with some classical or mythic prototype and thus endows it with a kind of cosmic regularity and inevitability. A natural correlative to this is in his rejection of the search for novelty and innovation, which I have already glanced at. It is given general force in the prologue to *The Unhappy Favorite* (1682):

> Tell me you Powers, why should vain Man pursue,
> With endless Toyl, each object that is new,
> And for the seeming substance leave the True?
> (12–14)

The erratic and perverted character of the crowd is emphatically expressed in these lines from *The Medall* (1682):

> Almighty Crowd, thou shorten'st all dispute;
> Pow'r is thy Essence; Wit thy Attribute!
> Nor Faith nor Reason make Thee at a stay;
> Thou leapst o'r all eternal truths, in thy *Pindarique* way!
> (91–94)

In such a mob doctrines and tenets can only be ephemeral:

> The common Cry is ev'n Religion's Test.
>
> And our own Worship only true at home.
> And true, but for the time, 'tis hard to know,
> How long we please it shall continue so.

> This side to day, and that to morrow burns;
> So all are God-a' mighties in their turns.
>
> (103, 106–10)

Dryden's most telling indictment of the sects is of course in *Religio Laici* (1682):

> The *Common Rule* was made the *common Prey;*
> And at the mercy of the *Rabble* lay.
> The tender Page with horney Fists was gaul'd;
> And he was gifted most that loudest baul'd:
> The *Spirit* gave the *Doctoral Degree:*
> And every member of a *Company*
> Was of *his Trade,* and of the *Bible free.*
>
> While Crouds unlearn'd, with rude Devotion warm,
> About the Sacred Viands buz and swarm,
> The *Fly-blown Text* creates a *crawling Brood;*
> And turns to *Maggots* what was meant for *Food.*
> A *Thousand daily Sects rise up, and dye;*
> A *thousand more the perish'd Race supply.*
>
> (402–8, 417–22)

Bernard Schilling, among others, has shown how extravagances of style were as much to be avoided as such moral or spiritual extravagances:

> A form that lacks discipline is then appropriate for expressing rebellious sentiments, and suggests how the desire for political and social order led to so much control of literary expression. Behind all the vast structure of rule and law there is a fear lest individual energy, if given any chance at all, will assert itself dangerously. Hence the attack on such displays of energy as eloquence, vigorous figurative language, powerful original thought or speculation, and, worst of all, the force of human imagination, which might lead into a whole complex of dangers suggested by the term "enthusiasm."

The conservative myth is celebrated in a style that avoids these pitfalls, a style which by its regularity and sobriety, its balance and rationality, and its irony and good humour enacts the meaning it expresses. In this neoclassical style wit is, in Dryden's phrase "a propriety of thoughts and words; or, in other terms, thoughts and words elegantly adapted to the subject" ["The Author's Apology for Heroic Poetry and Poetic License"]. Invention, for Hobbes (and Dryden would have concurred in this), carried little emphasis on creating something new, but was a matter of seeking and recovering something that was lost, a "calling to mind." In the preface to *Annus Mirabilis* Dryden describes the function of wit as searching "over all the memory for the Species or Ideas of those things which it designs to represent." Thus neoclassical style was undergirded by a neoclassical psychology of literary creation, and, like both the style and the conservative myth, focussed on the past, seeking what is lost. Ancient truths, the same *hic et ubique*, were to be expressed under the aegis of Homer, Virgil, Aristotle, Horace, and the Bible.

THE RESTORATION MYTH AND THE DEFENCE OF THE STUART SETTLEMENT

The weight of this formidable neoclassical machinery was employed by Dryden to persuade the moderate sort of people to accept the Stuart settlement. For Dryden the chief enemies of peace in church and state were those who, with the battle cry of "Popery and Tyranny," were seeking to disturb the succession in the Exclusion Crisis of 1681. It is appropriate that *Absalom and Achitophel,* a poem dealing with threats to the Stuart dynasty and to the principle of succession, should embody in every way the principles that underlie succession—all the conservative, retrospective principles that I have discussed earlier. The exclusive legitimacy of James as heir to the throne is an absolute right, not a relative one, and it is not negotiable. To tamper with it would be to tamper with the Law, which is divinely ordained: it would be to "touch the ark." Although Dryden goes to some lengths to present James as a worthy heir, his right to the throne is constitutionally independent of personal merit. I suspect that a corresponding function of the raillery with which Charles's various love-affairs are treated in the opening of *Absalom* is to undercut the notion of personal merit. Dryden enunciates (at least by implication) the doctrine of the king's two bodies—the natural and the politic—dealt with by Kantorowicz [*The King's Two Bodies: A Study in Medieval Political Theology*]. His basic assumption is that Charles, whatever his imperfections as a man, *is* the legitimate monarch, endowed with certain inalienable rights and corresponding responsibilities, chief among them in this crisis being the safeguarding of the succession to the throne.

Just as the Exclusionists would have threatened to destroy the succession and thereby the orderly continuity on which Church and State are founded so, in an earlier national crisis of war, plague and fire, the radical element threatened the continued existence of England by its apocalyptic interpretation of events. In *Annus Mirabilis* Dryden's strategy consists of deflecting the linear, eschatological view of events with which the sects hailed the end of the world in 1666—and sought, in Marvell's memorable phrase, "to precipitate the latest day"—into the familiar cyclical cosmos of loss and renewal. War, plague, and fire had, as dissenting prophets declared, been a judgment of God for sin, but the sin, in Dryden's view, was that of the rebellious citizens of London and not the allegedly profligate King and his court. So Dryden deftly turned the apocalyptic interpretation of events back upon the Dissenters and implicitly identified the origins of London's devastating fire with the career of the regicide dictator he had once celebrated in *Heroique Stanzas*:

213

As when some dire Usurper Heav'n provides,
  To scourge his Country with a lawless sway:
His birth, perhaps, some petty Village hides,
  And sets his Cradle out of Fortune's way:

214

Till Fully ripe his swelling fire breaks out,
  And hurries him to mighty mischiefs on:
His Prince surpriz'd at first, no ill could doubt,
  And wants the pow'r to meet it when 'tis known:

215

Such was the rise of this prodigious fire,
  Which in mean buildings first obscurely bred,
From thence did soon to open streets aspire,
  And straight to Palaces and Temples spread.

It is hard for me to avoid the idea that Dryden was alluding here to the Cromwell of Marvell's *An Horatian Ode,* who

like the three-fork'd Lightning, first
Breaking the Clouds where it was nurst,
  Did thorough his own Side
  His fiery way divide.

Then burning through the Air he went,
And Pallaces and Temples rent:
  And *Caesars* head at last
  Did through his Laurels blast.
'Tis Madness to resist or blame
The force of angry Heavens flame;
  And, if we would speak true,
  Much to the Man is due:

Who, from his private Gardens, where
He liv'd reserved and austere,
   As if his highest plot
   To plant the Bergamot,
Could by industrious Valour climbe
To ruine the great Work of Time.
                    (13–16, 21–34)

Nearly all Marvell's details appear in Dryden's stanzas: the obscurity of Cromwell's birth, his portentous role as a Heaven-sent scourge, his sudden attainment of power and his impetuous career, his "mighty mischiefs," the unpreparedness of his prince, and his rending of "Palaces and Temples." On the first of the stanzas quoted above the California edition notes: "Perhaps a reference to Cromwell, who came from the country and who was an obscure figure until the 1640s. The passage was probably in Gray's mind when he wrote II, 57ff. of the *Elegy*." If the three stanzas are taken together, however, we seem also to get a subtle allusion to the hero of Marvell's *Ode* and a rather surprising agreement between these two poets in their way of looking at the "dire Usurper" as a unique agent of apocalypse. Essential differences only begin to appear as the two poets develop in separate ways their estimate of the mighty mischiefs which are threatening "the great Work of Time." The differences are partly due to the circumstances under which the poems were written: in *An Horatian Ode* Marvell has to deal with the King's death as a *fait accompli;* in *Annus Mirabilis* Dryden is trying to ward off a repetition of the dire event predicted by the radical Dissenters. E. N. Hooker describes the polemical purpose of the poem thus:

> *Annus Mirabilis* is, in one sense, a piece of inspired journalism, written to sway public opinion in favor of the royal government, which dreaded a revolution—a revolution which, according to republican propaganda, was to be ushered in by omens and portents, by "wonders" signifying the wrath of God against the King and his party. Because of the mystic properties of the figure "666," expectations of revolution had centered around the year 1666; years before, William Lilly had prophesied that "in 1666, there will be no King here, or pretending to the Crowne of England," Fear was widespread. Pepys, recording a conversation with Lord Sandwich on 25 February 1666, reported: "He dreads the issue of this year, and fears that there will be some very great revolutions before his coming back again."

Hooker goes on to enumerate some of the pamphlets which attempted to exploit these fears: *Mirabilis Annus, the Year of Prodigies; Mirabilis Annus Secundus: or the Second Year of Wonders;* and so on. Not only did Dryden turn the enemy's guns upon them, but he adopted and modified the prophecies of the Sectarians about the impending end of the world and made it serve his view of restoration and renewal. Thus the stanza which precedes the passage quoted earlier includes one of Dryden's few eschatological references in the political poems:

> Yet *London* Empress of the Northern Clime,
>   By an high fate thou greatly didst expire;
> Great as the worlds, which at the death of time
>   Must fall, and rise a nobler frame by fire.

But once again the eschatological catastrophe has been deflected into the cosmogonic cycle of renewal.

EARL MINER

The Heroic Idea in Mac Flecknoe

CONFIGURING THE WHOLE

One thing in Dryden perpetually suggests another like it, may dissolve into it, and then emerge as itself or as something else quite different. Given his royalism, Dryden much favors using the figure of the king, kingship, succession, royalty, coronation, restoration, fatherhood, vice-regency under God, emblems of the king, and exemplary princes. The individual details enter, reenter, relate, and are distinguished in innumerable ways; however, seemingly very numerous and dispersed elements fit into a predication governed less by the narrative or other procedure than by the heroic idea. *Mac Flecknoe* and *To . . . Congreve* are astonishingly alike in dealing with drama, with king figures, with succession, with father and son artists, and with some of the same allusions. Here is Flecknoe:

> The hoary Prince in Majesty appear'd,
> High on a Throne of his own Labours rear'd.
> (106–7)

That obviously is picked up as a "High on a Throne" trope by Dryden out of the opening of *Paradise Lost,* book 2, describing Satan. Given Dryden's belief that panegyric and satiric topics can both take a likeness of nature and remain true, it is no wonder that years later he should prophesy of Congreve's success in the same terms:

From *The Restoration Mode from Milton to Dryden.* © 1974 by Princeton University Press.

> Yet this I Prophesy; Thou shalt be seen,
> (Tho' with some short Parenthesis between:)
> High on the Throne of Wit.
>
> (51–53)

(Recognizing the principle, Pope satirically reversed the trope again at the beginning of the second book of the *Dunciad*.)

The single trope tends to relate with others, and both in *Mac Flecknoe* and *To . . . Congreve,* we discover that the kingly detail and the images of art fall into relation with each other, producing what has been finely termed "Dryden's Poetic Kingdoms (by Roper as the title of his book). Any age tends to identify to some extent its systems of values. Nationalism may be related to agrarianism, capitalism, or socialism. That relatedness of values becomes to Dryden a systematic way of making his poems whole. The images of value cohere in themselves and relate to each other. Because Dryden believed so deeply in art and in monarchy, the relation of the two carried full conviction in his time and does still today. But it would not have carried conviction for an anti-monarchist like Milton or for a poet with a mind as divided as Marvell's. On the other hand, an earlier royalist, Thomas Carew, could anticipate Dryden in the epitaph concluding *An Elegie . . . upon Dr. John Donne.* I shall quote all four lines (changing to Roman letters):

> Here lies a King, that rul'd as hee thought fit
> The universall Monarchy of wit;
> Here lie two Flamens, and both those, the best,
> Apollo's first, at last, the true Gods Priest.
>
> (95–98)

Poetry and wit are honored by becoming a kingdom. The "kingdom of letters" also implies its complement, the art of kingship ("rul'd as hee thought fit," a true Stuart absolute monarch). And Carew's kingdom of letters yields at the end to another system of values, religion, giving us a religion of letters. Dryden does the same in *Mac Flecknoe.* Flecknoe prepares the anointing oil for his successor, playing the role both of Samuel the priest and Saul the king:

> The King himself the sacred Unction made,
> As King by Office, and as Priest by Trade.
>
> (118–19)

Dryden differs from Carew in moving beyond the use of superior values (monarchy, religion) for lesser ("wit") to the interchangeability of values. Flecknoe now offers his successor the regalia:

> *Love's Kingdom* to his right he did convey,
> At once his Sceptre and his rule of Sway;
> Whole righteous Lore the Prince had practis'd young,
> And from whose Loyns recorded *Psyche* sprung.
>
> (122–25)

The passage is not as obvious as may seem. Shadwell's opera, *Psyche,* is "recorded" both in the sense of having been "musically rendered" and "preserved in writing" (*Oxford English Dictionary*). That Psyche or soul came from the "Loyns' of *Love's Kingdom,* a play by Flecknoe. Since "Loyns" was pronounced like "lines," the literary descent works as well as the physical in the ambiguity of "Love's Kingdom." Sexual activity or practice of "Love's Kingdom" is in this context "righteous." Unhappily for those hasty Freudians who have recently discovered Dryden, the sceptre (a book) is not a phallic symbol, if anything a female symbol, but also part of the regalia, a Bible for the depraved, and a play, *Love's Kingdom.* In such fashion, Dryden's schemes of value relate and exchange functions: who could say finally what are the vehicles and what the tenors of the images here? The point really comes down to Dryden's values supporting each other by taking each other's roles.

Mac Flecknoe primarily concerns art, but the publisher, or whoever it was who supplied the subtitle for the surreptitious first edition, certainly understood what was going on; it was, he said, a satire on the true-blue Protestant Poet, Shadwell. The poem is about poetry (and other arts), particularly drama, but Dryden does not write of poetry in the abstract. There are particular plays produced in his own time, and the tinsel-and-cardboard romance of the poem is set in that present. Moreover, one can only understand the sense in which Shadwell is bad by attention not just to the good, but to the good in politics and religion as well as in art:

> *Heywood* and *Shirley* were but Types of thee,
> Thou last great Prophet of Tautology:
> Even I, a dunce of more renown than they,
> Was sent before but to prepare thy way.
>
> (29–32)

Flecknoe ("I") compares Shadwell (or Mac Flecknoe) to Christ (the "last great Prophet"), the fulfillment or antitype of such earlier types as Thomas Heywood and John Shirley. Shadwell can be termed the last prophet because he will fulfill the promises, and because he is the Messiah announced by Flecknoe as John the Baptist. A believing Christian cannot introduce references of this kind without expecting that they will take over what they are aligned with (literature) and totally evaluate it. Which is of course Dryden's aim: Flecknoe and Shadwell are respectively anti-Baptists and anti-Christs of wit. . . .

THE HIGHER MIMESIS

The turning of something absurd into a vehicle of meaning testifies to Dryden's faith in the reality of experience, both as we conceive that from our conscious selves and as we conceive it from external reality. His belief in the correspondence of those inner and outer worlds assisted him in acquiring the confidence that he maintained for all but a short period of his life, and the belief also permitted him to think of art in terms of a higher mimesis. Dryden's mimesis is "higher" not only because of its role in his heroic idea, but even more because of the evident reality he discovers to be shared by the subjective and objective worlds, by ancient and modern times, by religion and art, by pagan and Christian lore. At the center of all those things in *The Hind and the Panther* we discovered, perhaps to our surprise, that character was the important thing. Some two decades before, Dryden had defined drama (or rather art):

> A just and lively Image of Humane Nature, representing its Passions and Humours, and the Changes of Fortune to which it is subject; for the Delight and Instruction of Mankind.

The sense of what men and women are, the knowledge of what life is like, was as important to Dryden's art as his great idea, which told him what people and life might be. By enriching the real with the possible, Dryden heightens realism and makes life seem more valuable. Both his sense of "Humane Nature" and his hopes for it lead him into the preserves of narrative in most of his career, but both also lead him to swear a higher allegiance to matters that qualify—and make meaningful—the narrative he employs.

Mac Flecknoe offers us a useful early example, and a glance at the *Aeneis* will give us later evidence. Since I have found myself surprised on making a précis of *Mac Flecknoe,* I shall offer one here. The reigning emperor of the realm of Nonsense, Flecknoe, has grown old. He debates with himself as to which of his sons (in the Turkish fashion) ought to succeed him. He decides that it must be Shadwell, who most resembles his father in dullness. Flecknoe then (29) begins his first speech, the Thucydidean *logos* interruptive of historical narration. He tells how earlier dunces were only types of Shadwell, how even he himself merely prepared the way by making songs in Portugal, foretelling Shadwell's own recent lute-songs for water-music. His own raptures over his son lead him to weep for joy and to conclude that every reason, but chiefly Shadwell's plays, argue that he was destined to be prince of dullness.

The narrator then describes the locale where the succession ceremony is to take place: by the ruins of a Tower of the wall of the City, where now there thrive brothels, a school for stage-players, and other disreputably suburban activities. A prophecy by Thomas Dekker is recalled, naming a prince like Shadwell, a man prolific in the creation of characters. Now, hearing the call of Fame, unread authors appear, with a publisher leading the guard. Old Flecknoe appears on a throne made from his own books, and on his right hand sits Shadwell, his brows heavy in fog. When he swears the coronation oath, his father passes to him the regalia, a mug of ale and Flecknoe's own play, *Love's Kingdom*. Just then twelve owls hoot, and the crowd shouts three times.

At this Flecknoe delivers a prophetic exhortation. Beginning with a blessing on the prince, he evokes an Amen from the crowd. He urges his son to new depths of ignorance and impudence, to continuous nonproductive effort. Anything interesting should be left to others, and the fools in the plays should take their author as model. Above all, he should rely on his own talents for dullness, avoiding any claim to kinship with Jonson, life, or art. Jonson never reached such ideal stupidities as Shadwell, whose latest work is always more of the same dullness. The praise continues, mentioning Shadwell's grossness, his risible tragedy, soporific comedy, and toothless satires. The old prince particularly recommends leaving playwriting for acrostics, shaped poems, and torture of words. His last charge is muffled, however, for he is unceremoniously sent down a stage trap by two characters of Shadwell's dramatic creation. As the old man sinks, his prophetic mantle blows upward on a subterranean draft to Shadwell with the promise that he will be twice as dull as his father.

With omissions of detail not essential to the simple narrative line, that represents the plot of *Mac Flecknoe,* as anyone would recognize. The actual amount of plot surprises us, and I think that that helps account for the fact that we always remember the poem to be longer than it is, 217 lines. I take it of great importance that the poem in fact possesses a considerable measure of plot, and of equal importance that our impression runs quite contrary to the fact. If Dryden has provided us with more plot than we sense exists, that can only mean that his concern lies less with simple narrative than with other matters. As we have seen, Dryden's interest lies particularly in the evocation of a system of values interrelating the three principal ones: art, religion, and monarchy. Two other particularly Drydenian emphases fall on speech and place. Of course what is said carries the constant irony of praise for the wrong reasons. When so systematic, irony tends to take on some degree of unreality or of allegory: Pope's Sylphs, Swift's Lilliputians breaking eggs, or the Romantics designating the breach between symbol and reality. Dryden's irony creates no Baudelairean unreal city. It is the Thames that flows, well fed by the sewer ditches. A real place, the Barbican, provides the scene. Scholars have always assumed that Aston Hall must exist somewhere in London, although they have not identified it. So strong is the sense of London, or at least of suburban, extramural London.

The sense of reality, of the just and lively image of the known world, constitutes that higher mimesis of a truer, stable reality on which Dryden's poems are founded. His irony lacks what might be termed the metaphysical import of Swift's irony, because Dryden's metaphysics confirms the reality we feel. His irony is rhetorical in that it is rooted primarily in speech, the means by which individuals establish their relations with each other and express their understanding of people in their world. From *Mac Flecknoe* through the poems of the 1680s, skipping the period of crisis, Dryden's major poems use speech at great length. His trust in this capacity distinguishing men from beasts resembles his trust in those two other characteristics similarly distinguishing man: reason and laughter. Of course this satire orders things in gradations and contrasts. Shadwell is not quoted for a single word, and so becomes an inarticulate poet, whereas his reputed father seems garrulous to more people than the eager heir. Perhaps Dryden's higher mimesis can best be represented by his pretense to take as (unpleasant) realities the characters in Shadwell's own plays. Shadwell took great pride in them as humours creations in the tradition of Ben Jonson, and Dryden says in effect, yes, they are real: look what they do.

We must carefully consider Dryden's command of reality. It has long been assumed that Flecknoe was an Irish priest. In fact the only evidence for that assumption is provided by *Mac Flecknoe,* and a close reading of the poem does not support the assumption at all. Dryden symbolically equates Ireland with illiteracy and barbarism, dubs Shadwell "Mac" Flecknoe, and that is as real to the world as is the portrait of Shadwell in this poem. Dryden of course develops essential facts about Shadwell and uses traits of personality and character that can be verified. But Dryden also makes of Shadwell a literary character who varies considerably from the historical dramatist. One need only compare another "Shadwell," the Og of the second part of *Absalom and Achitophel,* or compare the "Shaftesbury" that is Achitophel and that who is the "Chief" of *The Medall* to see that Dryden's art creates the reality we presume so readily.

LAURA BROWN

The Ideology of Restoration
Poetic Form: John Dryden

Describing the fleet of ships that brought the royal party from Holland
to Dover in the spring of 1660, Dryden's *Astraea Redux* (1660) asserts a
confidence in the safety of the returning monarch:

> Secure as when the *Halcyon* breeds, with these
> He that was born to drown might cross the Seas.
>
> (236–37)

As a comment on the king's short trip across the Channel, this couplet is
at best problematic; as a celebration of his restoration to the throne, it is
ineffective and contradictory. The daring juxtaposition of the successful crossing and the image of inevitable death by drowning expresses the exuberance
with which Dryden's poem treats the occasion of the king's return. The radical
disparity between the two ideas illustrates the enthusiastic excess typical of
the tone and imagery in *Astraea Redux,* and the convergence of these con-
trarieties suggests a joyful reversal of fate, a resurrection, a triumphant defiance of history. But these lines deny as much as they affirm. They associate
the secure voyager with a man destined to drown, the restored monarch with
a victim of inevitable disaster, and the jubilant return of royal absolutism
with the prospect of its ultimate demise. In fact, drowning is a frequent
metaphor for historical cataclysm, and specifically for the revolution, in
Dryden's poetry. Here, the prediction of drowning is grammatically indicative,
while the successful crossing is conditional, deriving prominence in the couplet

From *PMLA* 97, no. 3 (May 1982). © 1982 by the Modern Language Association
of America.

solely from the extrinsic evidence of the king's actual return. The distinctive paradoxical structure of this couplet is characteristic of Dryden's major verse. These lines make an affirmation that they simultaneously fail to achieve. They reflect an unexpressed formal disjunction between celebration and anxiety. This essay seeks to explore that disjunction, to describe its centrality in Dryden's poetic corpus, and to define its ideological significance.

"Contradiction" and "paradox" have been staple terms for Dryden's critics since the modern reassessment and defense of his poetry began to gather force in the middle of this century. Studies of Dryden's imagery and appreciations of his poetic art have replaced the older consensus that dismissed Dryden's poetry as a form of rhyming prose. And at the same time, the earlier accusations of political opportunism and self-interested aesthetic pragmatism have given way to an emphasis on Dryden's divided consciousness, his skeptical temperament, and his consequent turn to the security of a principled conservatism. For recent Dryden criticism, the aesthetic and political poles of this revision are mutually dependent: the discovery of metaphorical complexity, irony, and imagistic richness in close readings of Dryden's poetry coincides with the documentation of various sources of ambiguity, division, and skepticism in Dryden's intellectual contexts. Louis I. Bredvold's influential study *The Intellectual Milieu of John Dryden* established the parameters of this new assessment of the poet, outlining the heritage of Pyrrhonism, the impact of the new science, and the resultant religious Fideism and political conservatism that characterize Dryden's "cast of mind."

The problem for this consensus begins with the breakdown of its intellectual component. Phillip Harth's *Contexts of Dryden's Thought* directly challenges the hypothesis of Dryden's Pyrrhonism and the assumption of a continual suspension of judgment in Dryden's most characteristic writing. Ironically, though most critics now accept this rejection of Pyrrhonism, recent readings of Dryden's specific works have increasingly discovered skepticism, paradox, subversion, absurdity, or irony to be their central aesthetic achievement. Such interpretations consistently disregard or dismiss the difficulties presented by the hypothesis of philosophical skepticism and stress instead the immediate and demonstrable intricacies of Dryden's style. Alan Roper's brief confrontation with the question in his "Characteristics of Dryden's Prose" typifies a decade of evasions:

> The *ignis fatuus* of scepticism flickers across almost the whole terrain of Dryden studies. . . . Was Dryden's scepticism real or apparent, dogmatic or probabilist; was he consistent or not? . . . Can sceptics, or can they not, have a preferred point of view, while recognizing others? Such questions, with their

answers, their distinctions, their refinements upon previous distinctions, usually derive from analysis which isolates ideas, intellectual positions, in Dryden's writings, often translating them into other terms, and then reads them off against a schedule of philosophical categories. If we restore Dryden's ideas to their context, responding to them in Dryden's words, the general problem disappears. Of course Dryden was a sceptic: the movement of his sentences declares him to be so.

Since at least 1968, then, Dryden studies have confronted a central critical contradiction, no less significant for being largely unacknowledged. Discussions and appreciations of the complexity of Dryden's language, the problematic intricacy of his metaphors, or the subversive irony of his allegory have come unmoored from an understanding of his intellectual, political, or social beliefs. Like Roper's simple dismissal of the intellectual context of Dryden's art, the current explication of Dryden's major poetry can give no account of itself. It can only valorize the ambiguity or the indeterminacy of the text as a source of aesthetic richness that, from the perspective of critical modernism, is its own justification.

For the theorist of Restoration poetic form, this contradiction in Dryden studies supplies both an interpretive fact and a critical goal. Recent readings of Dryden's major poems clearly show that these works share a tendency to attract imputations of irony or skepticism. An analysis of Dryden's poetry, then, must begin with the congruity of these interpretations, but it must do more than contribute an additional reading or an additional appreciation of the complexities of the text: it must explain the origin and significance of those complexities. In short, a full account will define the form of Dryden's poetry: the common structural core of his disparate works. But it will also define the ideology of this poetic form: the system of beliefs, assumptions, and ideals—conscious and unconscious, coherent and contradictory—that issues in the characteristic underlying shape of Dryden's literary production.

I

The sort of disjunction exemplified by the problematic praise of the royal fleet in the couplet quoted from *Astraea Redux* persists throughout Dryden's poetry. In *Astraea Redux* itself, the final welcome to the king as he approaches the cliffs of Dover raises a dichotomous image of disaster and success:

But you

.   .   .   .   .

> By that same mildness which your Fathers Crown
> Before did ravish, shall secure your own.
>
> (256–59)

Like the poem's other allusions to the errors of the revolution, these lines create an effect of celebratory contrast and extravagant compliment. Charles's "mildness" ensures the security of his reign; it also associates the king with Christ and the king's return with nothing less than the Resurrection. But matching this assertion of confidence is an anxiety evident in the juxtaposition of "ravish" and "secure." Both actions stem from the "mildness" that links Charles to his father, the present restoration to the past execution of the king, and this association implicitly overturns the future security promised in the second line. The couplet offers no reconciliation of past and future, nor even an explanation of their divergence. Like the earlier depiction of the king's security on the seas, these lines open a space between incompatible meanings.

In general, ironic reversal and subdued disjunction are among Dryden's most common local devices. They occur in the early panegyrical poetry as a softened version of metaphysical wit. *To My Lord Chancellor* (1662) juxtaposes martial strength with disarmament:

> Justice that sits and frowns where publick Laws
> Exclude soft mercy from a private cause,
> In your Tribunal most her self does please;
> There only smiles because she lives at ease;
> And like young *David* finds her strength the more
> When disincumberd from those arms she wore.
>
> (49–54)

"To the Lady Castlemaine" (1663) similarly equates shipwreck and success:

> As Sea-men shipwrackt on some happy shore,
> Discover Wealth in Lands unknown before;
> And what their Art had labour'd long in vain,
> By their misfortunes happily obtain:
> So my much-envy'd Muse by Storms long tost,
> Is thrown upon your Hospitable Coast;
> And finds more favour by her ill success,
> Than she could hope for by her happiness.
>
> (1–8)

The later poetry, less dependent on conceit, produces a comparable effect through allegory, oxymoron, and what Dryden terms "satire." The famous opening lines of *Absalom and Achitophel* (1681) implicitly oppose a present illicit promiscuity to a past pious polygamy:

In pious times, e'r Priest-craft did begin,
Before *Polygamy* was made a sin;
When man, on many, multiply'd his kind,
E'r one to one was, cursedly, confind:
When Nature prompted, and no law deny'd
Promiscuous use of Concubine and Bride;
Then, *Israel's* Monarch, after Heaven's own heart,
His vigorous Warmth did, variously, impart.

(1–8)

The numerous oxymorons of *Mac Flecknoe* (1678) juxtapose the contemptible talents of Flecknoe and Shadwell with the loftiest qualities of monarchy, religion, and art:

The rest to some faint meaning make pretence,
But *Sh——* never deviates into sense.

· · · · · · · · · · · ·

Besides his goodly Fabrick fills the eye,
And seems design'd for thoughtless Majesty:
Thoughtless as Monarch Oakes, that shade the plain,
And, spread in solemn state, supinely reign.
Heywood and *Shirley* were but Types of thee,
Thou last great Prophet of Tautology.

(19–30)

In "To Sir Godfrey Kneller" (1694) Dryden both demonstrates and admits his satiric propensity:

Our Arts are Sisters; though not Twins in Birth:
For Hymns were sung in *Edens* happy Earth,
By the first Pair; while *Eve* was yet a Saint;
Before she fell with Pride, and learn'd to paint.
Forgive th'allusion; 'twas not meant to bite;
But Satire will have room, where e're I write.

(89–94)

The comic irony of the preceding examples, in which the reversal tends to diminish or familiarize the subject, is matched by what some recent critics (Clark, Griffin) have described as a tragic ambiguity or contradiction in "To the Memory of Mr. Oldham" (1684). The opening Virgilian analogy of that poem—"Thus *Nisus* fell upon the slippery place, / While his young Friend perform'd and won the Race" (9–10)—equates victory with early death by identifying Oldham with Euryalus, the winner of the race, and by evoking the other appearance of the two friends, in which Nisus dies in a futile attempt to save Euryalus's life. Dryden's assessment of Oldham's verse in the body of the poem exhibits a similar dichotomy: the paradoxical conjunction of completeness and inadequacy, praise and criticism. Oldham's talent is both "abundant" and fundamentally lacking:

> to thy abundant store
> What could advancing Age have added more?
> It might (what Nature never gives the young)
> Have taught the numbers of thy native Tongue.
>
> (11–14)

His work is "ripe" (11), but also immature:

> Thy generous fruits, though gather'd ere their prime
> Still shew'd a quickness.
>
> (19–20)

And the poem ultimately combines a sanguine preference for the brevity of Oldham's career with a regretful sense that it was "ah too short" (23). Like the unreconciled triumph and disaster of Charles's sea voyage in *Astraea Redux*, the contrasts here—victory and death, poetic success and failure, triumph and regret—represent a formal contradiction that implicates all the poem's local allusions and images.

These details of Dryden's poetic language have a common structural core: the equation of drowning and the successful crossing of the seas, of ravishment and security, of strength and disarmament, of ill success and happiness, of whoring and pious polygamy, of prophecy and tautology, of painting and cosmetics, of triumph and regret—an equation that, for different reasons, in different contexts, and at differing degrees of conscious art, strives to join disparate and usually contradictory sentiments, qualities, or effects. In the satires, the equation is comic, deflating, and deliberate; in the panegyrical poems it is equally conscious, occasionally comic, but more often elaborately complimentary; in the political and religious poetry it is less clearly conscious, less elegantly controlled, but more assertive and more seriously subversive. Martin Price has described Dryden's verse as "dialectical," and analyses of the heroic couplet commonly refer to a balanced dialectical pattern of "proposition and completion" or "tension and release." But while the rhyme and meter of Dryden's verse clearly promote grammatical or syntactical equation, the distinctive quality of Dryden's semantic, imagistic, or thematic equation is its recurrent failure, a failure not merely of literal identity (which seventeenth-century poetics would in any case have proscribed) but of functional equivalence. The satirical or oxymoronic equation achieves its designed effect by failing; the panegyrical elevates by its very impossibility; and the political, historical, and personal equations acquire significance by the incompatibility of their terms. Dryden's form, then, in its linguistic and stylistic details, characteristically proposes an equation of irreconcilable terms, an equation that produces various kinds of poetic disjunction, and that reveals a deep and unexpressed contradiction.

II

In "To Oldham" the various local paradoxes of line and image merge to produce an extended paradoxical analogy in which the ripeness of Oldham's fall is both asserted and denied. This larger sort of disjunction, where the contradictory terms of the equation speak to each other across the whole poem and through a series of interrelated and extended metaphors, represents a more general variety of Dryden's characteristic form. The sustained and evolving analogy between the new science and the restoration of royal absolutism in "To My Honored Friend, Dr. Charleton" (1662) exemplifies this larger structure at its most artful. The political analogy of "To Charleton" begins as a subdued metaphor based on the description of the progress of scientific inquiry: the "Tyranny" of Aristotle, the voyages of discovery that "shook his Throne" (1, 9). It proceeds, by means of a description of Charleton's claim that Stonehenge was originally a Danish coronation site, to a direct association of the new science with Charles's restoration. And it ends with a turn to Charles himself, and to the particular historical moment of his "*Refuge*" at Stonehenge in 1651:

> These Ruines sheltered once *His* Sacred Head,
> Then when from *Wor'sters* fatal Field *He* fled;
> Watch'd by the Genius of this Royal place,
> And mighty Visions of the Danish Race.
> His *Refuge* then was for a *Temple* shown:
> But, *He* Restor'd, 'tis now become a *Throne*.
>
> (53–58)

The complex interaction of terms in this analogy is typical of Dryden's larger poetic equations, as other critics have observed. Earl Wasserman notes that "To Charleton" begins "with the political theme serving as the vehicle for the account of science" and ends "with the scientific treatise serving as the vehicle for the political thesis." For Wasserman the juxtaposition produces an ultimate synthesis. Such a synthesis, however, exists only in assertion. The equation of science with restoration or with absolutist prosperity is common in Dryden's poetry, frequently complex or vexed, and characteristically distinguished by an assertion of coherence that conceals an ultimate failure of congruity.

In "To Charleton" this failure is evident in the implicit stresses of the concluding metaphor, which sums up the analogy of the whole poem. As an object of scientific inquiry, Stonehenge celebrates the monarchy, just as Charleton's treatise and all the enterprises of the Royal Society serve Charles II. Thus Dryden's final couplet claims to rewrite history: in 1651, when Charles took refuge at Stonehenge, it "was" a Roman temple (the argument of Inigo Jones's earlier, rival treatise); in 1662, after the king's coronation, it "becomes" a Danish throne. The career of the monarch, not the argument of the scientist, explains and confers meaning on the past. Dryden's final couplet, however, proceeds no further than the rough temporal coincidence of the publication of Charleton's *Chorea Gigantum* (1662) with the restoration and coronation of Charles II. The metaphor itself admits that Charles came to Stonehenge as a fugitive, not as a monarch, and hence that the king is a victim of history, not its master. Neither Charles's restoration nor Charleton's treatise could make Stonehenge a throne, any more than the argument for Stonehenge's origin as a Danish coronation site could sanctify Charles's restoration or unmake the history of his refuge there.

Analogies of varying sorts occur throughout Dryden's poetry: *Annus Mirabilis* (1666) associates a present physical event, the great fire, with a past political event, the revolution; the contemporary panegyrics compare their subjects with the characters of biblical and especially prelapsarian history; and "To Dr. Charleton" and "To My Dear Friend Mr. Congreve" (1693) equate literary and political affairs. Alan Roper, like Earl Wasserman and David Vieth, identifies "a disparity between the nominal tenor and vehicles" in some of Dryden's characteristic analogies (*Poetic Kingdoms*). Though these critics explain the disparity differently and fail to specify its source, their common perception does suggest a recurrent ideological tension. Such a tension surfaces in the *Heroique Stanzas* (1659), where Cromwell's power and success are attributed both to divine appointment, with all its implications of public responsibility, and to individual, "private" usurpation, with its explicit challenge to the status quo. This dichotomy is directly linked to the poem's ambivalent treatment of the status and legitimacy of Cromwell's title (see Roper, *Poetic Kingdoms*). The characterization of Cromwell himself is similarly disjunctive. The poem presents him as an exemplar of implicitly individualistic bourgeois and mercantilist values and commends his successful implementation of an imperialist policy: his negotiations with Holland, his opposition to Spain, and his forays into the New World. But though Cromwell's virtues are recognizably those of a future social structure, the poem praises him in terms appropriate to a public hero of romance: he has the "Heroick haste" of an Alexander pursuing victory and a "Heröique Vertue" conferred by heaven.

Michael McKeon's suggestive outline of the historical implications of *Annus Mirabilis* defines a similar contradiction; in fact, McKeon's reading of this early work closely supports my assessment of Dryden's corpus as a whole. The poem's evident purpose is to defend the royalist status quo as a source of national interest and prosperity and as an expression of providential necessity. But in making this conservative assertion, the poem consistently evokes the progressive goals of the new science, with which it associates not only national prosperity but the monarchy itself. The "suggestive uneasiness" that McKeon rightly finds in the poem results from the historical incompatibility of these two objectives: on the one hand, the preservation of a royalist absolutism founded on feudal social structures and economic relationships and, on the other, the advocacy of scientific empiricism, material progress, mercantile nationalism, and economic individualism—the complex of ideas and practices associated with early capitalism. In short, the juxtaposed ideals of *Annus Mirabilis* are the polarities of seventeenth-century political, social, and economic history. Even as the poem expounds a conservative, royalist ideology, it transcends its local political reference, as well as its historical context, by presenting a vision of an imperialist future based on maritime capitalism:

> Instructed ships shall sail to quick Commerce;
>   By which remotest Regions are alli'd:
> Which makes one City of the Universe,
>   Where some may gain, and all may be suppli'd.
>
> (649–52)

Annus Mirabilis thus celebrates a contradictory equation of neofeudal absolutism and bourgeois imperialism, providential order and economic individualism, monarchy and empiricist science, the values of the past and the ideals of the future—an equation that is essentially parallel to, though locally distinct from, the analogies of "To Charleton" and *Heroique Stanzas*.

This equation, clearly a powerful formal force in Dryden's political and historical poems, also surfaces in the juxtaposition characteristic of his poems on the arts: that of absolute ideals and progress or change. In the poem "To the Earl of Roscomon" (1684), commending Roscommon's *Essay on Translated Verse*, the metaphor of translation is used to equate "Arts," "Science," Roscomon, restoration, and Charles II:

> Whether the fruitful *Nile*, or *Tyrian* Shore,
> The seeds of Arts and Infant Science bore,
> 'Tis sure the noble Plant, translated first,
> Advanc'd its head in *Grecian* Gardens nurst.
>
> . . . .
>
> The Wit of *Greece*, the Gravity of *Rome*
> Appear exalted in the *Brittish* Loome;
> The Muses Empire is restor'd agen,
> In *Charles* his Reign, and by *Roscomon's* Pen.
>
> (1–4, 26–29)

This summary of the progress of poetry is both encomiastic and ironic (Miner, "Dryden"; the virtues of a past ideal age implicitly qualify the accomplishments of the present real one. Significantly, the poem's vision of an ideal aesthetic future is expressed as the "translation" of Homer and Virgil from the past to the present, a conceit whose whole premise is a historical impossibility.

"To Congreve" contains a more overt contradiction between the virtues of the past age, represented as a lost ideal, and the accomplishments of the present, embodied in Congreve himself, who combines the political metaphor of legitimate succession with the religious one of atonement and redemption. Thus Dryden's famous rebuke of the present age expresses a clear distrust of the future:

> Already I am worn with Cares and Age;
> And just abandoning th'Ungrateful Stage:
> Unprofitably kept at Heav'ns expence,
> I live a Rent-charge on his Providence.
>
> . . . .
>
> Let not the Insulting Foe my Fame pursue;
> But shade those Lawrels which descend to You.
>
> (66–75)

But this sentiment is scarcely reconcilable with Dryden's opening millennial announcement that "the promis'd hour is come at last; / the present Age of Wit obscures the past" (1–2). The paradox here resides in the problematic relation between the past and the present, in which each is better than the other, in the tension between two views of history, one progressive and the other degenerative.

Dryden's complaint in "To Congreve" is reminiscent of his attack on the present age in the ode "To the Pious Memory of the Accomplisht Young Lady Mrs Anne Killigrew" (1685), and specifically on "the steaming Ordures of the Stage" described in that poem (65). Whether the work is read as a kind of travesty, as a straightforward—albeit generous—elegy, or as the translation of a minor versifier into the emblem of an artistic ideal, its distinctive quality is the incommensurability of its human subject with its transcendent claims. Anne Killigrew, Dryden volunteers in stanza 3, was never visited by the swarm of bees that endowed Plato with eloquence (50–53). Of art "she had none" (71) but made up the deficit with her "Noble Vigor" (75). She knew nothing of life (79) or love (83–87) but boldly wrote of both. She conquered the empire of "Painture" by force, as it lay "without Defence" against her "In-rodes" (99–100), and possessed enough skill to depict "The Shape, the Face, with ev'ry Lineament" (102) of her human subjects, and even the "Dress" of the queen (136). Her genius was so immoderate that "What next she had design'd, Heaven only knows" (146). In short, Dryden's poem is clearly conscious of the modesty of its subject's talents. One critic has even claimed that the singsong and rather mundane description of Anne Killigrew's paintings in stanza 6 parodies her own poetry, which was included in the volume to which Dryden's ode was attached (Hope; see also Vieth, "Irony").

But all these subtle ironies are balanced by the sincerity of Dryden's defense of poetry in stanza 4, by the apotheosis seriously evoked in the conclusion, and, most specifically, by the sustained imagistic structure that links Anne Killigrew's birth with the Incarnation and makes the "Sweet Saint" (193) herself an interceding virgin, a moral exemplar, a conqueror, and a monarch. The poles of this poem—the real identity of Anne Killigrew and the transcendent figure whose final ascension is fully affirmed in imagery and tone—are by definition incommensurable. Yet the ode's whole enterprise is their equation: the assertion of a functional identity between the mortal and the eternal, the translation of the local into the absolute. For Dryden this equation makes possible not only Anne Killigrew's personal apotheosis but the resurrection of the "Heav'nly Gift of Poesy" (57) from "This lubrique and adult'rate age" (63). The difference between this poem and "To Roscomon" or "To Congreve" is that the ideal is located in neither the past nor the future but in an inaccessible realm beyond the mortal.

The similarity of works as diverse as "Anne Killigrew" and *Heroique Stanzas*, then, like the recurrent structures of Dryden's lines and couplets, suggests a shared form characterized by disjunction and incommensurability, the failure of equation. Sanford Budick's reading of Dryden's religious poetry finds a comparable phenomenon in *Religio Laici* (1682) and *The Hind and the Panther* (1687): "From a formalist point of view, we might say that it is the planned leap or gap itself—the architectonic void supported between proposition and conclusion—which gives these works much of their power." In defining the attitude toward reason in *Religio Laici*—an issue that has con-

tinued to vex critics who insist on viewing the work's assumptions as static
and monolithic—Budick shows a tension between the use of reason as a
tool of empirical examination and the account of reason as innate revelation, a tension that reflects the contemporary conflict between the new science
and the old metaphysics. This conflict accounts for the contradiction between
Dryden's laborious argument, in the poem and its preface, justifying the salvation of those heathens who, lacking revelation, "follow'd *Reasons* Dictates
right" (208) and his peremptory rejection of the deist's apparently equivalent
reliance on reason:

> Vain, wretched Creature, how art thou misled
> To think thy Wit these God-like Notions bred!
> These Truths are not the product of thy Mind,
> But dropt from Heaven, and of a Nobler kind.
> *Reveal'd Religion* first inform'd thy Sight,
> And *Reason* saw not, til *Faith* sprung the Light.
> Hence all thy *Natural Worship* takes the *Source:*
> 'Tis *Revelation* what thou thinkst *Discourse.*
>
>   (64–71)

In Budick's view, though Dryden's material and sources are contradictory,
his poem is not; *Religio Laici* presents a theological paradox organically. But
Budick's own evidence suggests that the coherence asserted by the poet is
not demonstrated by the text. That *Religio Laici* reproduces a contemporary
theological paradox confirms rather than contravenes the poem's disjunctive structure.

Steven N. Zwicker, analyzing Dryden's political poetry, argues that in
the earlier poems metaphor is used to construct "an easy congruence" of
the past and the future, to bridge the gap between the ideal and the real.
Only in the poetry of the eighties, Zwicker suggests, does Dryden seem less
able to effect such a reconciliation, when he is confronted with the crisis of
the Stuart monarchy. The depictions of a utopian future, or ultimately of
any future at all, certainly diminish as the tone, the topics, and the conclusions of Dryden's poems evolve from *Annus Mirabilis* to "To Oldham" and
the Anne Killigrew ode. But the shared characteristics of Dryden's analogies
suggest that his basic poetic form is surprisingly constant from the earliest
years of his career to the latest, and that the constancy of his form lies in
the gap itself, in the unexpressed space between the terms of each equation.

III

This characteristic space is discernible not only in Dryden's lines and
couplets and in the larger images and sustained metaphors of his verse, but

also in the general shape of his most successful poetic works. The governing premise of *Mac Flecknoe*, for example, is the failure of congruence between Flecknoe or Shadwell and a genuine hero, a genuine monarch, or a genuine redeemer. The whole poem—from its "plot," the coronation, to the most specific aspects of its oxymoronic style—is ordered by the incommensurability of the two terms that it playfully equates. In fact, the greater the disparity, in plot as well as in style, the more fully *Mac Flecknoe* realizes its aim. In this respect, Dryden's mock-heroic mode is the most artful and conscious version of his disjunctive form as well as the version that most ostentatiously courts subversiveness. A travesty of monarchy, even one aimed at ridiculing the illegitimate hero, is a travesty of monarchy nonetheless.

In *Absalom and Achitophel* the disparity is neither so deliberate nor so near the surface. The explicit premise of the poem is the direct and even determinant conjunction between the contemporary exclusion crisis and the figural past of Old Testament history. The past is used to shape and explain the present and even, in the conclusion of the poem, to prophesy the future:

> Henceforth a Series of new time began,
> The mighty Years in long Procession ran:
> Once more the Godlike *David* was Restor'd,
> And willing Nations knew their Lawfull Lord.
> (1028–31)

The biblical analogy here enables Dryden to use the past tense to predict the future: Charles's settlement of the exclusion crisis will lead to a new age of prosperity and peace in England, just as David's restoration did in Israel. These lines echo the opening couplet of the climactic verse paragraph in *Astraea Redux*:

> And now times whiter Series is begun
> Which in soft Centuries shall smoothly run.
> (292–93)

But in *Astraea Redux* the prediction is made in the present tense: Charles's restoration has already initiated the "Series of new time" that, twenty-one years later in *Absalom and Achitophel,* is grammatically past and metaphorically yet to begin. The present is significantly absent from this affirmation of stability, and its omission is the direct product of the poem's analogical structure. Like *Mac Flecknoe*, this work proposes an equation, but here the significance of the equation resides, not in its own satiric reversal, but rather in the struggle to bring order and stability to historical experience.

The signs of this struggle appear in the ironies and anxieties implicit in the allegory. The characterization of Charles juxtaposes the image of the biblical patriarch and that of the contemporary rake. In the opening lines, as we saw earlier, this disparity is ironic, humorously admonitory, or disarming. In the concluding pronouncement of justice, it works as a dramatic reversal, supplying the poem's only semblance of a climax: the court rake's sudden turn to severity. Moreover, the plot of *Absalom and Achitophel*, like that of *Mac Flecknoe*, is abruptly truncated. The sudden denouement disrupts not only the poem's internal development—which appears to promise a conflict between the carefully delineated opposing forces of Achitophel and David—but also the much more smoothly symmetrical shape of the biblical source—which moves from tension to open conflict to tragic and inevitable resolution. In *Mac Flecknoe* the truncation of the coronation "plot" results from the priority of mock-heroic disjunction; the local effects of comic disparity take precedence over the continuity of the action. But in *Absalom and Achitophel* the truncation results not from the artfulness of the work itself but from the incongruity between contemporary events and biblical history. David's conflict with Absalom leads to actual usurpation, open battle, and Absalom's death; Charles's leads to the political maneuverings of the Oxford Parliament. But, ironically, the biblical story comes closer than Dryden's distortion to representing the actual shape of Restoration history: Monmouth was eventually executed, and the monarchical crisis ultimately led to the revolution of 1688. In effect, the assumption of security and order in Dryden's narrative contradicts both the biblical analogue and the contemporary course of events. In struggling to impose a conservative assertion of stability on the inevitably recalcitrant forces of history, the poem must falsify both the past and the present, the two terms that it endeavors to equate. In this sense, its disjunctiveness is double: the failure of its biblical analogy betrays the failure of its affirmation of contemporary order. And the analogy, in its very inadequacy, produces an insight beyond and even opposed to the poem's ostensible meaning.

Dryden's major heroic drama is notable both for its depiction of a radical, Herculean hero (to adopt Eugene Waith's term) and for its ultimate affirmation of a conservative status quo. In this respect, the action of a play like *The Conquest of Granada* (pt. 1, 1670; pt. 2, 1671) gives dramatic substance to a formal contradiction. Almanzor, the erratic, individualistic protagonist of that play, represents by his very nature a serious threat to social order, particularly to monarchy and even, ultimately, to the forces of European civilization and Christianity embodied in the invading Spanish army of Ferdinand and Isabella. But by formal fiat—the imposition of a fortuitous romance resolution on the hero's extravagant career—this radical challenge is turned to the service of royalist stability. When Almanzor is suddenly discovered to be a Spaniard and a Christian, the son of the noble Duke of Arcos, he and his lover are adopted by the kindly king and queen of Spain; and the radical hero, without ever revoking his individualistic assertion—"I alone am King of me" (pt. 1: 1.1.206)—accepts and celebrates the authority of the Spanish monarchy:

> Our Banners to th' *Alhambra*'s turrets bear;
> Then, wave our Conqu'ring Crosses in the Aire;
> And Cry, with showts of Triumph, live and raign,
> Great *Ferdinand* and *Isabel* of *Spain*.
>   (pt. 2: 5.3.345–48)

Almanzor's final affirmation of civic order attains legitimacy through another analogy characteristic of Dryden's poetry, that between private and public affairs. Though Almanzor himself always remains "a private man" (pt. 1: 4.2.474), fighting only for personal interests and at personal inducement, the play presents him as a public hero, a "Soul which Empires first began" (pt. 1: 4.2.475), and often dresses his love conflicts in the language of state affairs. Thus in the last scene, a character who has never taken a public stand and whose actions have consistently run counter to public order can speak for the forces of the public good without blatant implausibility, but not without underlying disjunction.

As the delicacy of these dramatic arrangements suggests, the royalist position in *The Conquest of Granada* is asserted, not won, and it is asserted in an action that presents its opposite, erratic individualism, with the full force of a radical challenge to social order. The specific ideology of this disjunction—royalist absolutism and progressive individualism—links it to works like *Heroique Stanzas*, "To Charleton," *Annus Mirabilis*, and even *Religio Laici*, while its formal control is perhaps more reminiscent of the carefully staged incongruities of *Mac Flecknoe*.

A somewhat different but equally characteristic paradox operates in the plot of *All for Love* (1667), where the action fails to substantiate the heroic virtues of the protagonists—Antony's epic valor and Cleopatra's enigmatic defiance and charisma. Though the play constantly refers to these virtues, and though the plot proceeds on the assumption that the characters resemble their Shakespearean precursors. Antony's heroism is wholly a matter of hearsay and Cleopatra's defiance only an elaborate lie concocted by Ventidius to lure Antony from his love. In fact, as represented in the play, Antony and Cleopatra are loyal lovers, pathetically devoted to each other, innocent of suspicion, of machination, and of public grandeur. Their conflict is artificially contrived by the subsidiary characters, Alexas and Ventidius, whose role is to give the play's evocation of pity the semblance of an action. *All for Love* thus derives its effect from a central dramatic disjunction: the protagonists' innocence and weakness produce pathos, while their implicit heroism gives that pathos an epic grandeur, a sense that empires and eternal glory are at stake. The drama's closing simile expresses this paradox succinctly: "See, see how th'lovers sit in state together, / As they were giving laws to half mankind!" (5.507–8). The Antony and Cleopatra of *All for Love* are only like those monarchs they mimic in their final suicide. In this play, the action is entirely incommensurate with its heroic claims. The resultant gap between asserted heroism and actual pathos produces the air of elegiac inadequacy and loss that is so notable in *All for Love*. Most notable in this connection, however, is the resemblance of the play's formal core to the disjunctive shape of "Anne Killigrew," "To Congreve," or "To Oldham."

IV

The illusory attribution of heroic stature to the tragedy of a "shrunk," "pitiful," and ruined lover (1.173–79) and a "weak, forsaken woman" (2.420) clearly differs from the ambiguous claim "with these / He that was born to drown might cross the Seas." These two problematic assertions occur in different kinds of works and at different levels of specificity—one structural, the other verbal—within each work. They serve different purposes by different formal means. They operate at different degrees of conscious artistry, with different materials, different assumptions, and different effects. But their differences illuminate the single quality they hold in common: the unexpressed space between the terms of an impossible equation—in *All for Love* the equation of heroism and pathos, in *Astraea Redux* that of security and doom.

The similarity of poetic statements as disparate as these makes it possible to penetrate to the core of Dryden's form, to define an essential structure that Dryden's individual poetic works realize in various ways. This structure, with its deep and unreconciled disjunction, reflects a continuous struggle to override a contradiction. Characterized by insufficiency, incommensurability, the failure of congruence, it represents the aesthetic codification of anxiety, the literary elaboration of an assertion at odds with itself.

This form is imprinted on the language, the couplets, the metaphors, the analogies, the actions, and the basic structural premises of Dryden's poetical works. In each of these aspects, of course, it appears in a different guise, and its distinctive generic manifestations give it even greater variety. The contrast between heroic drama and mock-heroic poetry, for instance, or between political allegory and pathetic tragedy suggests how much this form is mediated through the genres that embody it. But local manifestations only give substance to a structure that, in its characteristic disjunctivity, expresses the contradiction at the heart of Dryden's understanding of contemporary reality. Politically, Dryden favored royal absolutism and Stuart succession, the benevolent exercise of monarchical authority to preserve civic order and promote national prosperity. But in fact he fully accepted the terms and aims of the Restoration settlement, which qualified monarchical absolutism and formally instituted constitutional and legislative authority to counterpose that of the king. Socially, Dryden despised the "rascal rabble" and the common "mob" and celebrated the hierarchy of an aristocratic system, with its accoutrements of patronage and panegyric and its promises of continuity and stability. But he himself was one of England's first self-supporting literati; and his perpetual difficulties with patrons, pensions, and the shortfalls of the royal treasury, as well as his success in selling his talents for a living, especially as a dramatist and translator, testify to the presence, if not the predominance, of a different, even contradictory system. Economically, Dryden expounded the benefits of absolutist centrism while raising the possibility of a future individualist prosperity. Intellectually, he mixed a commitment to the new science and to the early manifestations of philosophical empiricism with an allegiance to the a priori stabilities of the old classicism. And theologically, he combined the old metaphysics with the new individual autonomy, the submission to a public, collective, or ancient authority with the discovery of a private faith, privately affirmed. In all these ways, Dryden's grasp of the reality of his age was paradoxical, repeatedly asserting a past ideal in terms of a contradictory present reality, shoring up the stability of an old system with the supports of an irreconcilable new one, and defending the stasis of history with the very evidence that marks its dynamism.

Dryden's lifelong literary production is the personal manifestation of these political and cultural contradictions. The defiance of history implicit in the description of the royal fleet in *Astraea Redux*, the oxymoronic incommensurability of *Mac Flecknoe*'s mock-heroic mode, the paradoxical equation of royalist and radical in *The Conquest of Granada*, and the central disjunctions of the allegory in *Absalom and Achitophel* all belong to the constellation of contradictory commitments and beliefs characteristic of Dryden's political, intellectual, and cultural position. This position is compatible with that of the other major Restoration court writers, and those writers share Dryden's tendency toward disjunction or reversal; the satiric comedy of Etherege, Wycherley, and Behn contrasts moral norms with social expedience, and Rochester's poetry consistently presents a cynical eternal regression, where every metaphorical vehicle deflates itself as well as its tenor. Dryden's poetic form, however, is distinctive because the polarities it presents are not solely the product of a satirical intention. While some specific poetic manifestations of Dryden's ideological disjunction are clearly artful and deliberate—the conceits of the early panegyrical poetry, the oxymorons of *Mac Flecknoe*, the ironic opening of *Absalom and Achitophel*, and the elaborate tours de force of the major dramatic actions—the ideology of Dryden's poetic form transcends deliberate artistry. What Dryden does carefully and consciously in one place or at one point in one poem is unacknowledged and unconscious in another. The irony in the opening of *Absalom and Achitophel* is as artful as any that Dryden produced, but the anxiety of that poem's final prophecy of "a Series of new time" is not part of a deliberate aesthetic elaboration. The congruence of conscious stylistic and structural effects with unconscious formal contradiction suggests a conjunction between deep ideological forces and studied art, poetic predisposition, and conventional trope. The use of the metaphysical conceit is for Dryden both a deliberate imitation of a successful seventeenth-century literary precedent and a signal of his own ideology, just as *All for Love* reveals, in its constrained and affective action, the influence of Racine and of the dramatic conventions of French classicism and yet retains its significance as a powerful dramatic manifestation of Dryden's peculiar disjunctive form.

In the past, critics have praised Dryden's poetry for its successful reconciliation of opposites—its artful joining of disparate images, perspectives, or experiences. This essay draws a very different conclusion. Dryden's form is not organic. It does not produce unity from disparity, though some individual poems claim to do so. It is defined precisely by its failure to reconcile, by its persistent reiteration of contradiction.

From a slightly different perspective, critics have also praised Dryden's expansive intellect—his willingness to examine all sides of an issue, to suspend judgment, or to recognize the ambiguities of a problem. While my definition of the ideology of his poetic form explains such interpretations, it does not support them. Dryden's form does not suspend judgment; it asserts a conviction. It does not generously offer the contradictory terms of an equation; it makes a claim that is inevitably subverted by its own assertion. It proposes perfect equivalence, but it produces only disjunction. In this respect, Dryden's poetic form is the opposite of expansive, generous, or open. In fact, it can more accurately be described as blind, just as Dryden's ideology can be seen to belie his own experience as well as the realities of his age.

But in failing to effect the reconciliations that it promises and in persistently subverting its own assertions, Dryden's poetic form knows more than it can say. It knows from the inside the anxieties of the Restoration settlement, and it reveals with unusual clarity and detail the contradictions of that moment in history. In its blind advocacy of a conservative and static ideal, it sees the realities of a progressive and dynamic historical process. Here is the prescience of a great poetry—not the impossible prophecy of the poet's "Series of new time," but the much truer vision of a future implicit in the contradictions of the present, a vision not asserted but irresistibly emergent in the disjunctive nature of Dryden's poetic form.

PAUL H. FRY

The Other Harmony
of Dryden's "Preface to Fables"

The prose style of the late Dryden cannot be praised too highly; the fine things that others have said about it would suffice, however, did it not remain to say that his style is in fact motivated by his views of literature and criticism. It is the nature of that motivation that will form the main concern of the present chapter. I shall take Dryden's *beau désordre* as a starting point for an excursion through every other dimension of the "Preface [to *Fables, Ancient and Modern*]"—its psychology, its natural philosophy, its view of other authors, its view of the self—in order to show that all these factors have a way of confirming and even changing places with one another: to show, finally, that in important ways the "Preface" itself is another Fable, is as much a translation as the ensuing translations are, and is very deliberately offered as a harvest, rivaling Chaucer's, of "God's plenty."

I

It is doubtful that the novelty of Dryden's later criticism is owing entirely to the appearance of Boileau's Longinus in 1674; but Longinus, who is quoted at a key point in the "Preface," certainly does encourage tendencies that appear in Dryden from the beginning. Consistently in the arguments of Neander, for example, but only in those arguments among many others in the *Essay of Dramatic Poesy*, we find Longinus unwittingly recalled and the author of the "Preface" anticipated—in the norm of the "large and com-

From *The Reach of Criticism: Method and Perception in Literary Theory.* © 1983 by Yale University. Yale University Press, 1983.

prehensive soul," for instance, that is applied to Shakespeare. But Dryden's two critical masterpieces are fundamentally different. The early *Essay*, a carefully constructed drama, is formalistic. It is wonderfully openminded, certainly, but in all its viewpoints it never strays far from the question of Rules. Its formality is most exquisite in the exordium, upon which I shall want to concentrate shortly, approaching the informal "Preface" by that route after a digression on the significance of beginnings in critical essays generally.

Formally preliminary and informally hazarded beginnings lead to two different kinds of coherence in the writing and the principles of critical theory. All beginnings, I have argued elsewhere, are insidiously proleptic. They not only outline what is to come but also anticipate it almost to the point of preemption through some figure, emblem, or anecdote that insinuates its relevance into every corner of the text. The point I want to pursue here is that formal beginnings are less prescient in their handling of anticipation than informal beginnings. The first monsters in the irregular-seeming but still immensely calculated beginning of Horace's *Ad Pisones* prefigure the many negative examples that further his theme of decorum as consistency, and lead in the end to his portrait of a monstrously shaggy poet. This much is plain, but there is also a less well-monitored side of Horace's prolepsis that becomes evident in one of those monsters, the woman who becomes a "dark, grotesque fish below" (*turpiter atrum / desinat in piscem*). She is one of "the dreams of a sick man" (*aegri somnia*) who cannot be distinguished clearly in this case from Horace himself. On the whole, though, one can only admire the casual shrewdness of Horace's beginning—the fact, for example, that his seemingly random first remarks have neatly exempted his poem from his own charge, a few lines later, that "Works with solemn beginnings" (*Inceptis gravibus*) usually fizzle out, while at the same time the very abruptness of these remarks, preceding even the address to the Pisos, suggests an unannounced rivalry with epics that begin *in media res*.

Despite Dryden's widely shared belief that Horace had "no method" ("Preface to the *Aeneis*," there is certainly a great deal of method in the beginning of the *Art of Poetry*. But the evidence of method appears to be indistinguishable from the evidence that Horace is keeping some things out of sight, in one instance perhaps even out of his own sight. This secondary, repressive function of form, which we first encountered in the *Poetics*, recurs in the exordium of Sidney's *Defence of Poetry*. The horse that Horace engrafted to a man's head at the beginning of the *Ad Pisones* was to have a long career; it can be linked even to Swift's man-like Houyhnhnms if we recall that Sidney, whose first name means "horse-lover," nearly falls victim, like Gulliver, to a strange encomium that he recalls at the beginning of his *Defence*: "If I had not been a piece of a logician before I came to [the Emperor's stable-master Pugliano], I think he would have persuaded me to have wished myself a horse." Here is the slip in Sidney's prolepsis, whether he be logician or no. It is true that he has not completely confused the horseman with the horse: having praised horsemanship, his spokesman Pugliano then turns to a distinctly new topic, the praise of horses, but that justification will not explain why Sidney delays his sudden outburst of identification—however ironic—until the topic has changed.

The explanation is, I think, that he is having a phil-hippine crisis. Afraid that his "self-love" ("Apology for Poetry") may not be legitimate, he undertakes the vocational defense to follow. What Sidney will wish to say is that poetry, "the companion of the camps," is as active, heroic, and "right virtuous" a calling as equestrian knighthood itself, that both callings are equally good at producing a Cyrus or an Aeneas, an Edward Wotton or a Philip Sidney. The slip about horses, however, which shows man aspiring merely to equal the noblest of animals, reveals that Sidney will be unable to refute *The School of Abuse* on its own terms. Despite his Platonic veneer, Stephen Gosson himself had had no notion of attacking poetry per se but only poets, as his title shows, and Sidney in his turn has little enough to say merely in defense of poets. Man's "erected wit," noble horseman that it is, may aspire toward what Shelley was to call "beautiful idealisms" ("Preface to *Prometheus Unbound*"), but the "infected will," itself as unbridled as a horse in clover, Pegasus with neither curb nor bit, raises up a cavalry of evils that "can do more hurt than any other army of words."

In the "Preface to *Fables*" Dryden dispels this secret fear, which is brought into the open in part by the formality of Sidney's extended comparison, by seeming frankly to concede whatever Jeremy Collier can allege against the theater and against himself. This relaxation is anticipated, as we shall see, by the opening sentences of the "Preface." Even in the *Essay*, however, which has a formal exordium and proceeds to canvass—if not precisely to defend—the advantages of various rules and forms, Dryden has already learned to disarm the more destructive tendencies of formal prolepsis, providing a model of cognitive flexibility that looks forward in some ways, again, to his final poetics. For one thing, unlike Sidney, Dryden is a "new man" (Ne-ander) who is not obliged to keep up Sidney's tense vigilance over his country and his class. Thus in the dedicatory epistle to Buckhurst (the well-born "Eugenius" of the *Essay*), he good-naturedly confesses the irrelevance of Sidney's gallant equestrianism to his own social standing: "Sometimes I stand desperately to my arms, like the foot when deserted by their horse."

Just as this dedicatory epistle features alternating figures of military combat and love, so the exordium to the *Essay* launches a combat between friends that echoes, or seconds, a dispute between equal navies: as in a dance, the "most mighty and best appointed fleets" approach each other "in parallel lines." The elegance of dramatic resolution that is thus anticipated on these two fronts, both forensic and military, encourages the reader to hope for a happy outcome on yet a third front: for the success, after a "dreadful suspense," of the struggle waged by the English theater to "restore" itself under the new monarchy and to reassert its claims against rival theaters. In all three of these struggles—the battle, the debate, and the restoration—England will triumph owing to the ascendancy of "new men." At certain moments the *Essay* seems to propose itself as a model for the new theater, as when the disputants wish to avoid suddenly reappearing on "the stage, . . . which is against the laws of comedy." Even Neander's defense of rhyme, which temporarily seemed important enough to start a family quarrel over but which Dryden painlessly recanted only a few years later, is pursued at least partly for the sake of a figure that exactly mirrors the relation set forth in the exordium between conflict and conciliatory balance. Speaking of the function of rhyme in stichomythic exchanges, Neander addresses Crites: "You tell us, this supplying of the last half of a verse, or adjoining a whole second to the former, looks more like the design of two than the answer of one. Suppose we acknowledge it: how comes this confederacy to be more displeasing to you than in a dance that is well contrived?" In short, conflict is everywhere staged in "parallel lines" and purified by artifice until the agony of actual violence is no longer evoked by it. (In just these cathartic terms, Wordsworth defended verse writing as opposed to prose in his 1800 "Preface.") Staged conflict is like "those little undulations of sound, though almost vanishing before they reached [the hearers], yet still seeming to retain somewhat of their first horror, which they had betwixt the fleets."

The formality of these figures is delicate and unobtrusive, but it still reveals the calculated restraint, or perhaps repression, that informs Dryden's early work and distinguishes that work from what I could almost wish to call the "release" of his last "Preface." To begin with rhyme itself: In proclaiming its virtues, Dryden must suppress the fact, as he does even more egregiously in the bad-mannered and badly conceived "Defence of an *Essay*" (1668), that the great Elizabethans rarely used it. Here in small is the dilemma of the *Essay*. Dryden can easily engineer an English victory over the Dutch in real life and over the French, the Spanish, and even the ancients in literature, but how, in literature, can he bring the English to conquer their own ancestors in "the last age"? At times Dryden cheerfully confesses that writers in the present age have fallen off but he always hopes that a new "confederacy" of rival playwrights can win this last, most elusive victory. Still, the problem causes anxiety. The three formal debates—Ancients vs. Moderns, French vs. English, blank vs. rhyme—are set in place to keep a debate between the English before and the English after the Commonwealth from materializing. Neander makes the possibility of such a debate still remoter by making his set contrast of Shakespeare, "Fletcher," and Jonson a matter of national pride and not modern envy.

Nothing he does can make the past seem less dominant, however. There is an occasional note of elegy in the *Essay*, especially in the exordium, which seems specifically to mourn the passing of the Elizabethans. The beauty of the prose in the first paragraphs comes from an apparently unmotivated surplus of pathos. In particular, this quality can be sensed in the prevailing silence. Getting away from the noise of the city (which Hobbes called the "scommatique" world of satire and comedy) and dropping below the natural noise of a waterfall (Hobbes's "pastorall" world of pastoral and pastoral comedy) in order to hear the "heroique" noise of epic and tragedy, all Londoners alike are said, in a remarkable phrase, to be "seeking out the noise in the depth of silence." In part this is just a matter of not talking ("every one favouring his own curiosity with a strict silence"), but the moment also involves a silence in the atmosphere that seems not to help people hear but to function, rather, as a kind of acoustic muffler. It is a silence that must be listened *through*: the descent down the river, "dropping below" the falls from city life toward the greater "depth" of heroic life, passes through silence as if through a time warp. That is just what it is; it is the silence of the interregnum when the theaters were closed. What is veiled by Dryden's opening scene, then, is the intense effort of modern wits to catch the accents of "the last age" but one, the age prior to the artistic silence that was compounded by an unregulated and unresolved noise resembling a "great fall of waters": the noise of civil strife.

By straining, the characters of the *Essay* can hear the noise of "the giant race before the Flood," hoping even as they listen that the time will soon arrive that is finally announced by Dryden in his "Prologue to Congreve's *Double-Dealer*" (1694):

> Well, then, the promis'd hour is come at last;
> The present age of wit obscures the past.
> Strong were our sires; and as they fought they writ,
> Conqu'ring with force of arms, and dint of wit;
> Theirs was the giant race before the Flood;
> And thus, when Charles return'd, our Empire stood.

If the unsung strife in the *Essay* occurs between Dryden's contemporaries and the age of Shakespeare, that may be why the navies at present are said to have "disputed the command of the greater half of the *globe*" (italics mine); and it may further account for the pathos of the prose. Like T. S. Eliot after him, Dryden nostalgically evokes the Thames of Spenser's *Prothalamion*. First he writes that the four companions "ordered the watermen to let fall their oars more gently," and then later, lest we miss his cue, he tells us that they have "given order to the watermen to turn their barge, and row softly."

This series of instances, including that of the misleadingly casual Horace, is meant to show that the formal beginnings of critical essays set in place the resistance to undigestible material that shapes them overall. The chef-d'oeuvre in this kind, the "frame-story" of Dryden's *Essay*, shares this tendency to conceal things with its predecessors and thus serves to mark the distance Dryden will have come by the time he speaks his last words in the "Preface," which are contrastingly uninhibited—and informal. Although he had always known Montaigne, one suspects that as he grew older and his essays more and more often included mock-apologies for haste, forgetfulness, and the garrulity of age, the taste for Montaigne, who began to affect senility not long after he turned forty, must have grown on him also. Montaigne complained, perhaps disingenuously, that he could never compose formally, not even a business letter or note of introduction, but it is clear, throughout his work, that he held this failing to be a virtue. Master of nonchalance himself, he advised other writers to follow him in doing without "exordiums and perorations." Eventually Dryden brought himself to take this advice. "The logical and Aristotelian arrangements are not to the point," Montaigne wrote elsewhere: "I want a man to begin with the conclusion" (*Complete Essays*). What Dryden learned from Montaigne, who was the first to have gone some way toward achieving Rousseau's wish to tell the whole truth about himself, and who talks on as cheerfully about incest and cannibalism as about anything else—what Dryden learned from him was an uninhibited manner which enables him in many respects to begin where others leave off.

To turn then to the informal beginning of his "Preface": in the past, Dryden had often had recourse to architectural expressions when he wished to affirm Judgment—the "master-workman"—or the regularity of art. Thus at the end of the *Essay* Neander argues that rhyme is "a rule and line by which [the poet] keeps his building compact and even." In the first paragraph of the "Preface," however, architecture begins, like the haunted houses of fiction, to ruin the composure of the builder:

> 'Tis with a Poet, as with a man who designs to build, and is very
> exact, as he supposes, in casting up the cost beforehand; but,

generally speaking, he is mistaken in his account, and reckons short of the expense he first intended. He alters his mind as the work proceeds, and will have this or that convenience more, of which he had not thought when he began. So it happened to me; I have built a house, where I intended but a lodge; yet with better success than a certain nobleman, who, beginning with a dog kennel, never lived to finish the palace he had contrived.

There is a certain contempt for this nobleman's bungling which is not surprising in a "new man" who has had to court the great more often than he could have wished. It would be just like a slovenly specimen of the class Arnold later called "barbarian" to want to live with his dogs, say, and to find himself living instead in the only completed wing of a palace that no one else could afford. The bourgeois, on the other hand, has extended himself to finish a sensible house. But if there is contempt in Dryden's simile, there is also an understandable measure of identification: A lodge might have sufficed Dryden himself, but he feels that a dog kennel has been his lot ever since 1688. He dares affirm, however, giving notice of the immense pride that increasingly shores up his serenity, that he has not only designed a palace but finished it.

Or rather, he has finished a facsimile of it. Underlying his pride, without necessarily undermining it, is the awareness that his edifice has got out of hand and built itself beyond the poet's—or essayist's—power to control it. The palace in any case is not the one he had wanted. Just as formerly he had meant to write an epic and instead translated the *Aeneid*, so now, failing to the same degree in a lesser ambition, he has meant to translate the whole of the *Iliad* and instead become distracted among other works. Like the *bricoleur* of Lévi-Strauss, an engineer in a time of dearth, he has learned to use what comes handiest, whatever is "lying next in my way," and trusts more and more to chance that the building will come out right. And that it will be finished in time: the nobleman "never lived to finish" his undertaking, and Dryden has just barely survived to finish his, he feels, having struggled through "several intervals of sickness." We cannot know his state of mind, of course, and indeed he speaks once of saving a quarrel until another occasion, but it is difficult not to feel that everything he says in the "Preface" has the ring of last words.

Although they are haphazard and although most of them are merely translations, the *Fables* are meant for neither a house nor a palace, after all, but for a monument. The entire volume, which is vast in extent, is a personal dwelling; everything in it is arranged to be "congenial" to the soul of the builder, to reflect him and his taste. He does not give the impression, however, that he has chosen his furnishings himself. They have chosen him. At large in his library, he is importuned by ancient voices and speaks them one after another. The builder "alters his mind," he says at first, but then on reflection he recasts the builder's role as a passive one: "So has it happened to me." The crowding in of last passages is so hurried that all distinctions based on judgment must be waived or run almost together: "Thoughts, such as they are, come crowding in so fast upon me that my only difficulty is to choose or to reject; to run them into verse, or to give them the other harmony of prose." Here, indeed, is God's plenty, with "such a variety of game springing up" that the author cannot "know . . . which to follow."

II

With this sketch of Dryden's prolepsis I "conclude," as Dryden says, "the first part of this discourse," having laid down "the dead-colouring" that can now be gone over again and placed in relief. To begin where we left off, with the subject of variety: For the aging poet, ripeness is all, and his "Preface" is a benediction upon final fruits and late "game." The imagery of hunting is not new to Dryden. In his first published prose, the "Preface to *The Rival Ladies*," the imagination is compared with "an high-ranging spaniel," and in his "Life of Plutarch" (1683), Dryden praises Plutarch as a master of the indirect approach in the handling of a topic: "the best quarry lies not in the open field." The aims and objects of literature offer a well-stocked preserve, then, but they cannot be expected to jump into one's net like the fish at Jonson's Penshurst or to wait submissively like the "painted partrich" that "lyes in every field." Dryden's is lively game "springing up" in profusion, not necessarily elusive but still difficult to flush out and snare in any consecutive order. It consists in a wealth of allusion, quotation, and translation, an excess flowing in from the literary medium itself, not unlike *auxesis* in Longinus or the "mathematical sublime" in Kant. Too many poets, too many ideas, too many characters in Chaucer; it is all charmingly too much.

Dryden's attraction to plenitude is spontaneous (and, quite precisely in the jargon of his day, against his better "judgment"). It is wholly natural that he would have little use for undernourished French plots, for Jonson's frugality of wit, or, we might add, for the lean prose of a Thomas Sprat or a Rymer. Much as he relies upon Scaliger for his etymology of "satire" in his *Discourse concerning the Original and Progress of Satire*, he still presents the alternative derivation from the *satura lanx* or "stuffed platter" of the Romans with evident relish. The dish is "full and abundant." It was "yearly filled with all sorts of fruits, which were offered to the gods at their festivals, as the *prémices* or first gatherings." Or again, the gods' plenty that satire holds out may be "a kind of *olla,* or hotchpotch, made of several sorts of meats." This pleasant attitude weakens the connection between satire and moral purpose that Dryden intends, on the whole, to promote. If satire turns out to be more like a good dinner than a bitter medicine for the vicious and foolish, Dryden can scarcely upbraid Horace, as he realizes, for not being as single-minded in his aim as Persius or Juvenal: "I know that it may be urged in defence of Horace that this unity is not necessary; because the very word *satura* signifies a dish plentifully stored with all variety of fruits and grains."

Unity is a virtue that Dryden always wants to praise, knowing that he should do so, but he has a difficult time fixing his attention, as a practical critic, on the notion of an organizing, purposive idea. His first "Preface," like his last, begins in disarray, with a "confused mass of thoughts" working their way "towards the light" of organization (*"Rival Ladies"*). It is the *mass* of this movement that is fascinating and must be resisted, not so much because it might prove overwhelming or because the evil that comes of excess is easy to identify and define, but simply because duty lies elsewhere in an age of French-import criticism. Thus despite the fact that stuffing is clearly the soul of satire, Dryden dutifully brings the foreign criterion of unity to bear on it. That his genius is for excess is clearest whenever he encounters meagerness, as when he allows himself a private joke as a holiday from the labor of praising the Earl of Dorset's trifling satires: "There is continual abundance" in Dorset's writing, he says, " 'Tis that which the Romans call *coena dubia,* where there is such plenty, yet withal so much diversity, and so much good order, that the choice is difficult between one excellency and another." Which is to say, Dorset's satires are dubious indeed.

It is the same with "Fars" (*ME* "Fars," stuffing; note that the French for *satura lanx* might be *écuelle farcie*), a word that Dryden appears to have learned from his kinsman Sir Robert Howard during their controversy over rhyme and then quotes against him in the "Defence of an *Essay.*" The context is certainly "derisive," as George Watson notes [in his edition of Dryden], yet there appears to be more fascination than condescension in Dryden's laughter. Howard had complained that people who make rules and distinctions "will grow as strict as *Sancho Pancos* Doctor was to our very Appetites; for in the difference of *Tragedy* and *Comedy*, and of *Fars* itself, there can be no determination but by the Taste" (Preface to *The Great Favourite*). Appalled by this passage, Dryden sarcastically quotes it again and again, but his fancy is caught by it nevertheless: "unless he would have us understand the comedies of my Lord L., where the first act should be pottages, the second fricasses, &c., and the fifth a *chère entière* of women." From the evidence of this well-stuffed dish, to which is added a dash of Restoration wit, it is clear how little Dryden himself cares for portioning out "rules and distinctions," and how much he is, after all, a creature of excess.

By 1700 Dryden knows that he loves plenty, excess, and every other sort of "hotchpotch," and loves them the more, perhaps, because they are bad for him. He scarcely bothers to conceal his irregular taste in the "Preface to *Fables*," even though it is just here that one finds his first unmistakably sincere apology for irregularity. Perhaps the reason for this anomaly is that he can turn this figure of thought, the apology for excess, to uses that in themselves offer a pleasant surfeit. For one thing, there are almost too many apologies. First he apologizes for such symptoms of senility as may appear in his writing—running afoul, once again, of Sidney's horsemanship: "I have the excuse of an old gentleman, who mounting on horseback before some ladies, when I was present, got up somewhat heavily, but desired of the fair spectators that they would count fourscore and eight before they judged him. By the mercy of God, I am already come within twenty years of his number, a cripple in my limbs, but what decays are in my mind, the reader must determine." Aside from the surplusage of weight and quantity, not the least excess in this passage is the protraction of gallantry into a time when it is no longer in character except as avuncular repartee, but even in that form it is just the sort of liveliness that draws comedies into censurable indiscretions. This apology precedes an apology for the author's failing memory—"which is not impaired to any great degree." That misfortune, such as it is, brings with it the compensation of yet another pleasing excess. The loss of memory is what makes room for the "thoughts" that "come crowding in." One sort of variety, that is, gives way to another, a garrulity that is no less copious than that of exact scholarship.

Possibly, though, it is not Dryden's memory for *fact* that is impaired: "Old men especially are dangerous," warns Montaigne, "whose memory of things past remains, but who have lost the memory of their repetitions." Later I shall take up the theoretical rationale for repetitiousness in Dryden's "Preface," noting only for the moment that a weak memory is a highly convenient pretext for the redoubling of abuse. The second time Dryden finds fault with Cowley, pretending to have forgotten that he did so before, he rejoices in the redundancy of the occasion by cross-examining his own love of plenty: "One of our last great poets is sunk in his reputation, because he could never forgive any conceit which came in his way. . . . There was plenty enough, but the dishes were ill-sorted." For the lover of clear contrasts, it must be disquieting that Dryden's stock figures can be applied so indifferently to the purposes of praise or blame, but we can also admire a mind so crowded that its possessor is obliged to reduce all rules to their exceptions and to convert all the preestablished tropes of evaluation into more adaptable formulas of description: *"Inopem me copia fecit"* is for him a highly ironic expression of modesty. Another excess anticipated by Dryden's apology for his impaired memory is the rather startling margin of error he allows himself. There is practically nothing he gets right about Chaucer, partly because he trusts in and repeats the errors of Thomas Speght's 1602 edition, but also because he simply forgets what he knows, as he disarmingly admits in the end: "When I had closed Chaucer, I returned to Ovid, and translated some more of his fables: and by this time had so far forgotten *The Wife of Bath's Tale* that. . . ." Not only Chaucer but also Homer (the "machine" of Agamemnon's dream comes *before* the Catalog of Ships), the Roman lyrists (he cites "Catullus" meaning Martial) and a good many others get mixed up in Dryden's immethodical progress. But unlike Aristotle's errors, for example those that concern the *Odyssey*, Dryden's forgetting appears not to serve as reinforcement for any systematic pattern of exclusion. It may not be forgetting at all—almost certainly it is not wherever there is a grievance to be repeated—but rather a skillful rhetoric of inadvertency, a show of confusion bearing witness to the author's easy familiarity with plenitude. In that case, it would bring one close to understanding the *consciously* revolutionary psychology of this, Dryden's last essay.

It is by pleading inadvertency (quite absurdly) that Dryden apologizes for the first of many times, each time seeming to have forgotten that he has done so before, for whatever there is that "savours of immortality or profaneness" in his writing: "If there happen to be found an irreverent expression, or a thought too wanton, they are crept into my verses thro' inadvertency." It is a little more to the point to argue, as he then does, that the authors of the indecencies he translates are the persons who should be held responsible for them, but that is scarcely an adequate excuse either. Dryden himself refuses to accept Chaucer's apology for "ful broad" speaking in the "General Prologue," which consists essentially in saying that it is not he, Chaucer, who speaks, but his characters. In Chaucer as well as in Dryden, this excuse is grossly sophistical in most respects. From one point of view, however, the modern one expressed in Rimbaud's *Je est un autre*, it is perfectly legitimate. It seems to me—and I shall try to show this more fully later on—that both attitudes coexist in Dryden's thinking, the one according to which he is a responsible speaker and the one according to which, in some sense inadvertently, he is spoken through.

Dryden's apology for past literary indiscretions is probably heartfelt, but still he is loath to part with his errors. To bid them farewell, as he must, is to write finis not only to his own high spirits but also, from the retrospect of "this concluding century," to the heyday of the Restoration itself. His clinging to gallantry in extreme age shows regret for a whole epoch, for the Cavalier horsemanship that has passed by. The culture of high-hearted profligacy had been literary as well as social and political. It had reached back to Montaigne—"I am one of those who hold that poetry is never so blithe as in a wanton and irregular subject"—and perhaps, through him, to Rabelais. To echo Bakhtin's treatment of Rabelais, "Preface to *Fables*" is a "carnival," a farewell to the flesh that becomes a last fling.

III

How is it that we sense Dryden's recantation to be sincere, even though it obviously resembles the sophistical apology of Chaucer's "General Prologue"? Dryden is convincing, I believe, because he seems so moderate in discriminating between his respectable critics and his traducers. "I shall say the less of Mr. Collier, because in many things he has taxed me justly." Collier seems to be cast as the "Good Parson" in Chaucer, while the execrable Luke Milbourn represents the bad divines. Nevertheless, Collier comes in soon enough for harsh treatment. The sentence I have just quoted is actually the only one that Collier would not have found offensive in one way or another. Dryden has said earlier: "Chaucer's Monk, his Canon, and his Friar, took not from the character of his Good Parson." But is this so? Does not the very quantity of rogues Dryden invokes here suggest that the few Colliers who exist are bound to be infected by the epidemic of Milbourns? "We are only to take care," he continues, "that we involve not the innocent with the guilty in the same condemnation." Collier is certainly the "religious lawyer" of the first digression on the clergy (this and the later ones really do put one in mind of the digression in *Lycidas*), and Collier as well as Milbourn must feel the sudden violence of a passage which should give one pause: "When a clergyman is whipped, his gown is first taken off, by which the dignity of his order is secured."

Like *Lycidas*, the "Preface to *Fables*" is a triumphant defense of an author's vocation, proceeding positively by identifying the self with departed genius and negatively by means of a satiric "underplot." Both interjected satires, Milton's and Dryden's, are aimed against the clergy—against the hypocritical formalism of the clergy—but Dryden's, understandably more than Milton's, expands through a subtle matrix of allusion to encompass every class of person by which Dryden had ever been tormented. Having already touched upon the elegiac qualities of the "Preface," I shall now try to bring out the element of satire as further evidence that the "Preface" is itself a fable, an exemplar of the kind of criticism that is deliberately cast in a nonanalytic mode. I shall make use of Frank L. Huntley's contention, in an ingenious essay (in *Essential Articles*), that the unifying purpose of the seemingly haphazard "Preface to *All for Love*" is to abuse Lord Rochester, in part by repeated quotation from Juvenal's satire against the well-born. Several of the details Huntley has configured reappear tellingly in the "Preface to *Fables*."

There are two points of special interest about the passage in which Dryden suddenly strips the clergyman and whips him: its sudden brutality and the accompanying detail of divestiture. Rochester is said to have instigated the cudgeling Dryden received in the Rose Alley in 1679, and though the culprit may not have been he, we have little reason to believe that Dryden did not think it was. As for the removal of the gown, Rochester was known to be an exhibitionist, as Dryden slyly intimates in the "Preface to *All for Love*" when he laments that noblemen "must call their wits in question, and needlessly expose their nakedness to public view." Now, although Dryden's violent outburst is nominally directed against the clergy, false priests and well-born prodigals are much more closely allied in his thinking than may appear. Shortly after this passage, Dryden turns to an analogous distinction between office and person: "Is then the peerage of England anything dishonoured when a peer suffers for his treason?" And when Dryden quotes Rochester—"*Not being of God, he could not stand*"—his acknowledgment of a witty enemy who had been dead for twenty years is qualified by "though somewhat profanely." Thus in turning against the nobility, Dryden himself plays the part of a respectable clergyman shocked by the Restoration court and perhaps not much mollified by Rochester's eleventh-hour religious conversion. The "new man" surfaces again. Although the "dog kennel" in the first paragraph is commonly assumed to be the duke of Buckingham's, it is hard not to think of Rochester as well in glancing back at it. No one had more notoriously made a kennel of his palace than the sodden Rochester in the last months of his life, the time of Dryden's beating. Those of lesser birth, whom Juvenal was at pains to praise, continue to live better, more exemplary lives, but also more straitened ones.

Dryden reinforces the link between clergy and nobility by securing it from the other direction. Milbourn was only one of the two criticasters who had most irritated him in recent years. The other was the parvenu wholesaler of epics Sir Richard Blackmore, the "City Bard, or Knight Physician" whom Dryden delights to exhibit as "this noble Knight." Clearly, "one M_____, or one B_____" are interchangeable vermin. Three of Dryden's four chief objects of aversion are now tied together by allusion: clergymen who try to legislate literature, noblemen who pull rank and patronize rivals, and literary hacks who attempt to ennoble themselves at Dryden's expense. To this collection of "parsons, critics, beaus" (Pope, *Essay on Criticism*), a fourth class of enemy, indifferent monarchs, is soon added. Advance notice comes with the allusion to William's debts, and from there the satire builds. Dryden soon casually remarks that Chaucer was "favoured by Edward the Third, Richard the Second, and Henry the Fourth, and was poet, as I suppose, to all three of them." He then extends the parallel between William and Henry, whose "title was not sound" and who was therefore happy to have Chaucer's voice in his service. But William joins the rogues' gallery in earnest when Dryden echoes his earlier violence against the defrocked clergy, this time in behalf of the murdered prelate Becket, and records "the whipping of his Majesty from post to pillar for his penance."

With these villains now set in place, Dryden contrives that all his enemies will be met, at the end of the "Preface," in the figure of Rochester. Huntley has shown that the quotation of Horace in the "Preface to *All for Love*" alludes unmistakably to Rochester. There Dryden says that Horace has no use for "Demetrius the mimic, and Tigellus the buffoon:

> Demetri, teque, Tigelli,
> discipulorum [*sic*: discipularum] inter jubeo
> plorare cathedras"

("You, Demetrius, and you, Tigellus, I bid you go and whimper by the lounge chairs of your girl students.") Admittedly, if Dryden's misquotation here is not a misprint (making the female students male), then my case is weakened because, as Dryden must have known, Demetrius the acting teacher trained women exclusively, just as Rochester had "trained" Mrs. Barry. Already in this passage, then, the bond is established between Grub Street curs and scurrilous noblemen. What Huntley does not mention is that this same passage, quoted anew, and this time accurately, constitutes the last words of the "Preface to *Fables*." Blackmore, miraculously both Grub Street *and* "noble," was formerly a schoolmaster; the connection with Rochester is preestablished; King William was known to be uxorious. It remains only to add the clergy: "As for the rest of those who have written against me, they are such scoundrels that they deserve not the least notice to be taken of them. B_____ and M_____ are only distinguished from the crowd by being remembered to their infamy:

> Demetri, teque, Tigelli,
> discipularum inter jubeo plorare cathedras."

Here too is God's plenty.

IV

As befits a volume of last poems that are mostly translated, the last words of Dryden's "Preface" are quoted words. Increasingly he has found it sufficient, perhaps even necessary, to speak the words of others: "*Facile est inventis addere* is no great commendation, and I am not so vain as to think that I have deserved a greater." And if translation is a modest enterprise, so too is the writing of critical prefaces. In the "Preface to the *Aeneis*" (1697), Dryden contrasts the essay he is writing with the essay of Jean Segrais from which he has taken much of his material. The preface of Segrais is "full and clear, and digested into an exact method; mine is loose, and, as I intended it, epistolary." But then, he says in the *Fables* preface, that is the way a preface should be: "The nature of a preface is rambling, never wholly out of the way, nor in it." The belief that nonchalance is the best style for a preface stems from the self-consciousness of Dryden's calling as a translator—from the conviction, that is, that there is no hope of rivaling or substituting for a text that is honored either by translation or by a preface: "My preface begins to swell upon me, and looks as if I were afraid of my reader, by so tedious a bespeaking of him" ("Preface to *Sylvae*").

Informality is thus a rhetoric of modesty, a mark of the sort of writing that is a satellite of the fully formed text to which it defers. Such writing is never far away from the text—because of dependence on it—but obviously is never "in it" either. Except for the *Essay,* which is composed as formally as a play (and has its own preface, the "epistle" to Buckhurst), all Dryden's *essais* are prefaces or postscripts. They are on a threshold and preserve the deference that suits their marginal importance, while at the same time they realize the freedom of a frontier, patrolling the border between form (the ensuing text) and formlessness (the arbitrariness of having been "prefix'd"). There is a hint of boasting in Dryden's modesty. Because they are "rambling," prefaces are uninhibited, he says: "This I have learned from *honest* Montaigne" (italics mine). It is owing to their honesty, their uninhibited frame of mind, that prefaces can begin to turn the tables on the texts to which they defer—and to restore the self-respect of translations as well. What makes the "Preface to *Fables*" unique is that in this, his last, essay, Dryden seems to have begun to notice that *all* writing is both preface and translation, in part because all writing of whatever "kind" is much more radically conditioned by the medium it shares with all other writing than commitment to generic norms had permitted his contemporaries to believe.

As we have mentioned, Montaigne discovers the privilege of age and of prefaces alike in their freedom from sanctions against repetition. He speaks of "handling . . . and going over" thoughts in order to "tame them"—to confine them to sense, presumably, as though they were Dryden's "confused mass of thoughts"—just as Dryden says, having finished his "dead-colouring": "In the second part, as at a second sitting, though I alter not the draught, I must touch the same features over again." It is easy to let an author's running commentaries on his own performance slip past when they are thus casual and not formally sustained like one of Fielding's interchapters, but it would be unfortunate to do so in Dryden's case, because in fact these particular touches in the building up of his self-image reveal an entire poetics based on premises that are rarely noticed in Dryden or any of his contemporaries—a poetics based on Associationism rather than formal composition. Although many scholars have concluded that Dryden was a Modern and a believer in progress (and certainly at times he was both) it is still undeniable that in passages like the one quoted above, which miniaturize a much broader idea, Dryden falls into a cyclic way of thinking. The "parts" of a text as he puts them together become superfices, mask upon mask, filter over ground, and no longer in the least resemble the consecutive but interlocking "parts" of Aristotle. The movement of composition is an overlay rather than an extension.

The late Dryden takes a similar view of movement in time, although he admits that the cyclic outlook can take a superstitious turn. Having heard that Mlle Scudéry is also translating Chaucer, he writes that "it makes me think there is something in it like fatality; that, after certain periods of time, the fame and memory of great wits should be renewed." His view of the individual life in turn reflects his view of history. In the best-known of the epistolary poems printed in the 1700 *Fables* he modulates a classical commonplace in a way that overturns any and all humor-psychologies based on the "Ages of Man." For an instant, at least, there is no question of second childhood or the coincidence of birth and death; more subtly, Dryden says that age repeats youth, although in a different key: "For age but tastes of pleasures, youth devours"—and then some game springs up, representing plenty this time as a type of overlay—"The hare in pastures or in plains is found, / Emblem of human life, who runs the round." Or again, in this same spirit but with reference once more to the scale of history rather than the span of life, Dryden remarks upon the shock of recognition with which we respond to Chaucer's cast of characters and then adds that "mankind is ever the same, and nothing is lost out of nature, though every thing is altered."

This is not a high Aristotelian physics but a kind of chemistry, a Dryden's law of psychodynamics that strikes me, at least, as being a more truly "organic" figure than anything in the *Poetics*. The stress in "every thing" falls on "thing," revealing the mobility of Dryden's phenomenal consciousness. Such a view of nature is very different from the radically ahistorical, uniformi-

tarian view of his rival Thomas Rymer, who argued that in Athens and
London, "*nature* is the same, and *man* is the same." As in a kaleidoscope,
everything in Dryden's concept of nature changes yet stays within the whirl
of the essential, which consists, I would suggest, in the primary instincts.
Here is a possible meeting place of Dryden's psychology, his understanding
of nature, and his theory of composition. There is a clue, as usual, to be
found in Montaigne, who offers this further apology for his casual approach
to writing: "Let me begin with whatever subject I please, for all subjects are
linked with one another." But the most significant source is nearer home;
Dryden identifies it outright in what I take to be the key passage in the
"Preface." It is carelessly planted near the beginning to justify one of Dryden's
first digressions: "In the mean time, to follow the thrid of my discourse (as
thoughts, according to Mr. Hobbs, have always some connexion) so from
Chaucer I was led to think on Boccace."

I have quoted this passage from an unmodernized text in order to call
attention to a mistranscription in Watson's modern edition which from my
standpoint is quite important. Dryden's spelling is "thrid," showing that his
one earlier use of this phrase ("I resume the thrid of my discourse," he says
again in the "Preface") should not read "where you break off the *third* of your
discourse," and so on. This expression occurs in a postscript to Dryden's
1691 letter to William Walsh on Walsh's verses: "Your apostrophes to your
mistress," writes Dryden there, "where you break off the [thrid] of your
discourse, and address yourself to her, are in my opinion as fine turns of
gallantry as I have met with anywhere." Only nine years before the "Preface,"
then, Dryden still understands digression to be a formal matter, a *parechasis*:
one sort of figure in this instance is cleanly interrupted by another, apostrophe.
Thus in the letter to Walsh, the "parts" of poetry need not be uniform but
their disparity, like the relation of a proper subplot to a main plot, has rules
of its own. Even in Dryden's second descent to the Labyrinth in the "Preface"
("I *resume* the thread") there is a relapse back to this more mechanistic
understanding of composition. But the passage referring to Hobbes places
Dryden the critical theorist on new ground altogether.

In the section of *Leviathan* to which Dryden refers, "Of the Consequence
or TRAYNE of Imaginations," Hobbes distinguishes two kinds of association, the first "*Unguided, without Designe*, and inconstant," and the second
"*regulated* by some desire, and designe." At first Dryden may seem to be
mistaken (though inspired) to have inferred from this conventional-seeming
analysis that one's thoughts are *always* connected. Another look at Hobbes's
"unguided" associations will show, however, that in his view also the mind
always harbors a network of connections from which, as Dryden would say,

"nothing is lost." In unregulated thinking, says Hobbes, the thoughts "*seem* impertinent one to another, as in a Dream" (italics mine), and he allows further that "in this wild ranging of the mind, a man may oft-times perceive the way of it, and the dependence of one thought upon another."

These passages constitute the origin of systematic modern Associationism (Aristotle's psychology had also been based on association, but that aspect of his thought was not to prove influential), a doctrine which in its essentials has continued to dominate psychological thinking to this day and remains nearly impervious to the succeeding waves of metaphysically grounded revisionism, like that of Coleridge in the *Biographia*, which arise to challenge it. It is obvious that *both* "traynes" in Hobbes are in fact motivated, or determined, to the same extent. Only an inattentive use of idiom causes him to mention the "way" of free association and yet still to reserve the notion of purpose for the regulated kind.

Whether one thinks of Dryden's "thrid," David Hartley's "vibratiuncles," or Freud's "neurones," there has always been plenty of determination beneath the surface. Scarcely anyone in Dryden's day paid any attention to it, however. Taking advantage of the almost universal belief that there is no rhyme or reason to most vagaries of the mind, Dryden frequently hints at the opposite of what he purports to mean without fear of being caught. Having labored to flesh out his eulogies of patrons all his life, Dryden in the end has ironic recourse to terms we have already discussed in his "Dedication" of the *Fables* to the Duke of Ormond: "I have sometimes been forc'd to amplifie on others; but here, where the subject is so fruitful, that the harvest overcomes the reaper, I am shorten'd by my chain, and can only see what is forbidden me [by the Duke's modesty] to reach." Tantalizingly close to open ridicule, this is the Dryden who elsewhere speaks, most uncharacteristically for his time, of ideas to be developed in translation that are "secretly in the poet." So where Chaucer writes in the "Nun's Priest's Tale,"

> This gentil cok hadde in his governaunce
> Sevene hennes, for to doon al his plesaunce,
> Which were his sustres and his paramours,
> And wonder lyk to him, as of colours,

Dryden's translation [in *Fables*] elicits the following:

> This gentle cock for solace of his life,
> Six misses had besides his lawful wife;
> Scandal that spares no King, tho' ne'er so good,
> Says, they were all of his own flesh and blood:
> His sisters both by sire, and mother's side,
> And sure their likeness show'd them near ally'd.

The jibe at King William is not gratuitous; for Dryden, it emerges from the secret meaning of *governaunce*, and surely his interpretation is valid. Chaunticleer *is* a foolish king who is led astray by eloquence, like Alexander in "Alexander's Feast," which Dryden reprinted in the *Fables*.

Because Dryden's underworld is unusually labyrinthine, he needs to provide both himself and his reader with a "thrid" from which there is no danger of separation no matter where it leads. Although I have had to do in these last paragraphs with deliberately filiated covert allusions of the kind that Dryden and his successors in satire perfected, I have also tried to show that Dryden's own philosophy of composition would encourage the discovery of meanings that are less calculated than these. For this reason it is difficult to accept T. S. Eliot's declaration that "it would scarcely have occurred to him that there was anything *irrational* in poetic imagination." In fact, unless we are content to let the "thrid" drop as an insignificant figure of speech— but where could it have come from?—the logic of the Hobbesian position must be pursued yet further, with the continued sanction, though, of Hobbes himself. Like Hobbes, though rather more cheerfully so, Dryden was on most occasions a determinist. In 1664 he was already writing of "the rational creatures of the Almighty Poet, who walk at liberty, in their own opinion, because their fetters are invisible." It is a creature of this sort who seems so much taken aback by the spontaneous growth of his house in the first paragraph of the "Preface to *Fables*," and who then writes very accurately in the passage referring to Hobbes with which we have been concerned: "From Chaucer I was led to think on Boccace"—led, no doubt, by the Almighty Poet who wrote them all.

V

There is more to say about the consequences of Dryden's determinism, especially for his theory of translation. But first one needs to understand the concept of "nature" against the backdrop of which his invisibly shackled creature appears. There are those who take it for granted that the Association of Ideas (the phrase was first used by Locke) is a mechanistic theory; Father Ong in particular has interpreted the Lockeian model of mind to be "quantitative," even "geometric." Indeed, within the clear and distinct intellectual horizons of what was once called the Age of Reason, this psychology could be shown to have accompanied the rise of Newton's mechanics and of Deism with its Divine Watchmaker. But we have just now seen Dryden, for one, writing of an Almighty *Poet*, not a technician. If it be argued, as it sometimes is, that it is just the function of the Divine Analogy to reduce poets to technicians, the sufficiently cautious assertion of E. L. Tuveson (in *The Imagination as a Means of Grace*) may be offered in answer: "The schoolmen had assumed that, since man is the center and the object of nature, the universe must present an analogy to the structure of the human mind and personality. Hobbes assumed just the opposite: the mind must be patterned after the physical universe. Particles of matter impinging on the organism give rise to modifications in the body which constitute the very substance of thought. Connections of these modifications, occurring in accidental sequences, in some way give rise to all our notions of relations." Hobbes's view, I take it, is materialistic but not mechanistic—and while it is true that mechanism has always been considered an outgrowth of materialism, the former term was not applied in biology, according to the *OED*, until the nineteenth century.

What I have been trying to demonstrate is that the "Preface to *Fables*," with its parts not laid out in sequence but threaded back upon themselves until they are tangled too densely to be sorted out again, furnishes strong proof by example that Dryden's poetics of composition cannot be accounted for by a mechanistic explanation. For Dryden, although the self is unwittingly deployed by a prior force, it is not thereby simplified or reduced. In the *Essay*, Dryden-Neander utters a commonplace in the course of praising Shakespeare which yet looks forward to later stages in the history of criticism: "He needed not the spectacles of books to read Nature; he looked inwards and found her there." If Dryden had truly wished in this case to be a "supreme conformist," as he has been called, he might better have said that Shakespeare looked outward. As it is, he subjects Shakespeare's "nature" to a secondary complication by confining it within the memory, the faculty that Hobbes had characterized as "decaying sense." Thus in Dryden's stock contrast between the imitation of books and the imitation of nature, which in itself would have passed current with any of his contemporaries, he nevertheless manages to commit Shakespeare to a measure of inwardness that is quite new. Dryden scholars who depict their author as a purveyor of elegant commonplaces will point out that nearly everyone in Dryden's day praised the genius of Homer and Shakespeare. That is true: but even in 1665 Dryden is trying to get at something a little more interesting, namely, the "nature" of genius.

The concept of a reproducible nature that is inward or psychological differs markedly from the "nature" that Pope was to equate simultaneously with "Homer" and the objective world. It was not possible for Pope to enforce the analogy between inner and outer without glaring catachreses. Addison's associationist division of the pleasures of imagination between the primary (sense) and the secondary (the comparison and contrast of sense with memory) is somewhat more circumspect because it shows, by a turn of thought that consorts wholly with Dryden's, that the genius even of a

Shakespeare is already a secondary process, more complex and in some ways superior to the primary pleasures of imagination but too much altered for analogies to be of much use in accounting for it. Hence it will appear that the "nature that is always the same" for Dryden is not that of the external world but instead that of the mind in its inmost workings. It is on these grounds that he responds to Rymer's notion that nature in Athens and London is the same in the unpublished notes called "Heads of an Answer to Mr. Rymer": "Tho' nature, as he objects, is the same in all places, and reason too the same, yet the climate, the age, the dispositions of the people to whom a poet writes," and so forth, are all different. "Climate" and "the age" were in the air, as the French critics had begun to export some rudiments of historical relativism; but the word *dispositions*, even if it only means something like "habits," is still so sweeping that it threatens the measure of stability that even Dryden claims for *nature* and *reason*.

Dryden's earliest and most startling discussion of nature is woven in and out of the *Essay*, beginning with Crites on the overthrow of Thomism: "Is it not evident in these last hundred years . . . that almost a new nature has been revealed to us?" Even if we suppose this new nature to be the one that is and all along has covertly been "always the same," the novelty of its bearing on knowledge must still discredit any appeal to fixed rules of representation. As Eugenius is quick to point out later, Crites can never defend the *mimesis* of the ancients once he has referred to ancient times, beginning with Aristotle, as "credulous and doting ages." The nature that now stands almost revealed remains somewhat wooden as a concept, as we shall see in a moment, but it is still too vital and variable to be represented adequately within any of the then-current literary formulas.

With the "new nature" to support him, Neander can proceed to defend the "tragi-comic" mixture; unlike Aristotle or Sidney, he recognizes that in the "variety and copiousness" of a plot dominant themes can be restated in different keys: "If contrary motions may be found in nature to agree, if a planet can go east and west at the same time, one way by virtue of his own motion, the other by the force of the First Mover, it will not be difficult to imagine how the under-plot, which is only different, not contrary to the great design, may naturally be conducted along with it." Again the Almighty Poet appears behind a similitude in Dryden. Whereas in Aristotle, whose terminology Neander borrows in this pasage only to subvert it, "art" is an external movement guiding that which lacks its own principle of movement, in Dryden the design of nature is twofold, not exactly a conflict between superimposed and inwardly dynamic forms but nearly that. The entire creative movement that Dryden has in mind reconciles the reasoned perambulation of a creature with the divine fetters that hold the creature back. It is very difficult to conceive of this reconciliation as a mechanical one, as the formalism of the *Essay* is, again, nearly imperceptible. Even during his defense of rhyme Neander admits that the formality of heroic couplets may be a hindrance, adding that breaks in the hemistich will make rhyme "as loose and free as nature."

Crites and his companions may possibly have believed that a perfect knowledge of nature was almost at hand. By the time of the "Preface to *Fables*," however, Dryden is likely to have arrived at the more uncertain feeling that truth in science "was farther off from possession, by being so near." He had become, in any case, the sort of critic who was known in the time of Horace as an "anomalist" with respect to words, one who believes, that is, that because there is no fixed analogy between words and things there is no warrant for the codification of a language. "Another poet, in another age, may take the same liberty with my writings," Dryden says, that he, Dryden, has taken with Chaucer's. Whether nature in its actuality remains the same or not, in any case, it cannot be expected to remain the same throughout the history of consciousness, and therefore the referents of words and the allegedly mimetic element in formal structures can no longer claim the authority of fixed objects. As the "new nature" becomes looser and freer, more various and atomistic, the individual comes into focus and the class, or species, becomes increasingly blurred at the edges. Nature ceases to be nature (*phusis*) and becomes reality (*natura*: the swerving atoms of Lucretius). Even in the *Essay*, the fragile formalism of Neander's defense of rhyme and his sense that "A play . . . , to be like Nature, is to be set above it" should not prevent one from seeing what has already happened. A "play," according to Lisideius, who does not even find generic distinctions interesting enough to speak of "tragedy" or "comedy," is "*a just and lively image of human nature*," and so on. What Aristotle had called the "soul of tragedy," the *muthos* or archetypal representation of action, is mentioned only in passing toward the end of this definition.

From time to time later in his career, and in certain passages even in the "Preface to *Fables*," Dryden will try to resurrect "invention," and he will never cease to rate the power of invention first among the attributes of the authors he discusses. This is the sort of evidence that is carefully documented by his neo-Aristotelian commentators, but neither they nor Dryden himself can explain *why* he revives the "invention" topic, in which, manifestly, he has little or no interest as a practical critic. He rarely discusses the architectonic aspects of literature. On the contrary, his main concern, early and late, is with character, both the characters in plays and the character of authors.

Beginning in the *Essay,* this interest may be said to have carried Dryden in two opposite directions. One of these, which led to his conception of the larger-than-life "heroic drama," did not prove fruitful. It is misleading to assume, however, with the authors of *The Rehearsal,* that even this tendency is wholly opposed to the spirit of realism. When Neander says, "A play, to be like nature, is to be set above it," it is much likelier that he has in mind the verisimilar illusion created by exaggerated perspective in the visual arts (hence the ensuing comparison with sculpture) than the idealized "nature" of Neoplatonism.

The second direction in which his interest in character leads Dryden is the more openly realistic course he was to pursue to the end. It will be found in his somewhat novel alertness to nuance and detail and also in his individualism, which is what essentially distinguishes him from the Court Wits. The simplicity of Rochester's "Satyr Against Mankind," with its exuberantly cynical reductions, is unavailable to Dryden, who is schooled rather by honest Montaigne, author of "De l'inconstance de nos actions." Owing to the intervening influence of Hobbes, however, Dryden differed from Montaigne on human inconstancy without perhaps knowing it. Whereas it is the purpose of Montaigne's essay to maintain that there is no underlying principle guiding our behavior, Dryden recalls Montaigne specifically in order to defend the *unity* of a characterization in one of his own plays. The critics, he says in the late "Preface to *Don Sebastian*" (1690), "maintain that the character of Dorax is not only unnatural but inconsistent in itself; let them read the play and think again, and if they are not satisfied, cast their eyes on that chapter of the wise Montaigne which is intituled 'De l'inconstance de nos actions humaines.' " In Dorax, in other words, there is a Hobbesian "thrid" everywhere to be followed. This is the theory of characterization that was to continue unchallenged in literature until the "decentering of the human subject" began to preoccupy the New Wave novelists in France.

VI

What I am here calling Dryden's "individualism" is not a late development; it makes an important appearance in the *Essay* when Neander programmatically revises the psychology of humors that the English had taken over from Roman comedy. As Neander complains, such a psychology can accommodate "only the general characters of men and manners." In reaction to this generality the New Man undertakes to match his own identity with the New Nature. He discovers "humour" in that quality (or those qualities, in the case of Falstaff) "wherein one man differs from all others."

In practice, Dryden succeeded little better than the humor-fanatic Shadwell in freeing himself from the principle of the "ruling passion," which lent itself to extravagances of portraiture and fostered its own sort of rigidity. If Jonson's Morose hates noise, there is little that he can be permitted to say on any other theme. In theory, however, this concept opens out upon that novelistic fullness of presentation that was later to be called the comédie humaine, and leads directly to the appreciation of Ovid and Chaucer in the "Preface": "Both of them understood the manners; under which name I comprehend the passions and, in a larger sense, the descriptions of persons, and their very habits" (*very* means that which belongs to the individual and *habits* means bearing or outward appearance). It is the "plenty" in Chaucer's characterizations that finally earns Dryden's famous benediction, and while it is true that he took much of the material in his appreciative roll call from the elder Francis Beaumont, the precision of his individualism goes far beyond any earlier Chaucer criticism. What is new and admirable is his conviction—the same conviction that Johnson was to query in Pope's judgment of Shakespeare—that no voices in Chaucer are quite interchangeable: "Even the grave and serious characters are distinguished by their several sorts of gravity. . . . Even the ribaldry of the low characters is different."

The "Preface to *All for Love*" is the response of a professional writer to the condescension of aristocratic dilettantes; this conflict also appears in the contrast between Neander's evidently recent standing and the established character of the Court Wits in the *Essay*. A recent writer on the affective qualities of Dryden's prose has shown how much his style varies with the degree of subservience in his address. Dryden's was a landed family, and I do not mean to suggest that his individualism and his sense of being self-made reveal him to have been, as it were, a suburban writer—or a "City Bard" like Blackmore. All the same, would Buckingham or Rochester, adding to their palaces, keep wishing for "one convenience more"? Dryden's rank is essentially that of those who have most admired the fitness and naturalness of his prose, from Johnson ("every word . . . falls into its proper place") to Eliot ("every blow delivered with exactly the right force") to most of his admirers in the universities today.

Middle-class criticism invented and first exemplified the notion of the verisimilar (the completely unreal "nature" of the patrician Sidney can be alleged in contrast), and it also pioneered the idea that a responsive criticism should be flexible. More than the upper class with its spontaneous code of belonging and the oppressed classes with their spontaneous calculus of need—neither of these being structures of consciousness that can be deliberately "learned"—the middle-class tends, comparatively speaking, to improvise its values ac-

cording to every socioeconomic trend, veering, for instance, between
hedonism and austerity. Classical Marxist analysis may be wrong to confine
its critique of reflexive ideology chiefly to the middle class, in which behavior
is not "free," to be sure, but is more subtly mediated by a sense of alternative
than it is in the upper and lower classes. This idea is implicit in the writing
of a recent snobbish reviewer of Evelyn Waugh's letters: "[Waugh] thought
more of aristocrats than of artists. This viewpoint had its limitations but at
least it saved him from the folly of imagining that behavior could be much
influenced by intellectual fashions."

The con man, the bricoleur, the tricky slave (paradoxically), the literary
hireling, the "Renaissance Man" (paradoxically: but it was not a fully
recognized type until burghers like Franklin signaled the end of the breed),
and Keats's brilliantly conceived "chameleon poet": all these characters are
bourgeois self-conceptions made possible in the democratic atmosphere so
much deplored by the virtuous philosopher Plato, whose "one man, one job"
is possibly the most important root idea of the *Republic*. In Dryden's time,
however, it is not surprising that "virtue" would seem to belong to another
sort of sensibility, to be invested by a "new man" in the new class that had
discovered a "new nature" in which that class could see itself reflected quite
apart from the monotonously inflexible nature of the debauched court. So
in the "Preface to *Fables*" Dryden pauses over "The Wife of Bath's Tale" to
concentrate on the old crone's nuptial oration against "the silly pride of
ancestry and titles without inherent virtue, which is the true nobility," and
it is to this theme that Dryden's sly forgetfulness quickly returns him: "When
I took up Boccace, unawares I fell on the same argument of preferring virtue
to nobility of blood and titles"—so revealing is the "thrid" of thought.

In the context of this discussion it should be clear that Lisideius's "definition of a play" revises Aristotle's definition from an essentially social standpoint. (As I have noted, Dryden's experiments with "heroic plays" in the next
decade represent a separate tendency in his thinking, one that is not dominant in the first and last phases of his career.) The only trace of "action"
in Lisideius's definition is the belatedly mentioned "changes of fortune"—
into which phrase there has crept a decidedly commercial flavor. Since the
time of the *Mirror for Magistrates* the wheel of fortune had come to turn
most conspicuously for the merchant-princes, and in the time of Dryden the
middle-class dramas of Lillo and Lessing in the next century were already
theoretically possible. Even during Dryden's period of involvement with heroic
plays there is evidence of apostasy from the focus on "action." "The story,"
he says in the 1671 "Preface to *An Evening's Love*," "is the least part" of
the poet's artistic investment, and he declares again in the newly Longinian

"Preface to *The State of Innocence*" (1677) that "the fable is not the greatest masterpiece of a tragedy, tho' it be the foundation of it." Such opinions as these are profoundly anti-Aristotelian.

VII

One begins to see how Dryden could adjust to his final vocation as a translator. Once *inventio* has been taken down from its pedestal, there must be a reconsideration of the basis upon which poets can lay claim to originality. (Note that originality is not entailed in what I have been calling "individuality," a concept which arises, perhaps, only in homogeneous cultures where there is an eye for small differences and atomistic variations.) Both Ovid and Chaucer "built on the inventions of other men," says Dryden, but it must come as a surprise, given his critical milieu, that he does not hold this shortcoming to be important. The vocational pride of Dryden himself is at stake, and he protects it by shifting his attention and praise away from the Sidneyan "fore-conceit" toward the more palpably verbal elements of composition. In the passage quoted above, the poet rests content to use someone else's "story" or "fable," trusting in his ability to work up the material better. In this attitude it is evident that the high calling of mimesis has already been forsaken; soon enough it will seem sufficient simply to repeat, with modernized eloquence, the works of the past.

As Earl Miner has shown, there is a play on the term *translatio* in those "progress poems" by Dryden that are based on the Humanist theme of the *translatio studii*. Translation clearly has a very broad meaning, for instance, in Dryden's poem (1684) in praise of Roscommon's *Essay on Translated Verse*:

> 'Tis sure the noble plant, translated first,
> Advanced its head in Grecian gardens nursed
>
> . . . .
> Nor stopped translation here.

If the evidence of his criticism can be credited, Dryden began to assess the presence of the past in the work of current poets only after he took up translation. From the standpoint of the translator, the "Almighty Poet" who controls his actions is the poetic tradition itself. Having resigned himself to speak the thoughts of others, the translator carries out his task like the medium at a séance, solicited by the mighty dead: Dryden "could not balk" the speeches of "Ajax and Ulysses," and he is "taken with" a passage in Ovid.

However, the translator's labor is no less a "pleasing task" for being indentured, and in fact there are certain consolations available to him. If he adopts Dryden's technique of "paraphrase" (which is midway between a closely rendered "metaphrase" and a loosely adapted "imitation" [see the "Preface to *Ovid's Epistles*"]), the translator can improve the authors who importune him, not only by refining their diction but also by smoothing out their argument: "I have . . . added somewhat of my own where I thought my author was deficient, and had not given his thoughts their true lustre, for want of words in the beginning of our language." The business of a translator is to realize what is latent or evasive in his author. The authority of the master is absolute, but the servant is a good steward and knows the master's business better than the master does. This is possible, of course, only when a rare clairvoyance exists between author and translator; hence in Dryden, as so often in Longinus, what is happiest in discourse comes from being haunted by an alien voice. What Longinus calls a flooding, or "effluence," Dryden with equal vividness describes "in all transfusion, that is, in all translations."

These terms of transmission can be applied to the idea of literary tradition quite apart from the relationship between authors and translators. A curious effect of uneasy conscience in having diminished the importance of *inventio* is the tendency Dryden shares with many others in his century, from Jonson to his own contemporaries in France, to assume that every author has his source. In the "Preface to the *Aeneis*," in which he promotes Virgil in every way he can think of, Dryden echoes the widespread opinion that Homer himself had as many sources (now lost to the world) as Virgil had. Similarly in the "Preface to *Fables*," he avoids saying that Chaucer had no source for "The Knight's Tale" although he, Dryden, has no evidence to the contrary. What he says is that the source must be lost and that the service Chaucer performed for it must have been the same service, neither greater nor less, that Dryden's translations perform in the present volume: "The name of [the author of *Palamon and Arcite*] being wholly lost, Chaucer is now become an original; and I question not but the poem has received many beauties by passing through his noble hands."

Apparently the spirit of literature, like the sublime in Longinus, is a quality that gets translated from source-text to source-text. For the integrity of this idea, which implicitly denies the autonomy of the *cogito*, one can look again toward Hobbes, who insisted that the imagination is as closely bound to experience—to the past—as any other faculty. Imagination is furnished solely by the "decaying sense" of memory (*Leviathan*). Thus the imagination posits its originality in the moment of forgetting the past by which it is constituted. In common with some of his contemporaries, as we have seen, Dryden calls translation "transfusion" in the "Preface to *Fables*." This word also appears in an earlier passage: "Milton was the poetical son of Spenser, and Mr. Waller of Fairfax; for we have our lineal descents and clans as well as other families: Spenser more than once insinuates that the soul of Chaucer was transfused into his body; and that he was begotten by him two hundred years after his decease." Dryden here returns to an idea he had already expressed in the "Ode on Mrs. Killigrew" (1685), where yet another word for translation marks one of the moments when the lady is praised less fulsomely than she seems to be:

> If by traduction came thy mind
> Our wonder is the less to find
> A soul so charming from a stock so good.

Dryden of course continues to distinguish between translation and original composition. But still, the outlook of Hobbes, with its reduction of the distance between originality and reproduction, must greatly benefit the self-esteem of a writer who is no longer free to do as he pleases. Perhaps recognizing a closer kinship with Hobbes than he cares to acknowledge, Dryden uncharacteristically chides the philosopher for his apparent neglect, in *his* preface to a translation written in old age, of original invention as the foremost among poetic values: "He tells us that the first beauty of an epic poem consists in diction," whereas "the design, the disposition, the manners, and the thoughts are all before it." But the passage on "lineal descent" is more representative of the late Dryden. Not only does it sketch a theory of authorial transfusion, but it also calls attention to itself in a special way simply in seeming to be the least motivated of all the digressions in the "Preface." Other than by the circuitous route I have just followed, the reader will be hard put to make the transition between Dryden's praise of himself as a translator who can capture the spirit of his original—"and this, I may say, without vanity, is not the talent of every poet"—and the passage on the ancestry of great poets, which concludes in its turn with the subject of actual translation: Waller learned "the harmony of his numbers from *Godfrey of Bulloign*, which was turned into English by Mr. Fairfax." Only with reference to Hobbes can one find the thread of Dryden's discourse. The decision to begin with "diction" indulged by an old man in a new vocation (translating Homer) is just the decision to which, for the most part, Dryden himself had come to be committed.

Although he refuses to identify himself with Hobbes, Dryden takes every opportunity to compare himself with the authors he has translated, perhaps in order to show that the process of "transfusion" is reciprocal. Deservedly, Dryden's power of empathy is the quality for which the "Preface" is best remembered. Not only is Chaucer Dryden's "predecessor in the laurel," but it was Chaucer's peculiar strength as a poet to be able to transport his reader—or translator—into his own place and time. Owing to this gift, which resembles the power of "visualization" in Longinus, Dryden knows the Canterbury pilgrims "as distinctly as if I had supped with them at the Tabard in Southwark." In this convivial reaction Dryden finds a way of transcending time that resembles the First Circle of Dante or the symposium of the dead in other writers. At the Tabard the pleasure of the banquet consists in its "plenty," a collation shared by elected souls which are each in themselves storehouses of plenty, like Shakespeare's "largest and most comprehensive soul" in the *Essay*. "I found I had a soul congenial to his," says Dryden of Chaucer, having already announced that he finds translating Homer "more suitable to my temper" than translating Virgil. In seating himself at this banquet of souls, Dryden recoups whatever loss of pride he may feel as their translator. In the company of such writers, the excellence of whom his audience either knows or can be taught to perceive (to this latter end, he devotes most of his attention to Chaucer), Dryden can defy his petty detractors, again like Dante in the First Circle, as though he too were already canonized by posterity.

For the reader who knows both authors, an affinity between Dryden's "Preface" and *The Pleasure of the Text* by Roland Barthes should be evident. Of all the authors in his day who were willing to accept *prodesse ut delectare* for their mandate, Dryden keeps pleasure most in view. As he admitted long before the "Preface," "to my shame . . . I never read any thing but for pleasure" ("The Life of Plutarch"). Soon enough the formality of shame will be abandoned and pleasure will be its own excuse; it had always been his contention that whatever the purpose of tragedy may be, the purpose of comedy "is divertisement and delight." This heretical assertion was avidly seized upon by Collier in his *Short View*, as Dryden doubtless remembers in the "Preface" when he alleges as reason sufficient that he has found in Homer a "more pleasing task" than translating Virgil, and then repeats his pleasure almost verbatim under the cloak of forgetfulness: "I have translated his first book with greater pleasure than any part of Virgil." What strikes one as Barthesian is the presentation of this task as an erotics, an Aretine for the Aging: "It was not a pleasure without pains: the continual agitation of the spirits must needs be the weakening of any constitution, especially in age; and many pauses are required for refreshment betwixt the heats."

There is undoubtedly an aristocratic literary hedonism, though often it is a bourgeois projection like the one lavished on pedigreed detectives in fiction. But that sort of "taste" is in any case not at issue here. The savoring of first editions and crusty port is a ritual of exclusion and not a celebration of plenitude like that of Dryden. This is an important distinction, I think, which should qualify the implicitly Marxist austerity of writers who complain, with Frank Lentricchia, that some contemporary criticism recommends "a new hedonism." That is true enough, but the recommendation is in fact perfectly democratic. The best remembrancers of Dryden's pleasure are the pleasure of Barthes and the ironically self-excluding apostrophe of Walter Benjamin while unpacking his library: "O bliss of the collector, bliss of the man of leisure!" Perhaps Freud's alertness to the eroticization of writing belongs here as well. There is not a little of the homme moyen sensuel in Dryden's pleasure, and in the pleasure of those I have just mentioned, in that it seems so indifferent to Platonic or puritan objections. When Dryden at first feels called upon to defend himself in 1685 for "the englishing of the *Nature of Love*, from the fourth book of Lucretius," he soon quite simply decides that no defense is necessary: "Without the least formality of an excuse, I own it pleased me: and let my enemies make the worst they can of this confession" ("Preface to *Sylvae*").

VIII

Not until Keats, Hazlitt, and De Quincey will any writers about books evince the literary hedonism of Dryden. It is no great paradox, despite this unusual element in his criticism, that Dryden especially enjoys *purity* of style. Everywhere in his work, and most of all in his occasional outbursts of grammatical or tropical nicety, Dryden revels in the mastery of composition. In this pleasure, the pleasurable pride of *having learned* to write—so obvious is it that his friends, Howard and Walsh, and the neighborhood bully, Elkanah Settle, do not yet know how—there is a childishness which is not unattractive. In writing and the judgment of writing Dryden expresses the pleasure of retention and control. Perhaps the awareness of this sophisticated regressiveness in himself is what makes him more than usually attentive to the childhood of man and of culture.

As a creature of his age he of course takes a condescending view of everything childish, as when he calls Ovid's rhetorical extravagances "boyisms"; but Dryden returns more frequently to those things that are crude, archaic, or unmastered than is usual in his era, and his attitude toward them is actually ambivalent. Although he can say, sententiously enough, "We must be children before we can grow men," the subject is never quite closed. His most predictably negative opinions about the past will be found to issue from the critically unprofitable period of the 1670s, when he was attempting to raise his contemporaries above the Elizabethans. It is at this time that he anticipates the apology of Johnson's "Preface to Shakespeare," viz., that "the times were ignorant in which they lived," and follows that assertion by transposing the attributes of the two periods so unwarrantably that I suspect not even Rymer could have agreed with him: "Poetry was then, if not in its infancy among us, at least not arrived to its full *vigour* and maturity" ("Defence of the Epilogue"; italics mine). This way of putting the contrast is so clearly tendentious that it betrays uncertainty, the same uncertainty that appears in Dryden's first published reference to Chaucer as "our English Ennius" ("Postscript to the *Aeneis*").

One could draw a rough parallel between Dryden's alleged formalism and his alleged belief in progress. In both cases to some extent the characterization is undeniable. Dryden is certainly at home with all the dramatic and other generic prescriptions and invokes them on cue for arguments of all kinds, and by the same token he is constant in his praise of the refinement of modern poetry; he is chiefly responsible for the over-praise of Denham and Waller that was to echo throughout the next century. It could be said, in sum, that Dryden was a formalist and a Modern by design, but an impressionist and an Ancient by instinct. I do not mean to say that he was an Ancient like Crites in the *Essay,* who by a sleight of argument substitutes the *Poetics* for the Greek dramas themselves and is able to conclude on that basis that the Ancients are not only more civilized than the Moderns but also better formalists. Dryden's tendency to prefer old things to new has rather to do with his having recognized the intrinsic value of imperfection. Thus Chaucer's versification, of which Dryden of course knew nothing, has "the rude sweetness of a Scotch tune in it, which is natural and pleasing, though not perfect."

In this typically casual observation, which may have provided Addison with the precedent he needed for his appreciation of "The Ballad of Chevy Chase," there stands embodied an aesthetic of the primitive which has far-reaching implications and constitutes yet another challenge to the hegemony of established norms and forms. It is also closely allied to the nostalgic linquistics of the primitive that was to be developed in all the treatises on the origin of language and metaphor in the next century. This view of language is anticipated almost by accident in Sprat's *History of the Royal Society.* Even though in the previous chapter Sprat has argued that in every culture language reached perfection when civilization was at its height (the standard assumption in Dryden's milieu), Sprat then becomes so incensed at the "specious Tropes and Figures" of modern usage that he announces, as the program of the Royal Society, a "return back to the primitive purity and shortness, when men deliver'd so many *things* almost in an equal number of *words*." This extreme of thought, which was soon to be put into practice in Swift's Academy of Lagado, represents another part of Hobbes's legacy. The Hobbesian outlook holds good for either of two complementary worlds which are indistinguishable in experience: an altogether material world in which mind itself and its symbols are atomistic and words are really objects; or else a world that is no different in structure from the other one, a world in which each phenomenal thing is a sign—an index, a symptom, or a cipher of some thing other than itself—but in which words are still understood to belong in the same medium with, say, sticks and stones. Thinking that is at home in either of these worlds remains steadily on the border between nature and its representation. . . .

One happy consequence of this habit of thought is that it instantly shows up the inadequacy of the primitive-vs.-modern formula as a scale of aesthetic value—whether the formula be typically stated by Puttenham in his contrast between "monstrous . . . conceits" and the civilized virtue of a mind that is "very formall, and in his much multiformitie *uniforme*," or less typically by Wordsworth in his evaluatively opposed contrast between language "derived from the best objects" and the "arbitrary and capricious habits of expression" fostered by advanced cultures. For the most part, in both precept and practice, Dryden is undecided between these versions of the formula because he seems to see the futility of the double standard on which both are founded. In order to defend this assertion, I turn now to consider several other aspects of Dryden's casual but telling evasion of dualistic thought.

We have seen how regularly Dryden affirms a festal communion between himself and the authors he admires, loosely translating them as if to imagine, as Longinus would have it, that he himself has written what they wrote. He collapses other conventional distinctions as well. Just as the authors Dryden translates are the heroes of his "Preface" and resemble him, so in turn "The very heroes show their authors." Here follows the well-known passage about hot Achilles and patient Aeneas. Of a piece with his readiness to admire self-portraiture in fiction is Dryden's earlier contribution to the theatrical dispute between "wit" and "humor" in comedy. Proponents of humor-comedies insisted that there be a strict demarcation between authors—guarding their impersonality—and their objectively conceived eccentrics. Dryden saw that characterizations of this sort would have to be "forced" and would scarcely be recognizable in an educated society with more or less uniform manners. He preferred that the whole fabric of dialogue in a comedy be suffused, instead, with the "wit" of the author. Such unconcealed evidence of the dyer's hand, recalling the "confederacy" between antagonists effected by rhyme in the *Essay*, parallels the tendency of epic authors to write themselves into their heroes. Herein Dryden differs notably from the major critic who perhaps most resembles him, Hazlitt, who loved Shakespeare's impersonality and deplored the loss of the "distinguishing peculiarities of men and manners" that makes a "modern comedy," as he believed, impossible. It remained for Wilde and Shaw to prove Hazlitt wrong and Dryden right. As a basis on which criticism can proceed without being forced on the rack of presupposition, I think that in general Dryden's view is far preferable, together with nearly all pre-Kantian criticism in this respect, because it avoids the fallacy of autotelic form.

For reasons similar to these, Dryden shares with Longinus the tendency to let his criticism merge with its object—writing an essay on drama, for example, in dialogue. In the "Preface to *Fables*," Dryden writes a fable about a banished, diversely maligned but supremely insouciant poet who is forced to "build" anew and lives to consecrate his monument. (Having come so cheerfully to terms with his "lineal descent," Dryden not surprisingly appears, with Longinus, at the Colonus phase of the oedipal progress.) Arguably there is some trace of imitative form in everything he wrote, and a corresponding lack of attention to the requirements of the traditional, impersonally constituted genres. This Longinian blending of forms accompanies the relativism of Dryden's thinking generally. To be sure, much of his criticism goes forward by appealing to principles of genre and decorum. At the same time, however, as Irvin Ehrenpreis has argued, Dryden tests the edges of genres, mixing and "coruscating" their surfaces.

If Dryden's epistemological categories are provisional, his judgments are even more so. Neither the designer of a work nor the judge of its merits can be "very exact" except "as he supposes." Even with a carefully constructed groundwork all comparisons must be tentative: "By this means, both the poets being set in the same light and dressed in the same English habit, story to be compared with story, a certain judgment may be made betwixt them"— not by the translator himself, even under such careful controls, but only "by the reader." To form any kind of judgment at all, one needs some standard of comparison; ex cathedra principles like those of Rymer are simply unavailable. Dryden typically apportions values between two objects. This technique is not at all new; and the majority of the insights Dryden gains from it are not new either. His comparison of Homer and Virgil is for the most part commonplace, and its values are distressingly unstable, as the reader of the parallel but evaluatively inverted comparison in the "Preface to the *Aeneis*" will discover. However, although such considerations as these certainly undermine the notion that Dryden was "the father of comparative literature," they should not obscure what remains unusual in his handling of comparisons in the "Preface to *Fables*." For one thing, no literary essay had ever before arrived at its judgments *exclusively* by means of comparison, and this innovation actually reflects a major epistemological shift. For the first time comparison is no longer an alternative form of judgment brought in to reinforce positive certainty; it has become the only form of judgment and seems in fact to have acquired the function of challenging autocratic pronouncements. The modification of judgment by comparison brings with it a new diffidence; the poet's boast that his soul is more congenial to some authors than to others is also the critic's modest admission, at every turn, that he is probably biased.

Another unusual aspect of Dryden's comparisons is his fascinating use of syncretistic reduction to create a kind of myth-criticism in which, for provisional purposes, all texts are similar. Here is the one facet of "invention" as a critical topic that seems to interest him, at least when he is not trying to minimize similarities. "I say not this in derogation of Virgil," he assures us in the "Preface," "neither do I contradict any thing I have formerly said in his just praise"; perhaps not, but what he *had* formerly said and now seems to deny is that "the designs of the two poets were as different as the courses of their heroes." What he seems newly to appreciate in 1700 is the degree to which inventions repeat themselves: "The adventures of Ulysses in the *Odysseis* are imitated in the first six books of Virgil's *Aeneis*; . . . the seas were the same in which both heroes wandered; and Dido cannot be denied to be the poetical daughter of Calypso. The six latter books of Virgil's poem are the four-and-twenty *Iliads* contracted: a quarrel occasioned by a lady, a single combat, battles fought, and a town besieged."

Much of this too had been said by earlier commentators, but it was the sort of material that had always been invoked solely for the purpose of vindicating the character of one poet or another. Dryden is conventional enough to write his comparison in that same context, but it is not fanciful, I think, to detect in him a delight in the comparison undertaken as its own reward. To say that Dido is the "poetical daughter" of Calypso is much the same as to say that Milton is the poetical son of Spenser; authors and characters merge once again, this time not only to confirm the priority of the past but also, without contradiction, to intimate the uniformity of all invention in the timeless narrative present which transcends chronicles of "lineal descent." "The seas are the same": there is but one oceanic stage on which the story of *Totem and Taboo*, or some rough equivalent, is endlessly enacted—a dispute over a lady in the primal horde resulting in the foundation of society. "Invention" appeals to Dryden in this context precisely because it is no longer an object of dissimilative, or categorical, thought. As a single "fable"

inevitably to be repeated, that which is invented stands at the opposite extreme from the affection for the self-identity of things which likewise
discourages—though it cannot prevent—the formation of categories. Dryden's
critical interest, then, like that of Longinus, is most active at just those liminal
regions of significance in a text that escape the attention of Aristotle.

IX

The microcosmic extreme includes diction and words generally. On this
topic especially Dryden supposes himself to have orthodox opinions. Eliot
approvingly quotes a passage from the early "Preface to *Annus Mirabilis*"
(1667) which is certainly conventional but is not in fact typical of Dryden.
Here is part of the passage: "The first happiness of the poet's imagination
is properly invention, or the finding of the thought: the second is fancy, or
the variation, deriving, or moulding of that thought . . . ; the third is elocu-
tion, or the art of clothing and adorning the thought." In the long run, Dryden
proves to be dissatisfied with this settled dichotomy of thought and words,
which he expresses, like most other writers, in metaphors of clothing. As
long as the image of outer-wear seems adequate for it, language will certainly remain less important than whatever it is one supposes thought to be. But
at some time the question will arise, as it did more insistently for the New
Critics: Where is thought located and how can it be identified apart from
words? As Lévi-Strauss definitively reminded the present generation, the
"myth" to which its descriptions refer is another description. While Dryden
cannot be said to have deliberately entertained this idea, he does appear to
have found the notion of words as dress a little threadbare. In the "Preface
to *All for Love*," again, he reserves that trope for the specifically satiric purpose of exposing Rochester: "Expressions therefore are a modest clothing
of our thoughts, as breeches and petticoats are of our bodies."

In the "Preface to *Fables*" there is another passage in which invention
is given precedence over language, but with obvious misgivings. Dryden has
just criticized Hobbes, as we noted, for putting words before invention, which
is "the first virtue of an epic poet." Still in disparagement of words, he continues as follows: "Now the words are the colouring of the work, which,
in the order of nature, is last to be considered. . . . Words, indeed, like glaring
colours, are the first beauties that arise and strike the sight; but if the draught
be false or lame, the figures ill disposed, the manners obscure or inconsistent, or the thoughts unnatural, then the finest colours are but daubing, and
the piece of a beautiful monster at best." Dryden still strains toward the
Aristotelian outlook in this passage, or more specifically the Horatian one,
but the strain is apparent. Colors are not as easily removed as clothes. *Col-*

ouring remains primarily a rhetorical term for Dryden (the tropes and figures were traditionally "colors"), but it already looks forward to its crucially important position in the theoretical works of Wordsworth and Shelley. How can the "work," or even the "draught," be imagined apart from its coloring? The latter distinction is conceivable in the case, say, of an architect's plan, but plans, as the first paragraph of the "Preface" demonstrates, are irrelevant to the growth of forms. The example of an artist's cartoon would be even less apropos for one who has already said that the "first part" of his preface, before which there was nothing, is simultaneously comprised of a "draught" and of the "dead-colouring of the whole," as in a sepia wash. By Dryden's reckoning, then, an artist's first lines and first colors come into being interdependently, and his own "Preface" is a beautiful monster.

Because translation is chiefly a matter of choosing words, Dryden in his late prefaces may have had an especially difficult time keeping words from usurping the whole domain of "thought," or of his own thought in any case. He had always had an almost unseemly regard for verbal surfaces—quite apart, that is, from his indulgence in the respectable form of sneering known as "verbal criticism." In the unpublished "Heads of an Answer to Rymer," which is certainly his least Aristotelian essay, Dryden argues quite unusually as follows: "Amongst us, who have a stronger genius for writing, the operations from the writing are much stronger: for the raising of Shakespeare's passions are more from the excellency of the words and thoughts than the justness of the occasion." "Words and thoughts" are here nearly appositive, like Wordsworth's "rocks and stones": there may be a difference, but we are not sure what it is. The closeness of these conventionally opposed terms in such phrases may suggest that there is a noncommital, even evasive element in Dryden's well-known definition of wit as "a propriety of thoughts and words."

Although he never cancels the distance between thoughts and words altogether, it remains an extremely narrow distance which can be gauged with some accuracy in the following passage on the efficacy of translation: "I grant that something must be lost in all transfusion, that is, in all translations; but the sense will remain, which would otherwise be lost, or at least maimed, when it is scarce intelligible, and that but to few." This passage appears at first to turn on an implicit distinction between words and "sense": words change, while sense, like nature, stays always the same. But if that is so, if sense being always the same can never change, it must be something *verbal* that is "lost" in translation, as of course it is. But if what is lost is verbal, then it must also be the sense, which is said to be lost or maimed altogether where no words are used—and is not a fixed entity in that case after all. On Dryden's own showing, in short, sense and language are not differential but interchangeable terms.

Nevertheless, if we fall back on the meaning of this passage that was no doubt intended, an opposition does remain between sense, which is permanently given, and words, by which sense is new-made. Dryden is neither an Ancient nor a Modern, finally, because his belief in the priority of sense to language—of Homer's having exhausted invention, for example—is more or less evenly balanced by his unswerving faith in the progress or "refinement" of language, with the help of which he has "improved" Chaucer. It is too readily assumed that all Dryden's contemporaries shared his belief in the continued progress of language. Dryden himself admits that they did not: "Many are of a contrary opinion, that the English tongue [in Jonson's time] was in the height of its perfection" ("Defence of the Epilogue"). It may well be asked, then, why it is so important for Dryden to insist that English is improving, that Denham and Waller are new benchmarks, and so on.

These opinions constitute Dryden's last formalism and serve, like the formality with which the *Essay* was composed, to salvage the self-respect of the author and his contemporaries. The equilibrium between the vigor of the past and the refinement of the present is actually very precarious. Dryden reveals the weakness of his case in the difficulty he has maintaining it. He insists, for example, that Chaucer will not scan, despite Speght's warning in the 1602 edition that probably Chaucer would scan if only we understood his system. By expressing this conviction, Dryden commits himself to the lame idea that a person whom he credits with the highest intelligence and with proficiency in all the arts and sciences is unable to count feet or to invent a means of doing so. Dryden has no choice but to find Chaucer wanting in this respect; otherwise there would be nothing left to say for modernity, and in that case the reciprocity of benefit between past and present souls, on the strength of which Dryden justifies his own election to the symposium of his "Preface," could no longer be demonstrated. Thus the assertion that "our numbers were in their nonage" until Waller and Denham appeared must be made by any handy means to seem stronger and more conclusive than it is.

It is not only a matter of saving some few scraps of honor for the Moderns, but of affirming what the Hobbesian Dryden had always helplessly denied: the freedom of the will. Having yielded priority in invention, characterization, and copiousness of thought—all draughts of dead-coloring that can only be retouched once they are laid down—Dryden then retrenches and maintains that his own authority, his originative exercise of will, is directed toward the refinement of the heroic couplet. But if this refine-

ment is a worthwhile accomplishment, why not praise other sorts of refinement as well? Dryden boasts of having improved a system of versification,
yet disparages Virgil for having *merely* improved Homer's plot. In every
respect—and there would be no harm in this if the stakes were lower—the
secondariness of the Moderns is elaborative, interpretive in nature. It is an
art of variation within limits prescribed, not prescribed in this case by an
Almighty Poet but by the poetic tradition, a "thrid" of yet another kind that
keeps one from going astray even when one hopes to do so.

   In the "Preface to *Fables*" Dryden relaxes. Forsaking or modifying nearly
all the categories of his age and of his own earlier thought, he is an exemplar,
in this one essay, of criticism without the ballast of "methodology." Only
two categories remain, concerning the need for which we might expect Dryden
to remain adamant, namely, the categories of poetry and prose. After all,
Dryden stakes his whole claim to originality upon the very feature, versification, which defined *poetry* for his contemporaries. Thus the young Addison
would insist, in his "Essay" prefixed to Dryden's *Georgics* (1697), that "to
choose the pleasantest [way of conveying truth] is that which chiefly
distinguishes poetry from prose." Here in vague outline is the formalist doctrine of the "poetic function," so worded that it may surely appeal to the
literary hedonist in Dryden. Nevertheless, in the "Preface to *Fables*," Dryden
seems to treat even this distinction very casually. Chaucer wrote "novels in
prose, and many works in verse," it hardly seems to matter which. Nor does
it matter any longer in Dryden's own practice, which he describes in the next
paragraph: "Thoughts, such as they are, come crowding in so fast upon me
that my only difficulty is to choose or to reject, to run them into verse or
to give them the other harmony of prose."

   For Dryden at the end of his life, fully in the habit of alternating translations with prefaces, verse and prose have come to be more similar, as habits,
than any formal distinction can suggest. As early as the "Prologue to *Oedipus*"
(1679), Dryden seems not to feel the need for a distinction:

>   Then Sophocles with Socrates did sit,
>   Supreme in wisdom one, and one in wit:
>   And wit from wisdom differed not in those,
>   But 'twas sung in verse, or said in prose.

It cannot be supposed that Dryden late in his career, if anything more securely
in possession of the critical laurel than the poetic one, would endorse the
separate and inferior status we assign to our critical prosings today, although
he would know that they must always be secondary and elaborative. The

"Preface" offers pleasures and complications very near those of verse and is certainly, itself, one of the more important fables. It is a late variant on the plots of Homer and Virgil: all at sea at first, the author settles down to quarrel over the effects of literature on the "beaux and ladies of pleasure in the town," engages in single combat with Collier, extends the combat to encompass all his enemies, and all the while defends the fortress of his art.

MICHAEL McKEON

Marxist Criticism *and* Marriage à la Mode

No experience of *Marriage à la Mode* (1672)—as a text or in performance as the vocational business of the literary critic or the avocational pleasure of the literary consumer—is likely to persist for long without a sharp awareness of Dryden's enthusiastic dedication to the formal device of the double plot. What are we to make of the device as Dryden uses it? How does it affect our experience of the play, and how does it contribute to our general understanding of the play's significance once the immediate experience of it has ended? Dryden himself remarked of the drama that "*there are manifestly two Actions, not depending on one another*," and some critics have wondered if the extreme independence of the two plots may sacrifice the Aristotelian principle of the unity of action. If so, to what end? The rich tradition of English drama has taught both Dryden and his audiences that double plots may be unified not only by the interaction and contiguity of plot lines, but also by their similarity, by the way actions, characters, language, and ideas may reflect each other in plots that, as structures of events, remain unrelated. It has not been difficult to discern, on several levels, this kind of foil correspondence between the high plot of Leonidas and Palmyra and the low plot of the Rhodophil and Palamede. To cite only one very obvious example, Melantha repeats her cant but suggestive ejaculation "Let me die!" several times just before we hear the heroic Leonidas earnestly exclaim of his own beloved's proposed sacrifice: "but let me die before I see this done." Is the general effect of this sort of foil correspondence to unite actions which at

From *The Eighteenth Century: Theory and Interpretation* 24, no. 2 (Spring 1983).

first appear only to proclaim their separateness? What sort of formal or conceptual rationale might justify the internal comparison of actions which are
so strikingly divided from each other?

By this point in our thoughts about Dryden's double plot in *Marriage
à la Mode* it becomes difficult to ignore the relevance to it of the traditional
doctrine of the separation of styles, a notion of decorum that distinguishes
literary forms according to their correlation with particular levels of social
content. For the doctrine of the separation of styles helps to rationalize our
experience of Dryden's play by formulating an ideal of division within unity, an "ideological" vision of the hierarchical segregation of social categories
within a greater, harmonious whole. The high and the low, the heroic and
the comic, those possessed of aristocratic blood and those without it, show
themselves to be analogous links in the same ordered chain, even as the hierarchical distinction between the links is evident in the fact that they scarcely
come into contact with each other. Now it would seem a remarkable confir-
mation of this ideological rationale for the formal features of Dryden's plot
that on the only two occasions when the bifurcated lines of action momentarily converge both encounters serve explicitly to reinforce that sense of the
social distance between high and low plot characters which customarily is
achieved by their strict segregation. (see 5.1.80–125, where the princess
Palmyra disdains the socially ambitious Melantha as an "impertinent," and
438–52, where Rhodophil and Palamede show their deferential "loyalty"
to their "long lost King" Leonidas by rushing to his defense.) And we may
recall as well that Dryden's separation of styles in *Marriage à la Mode* is
ostentatious enough to entail the alternation between elevated pentameters
and the bantering prose of the Restoration courtier, a quite explicitly stylistic
signification of the difference between high and low dramatic action. Form
and ideology, in short, appear mutually reinforcing. The double plot of *Marriage à la Mode* expresses a traditional or "aristocratic" ideology according
to which those who lack noble blood pursue their mundane and diverting
entanglements quite apart from their betters, but following a model whose
sharply diminished scale cannot hide the fact that it ultimately owes to
aristocratic example.

The weakness of this traditionalistic solution to the problem of Dryden's
double plot as we first experience it as that it seems to have found no takers
among viewers, readers, and critics, among whom major disagreement has
persisted since the first performances of the play. True, most critics would
agree with the general view that *Marriage à la Mode* embodies not only a
formal division, but a decided thematic opposition that is, in some fashion,
"resolved" during the course of the action. Most would concur, moreover,

that the opposition is sharp enough to be felt as a conflict between competing philosophies that possess clear social implications: between the feudal-aristocratic, heroic, idealistic, and hierarchical values of the high plot and the individualistic, mundane, skeptical, and empiricist values of the low. But the range of dispute over the nature and extent of resolution is very broad.

By some accounts, the extremes of each opposed perspective and its sociodramatic conventions are to a degree cancelled out through the very act of structural juxtaposition. By other accounts, conflict is mitigated through the timely removal of support for the modern ideology of the low plot. Yet the edge and vibrancy with which Dryden has invested that ideology may make it hard for us to be certain that (for example) Melantha's "Let me die!" is a vulgar adulteration of Leonidas' idealism rather than a parodic demystification of it. And in the end it may even appear that the only convincing demonstration of the play's unity demands a candid acknowledgment that its ideological conflict never is resolved, that the foil relationship between the two plots is a strictly formal symmetry that thrives on the very absence of ideological resolution. In short, critical consensus exists only on the fact of a socially significant and volatile conflict between the two plots. And we turn to the history of literary form to support the view that an overarching unity is entailed in the separation of styles, we are obliged to admit that the prevalent destabilization of heroic form by mock heroic impulses in this period is no less persuasive, as a formal argument, than the frequent persistence of heroic and aristocratic models. Nor is the apprehension of conflict dissipated by recourse to contemporary response. For the first viewers of *Marriage à la Mode* had no doubt that it depicted modern and controversial attitudes, especially on sex and marriage; but they were very sharply divided regarding which side of the controversy, the modern or the traditional, Dryden seemed to support.

We are left by all of this in a rather odd position. The argument from ideology, introduced on the coattails of the doctrine of the separation of styles in order to rationalize the apparent instability of Dryden's dramatic form, has itself been divided and destabilized. No sooner do we seek to understand the play as an expression of ideological integrity than its ideology begins to look like an amalgam of contradictory postures. What are we to make of a putatively unifying impulse that persists in separating its formal components like a centrifuge, of a harmonious and inclusive ideology which is internally divided and truculently requires that we choose sides? What are we to make of the ideology of the play "as a whole"? And what can we still hope to achieve by a soberly definitive specification of the ideology of so protean an experience as *Marriage à la Mode*?

II

Marxist criticism is closely associated both with the term "ideology" and with the view that it is not in the nature of ideology to be quite so definitively specified as some have thought. Marx's own use of the term is inconsistent. At times he speaks of ideology as though it were a mere "reflex" or "echo" of reality, the passive product of an iron, material determinism. But against this harsh causality he also places the more complicated model of dialectical relations, whereby all human reality is seen to be in perpetual process, momentarily unified by the contradictory movement of parts which themselves attain unity through the force of what they are not, through their negations. Because it was born in the criticism of contemporary political economy and in the negation of other intellectual systems, Marxism itself evinces, in its origins, this dialectical model of human reality. And once born, Marxist thought has retained its integrity through the ongoing, dialectical encounter between its materialistic and its dialectical components, tendencies whose fundamental antagonism is the cement by which Marxism is bound into a dynamic whole. This may be seen in the history of modern Marxist criticism, which consists of a series of self-conscious efforts to regenerate its subject through the negation of orthodox or "vulgar" Marxism and what are thought to be its several failings—determinism, mechanical materialism, the metaphor of base and superstructure, reflection theory, the idea of false consciousness, even the idea of ideology—an exercise which may or may not appear to negate large fragments of Marx's thought as well. In the following discussion I will focus my attention on the writings of Marx and Engels [in particular, *The German Ideology*, except where noted otherwise], but I will suggest in passing some of the ways in which modern Marxists have sought to revise or to revive Marx himself in response to what are seen as his own or others' excesses. My aim in this discussion will be to suggest why I think the destabilizing of Dryden's ideology as the definitive product of aristocratic society, although disconcerting, does not so much invalidate the notion of "ideology" as provide a fleeting evocation of what it really means. As everyone knows, Marx was both a materialist and a dialectician, and both of these commitments can become intelligible to us only in their inseparability. But as an intellectual if not an experiential task, this can be genuinely difficult and demanding. Often it has seemed much easier to come to terms with Marx's materialism "itself" in the rigid isolation of some great monolith deposited by the flow of a dialectical movement which now unaccountably has melted into the ground. From this attempt to understand Marx's materialism apart from his dialectics has emerged the view of ideology as a static, self-consistent, and consciously propounded representation of abstract political and social interest, a view whose clarity cannot compensate for its incapacity to describe how people really think.

Marx's most concentrated attempt to expound the nature of dialectical method occurs in the "Introduction" to the *Grundrisse*. The exposition of method proceeds, as we might expect, as an effort simultaneously to practice it. On both levels of the exercise, Marx is concerned with understanding how dialectics may be consistent with materialism, a relation of parts which itself appears to strain toward dichotomous opposition but which Marx would comprehend as a contradictory whole. He achieves this comprehension by pursuing the implications of his first premise: that, as a human process, material production of whatever sort is a historical process and that history is defined by its dialectical character. Because it is tacitly divided into two parts, Marx's argument in the "Introduction" allows us to consider historical materialism from two different perspectives. In the first part he abstracts from the movement of history what might be seen as a vertical cross-section in order to ask how the material nature of a hypothetically single and static slice of human experience is dialectically comprised. In the second part he abandons this experimental abstraction, returning the "vertical" slice to the horizontal continuum of history and to the complicating dialectics of historical process. I will take up these complementary accounts of dialectical relation in the order followed by Marx's own exposition.

In the first part of the "Introduction," the contradictory whole of which our cross-section consists is constituted from the dialectical relation of four opposed parts: production, consumption, distribution, and exchange. Marx manipulates the interrelations between these parts along a complexly articulated spectrum, ranging from identity to difference, in order to establish that the "decisive" priority of the productive moment in "determining" the other moments is a basic condition of its determinant status, setting the general limits within which a reverse and reciprocal influence also is exerted upon production itself. This notion of causality as a setting of limits, as a "determinant" rather than a "determinism," suggests a fundamentally limiting field of force which encloses a contradictory and correlative energy. And in other writings, the metaphor of determination subtly informs Marx's elaboration of the more celebrated metaphor of "base" and "superstructure." Human experience is conceived as a dynamic totality held together not only by the unity but also by the antagonism of base and superstructure, each of which delimits the powers of the other through respective acts of regulation. Yet even to speak now in terms of base and superstructure discloses another way in which method is obliged by the nature of reality to become dialectical.

So far our focus on the vertical slice of history has taken in the four part, dialectical totality of economic activity, what Marx would call the economic or productive "base." But by no more than a slight adjustment of our analytic lens, we also may expand our view of "totality" to include not only base but superstructure, not only the four economic parts but also a new one that comprises social institutions and even consciousness or ideology. This expansion of focus, this "totalization" of our previous totality, amounts to a dialectical leap of a sort that is central to Marx's method, and it affords us a parallel dimension in which the dynamic process of dialectical movement may be felt. For it is not as though our former access to dialectical relation—the notion of reciprocal influence within determinant limits—now becomes inconsequential. On the contrary, the relation between base and superstructure is similarly determinant, and Marx often prefers to divide this more inclusive totality into a threefold relation the better to manifest both its materialistic and dialectical character. Thus on the one hand it is "the totality of [the] relations of production" that provides "the real foundation on which legal and political superstructures arise and to which definite forms of social consciousness correspond" ("Preface" to A Contribution to the Critique of Political Economy). But if it is the first of "these three moments"— "the forces of production, the state of society, and consciousness"—that determines the general character of the others, on the other hand "the whole thing can [also] be depicted in its totality (and therefore, too, the reciprocal action of these various sides on one another) (The German Ideology).

What is important, first of all, about this leap from base to base and superstructure, from four parts to three, is not the positive knowledge that it yields, but the fact of the movement itself—the differential between part and whole, totality and new totality—whose comprehension is the essence of dialectical method. Within the broadest limits of that "realm of material necessity" in which all human freedom finds its meaning, our understanding of the relationship between the "moments" that constitute our historical cross-section depends upon the perspective in which it is "depicted," and our perspective will depend, in turn, on the particular sorts of questions that we wish to pose. From the most abstract and comprehensive perspective, as though viewing human experience from an immense distance, it is possible (as we have seen) to reduce the number of essential moments even to two. And here, as we might expect, we sacrifice in truth of detail what we gain in bold accuracy of outline: "life is not determined by consciousness, but consciousness by life." "It is not the consciousness of men that determines their being, but, on the contrary, their social being determines their consciousness."

Yet even from this extreme and dizzying altitude it may be instructive at times to recall the reciprocity of the relation that is implied in the dialectical notion of determination. In fact, within some argumentative contexts it may even be necessary to insist upon the real efficacy of consciousness. Thus in countering what he sees as the insufficiently dialectical materialism of Ludwig Feuerbach, Marx argues that "the materialist doctrine concerning the changing of circumstances and education forgets that circumstances are changed by men and that the educator must himself be educated. This doctrine has therefore to divide society into two parts, one of which is superior to society." Of course dialectical method as well cannot proceed without dividing wholes into parts. But its abiding assumption is that none of the parts which result from such divisions can be "superior to society" because the act of division itself always is understood to be provisional, an operational deployment of method which is partial and incomplete without the reciprocal movement of unification. The great aim and enabling condition of dialectical method is, in fact, to incorporate within itself a recognition of the conditionality of its own definitional operations. And it is with this tacit understanding of provisionality that Marx is able to disclose the determinant efficacy of "consciousness"—from a certain perspective its own effectual "priority"—even within the close economic focus of the discussion in the *Grundrisse* with which we began. For "consumption *ideally posits* the object of production as an internal image, as a need, as drive and as purpose. It creates the objects of production in a still subjective form."

Thus the creative power of consciousness may be acknowledged even in argumentative contexts that emphasize the circumscribing dominance of the base. More often, however, it is when the perspective narrows to concentrate on the category of superstructure, or on that imaginary conjuncture where social being bleeds into consciousness, that the efficacy of ideology is likely to come into view. One line of thought, seeking to counter the reductive bird's eye view of ideology as a reactive and distorting mechanism, has proposed instead that the creation of ideology be understood as a process of interpretive representation, in which "symbol systems" are constructed as models in order to be matched experimentally with other systems encountered in the course of social experience. Thus intellectual "systems" work as "paradigms," providing models from which a complex method of "placing" the world may be generated, but which may themselves be remodeled in response to anomalous developments that resist systematic placement. But how, and where, do anomalies develop? It is possible to pursue the fruitful notion of ideology as system in such a way that questions like this begin to appear tautological. At such a point, "ideology" has begun to court the status of a self-sufficient perpetual motion machine for the generation not only of itself but of what it is not—that is, of material reality. Some theorists have pursued this line of thought to the conclusion that not only superstructure but base (or "infrastructure") is modeled according to a vast, overarching structural paradigm, a system sufficiently broad and pervasive to provide the ultimate totalization of both consciousness and social being. In earlier ages, the model for such a totality would be divinity; in our fallen theology it can only be the secularized systematics of language. And in this respect the phenomenon of "structuralism" may be most intelligible not simply as idealism but as the product of a reifying reversal, of a dialectic that has become permanently stalled at the "moment" of conceptual reality. For it is not only that consciousness now usurps the "decisive" priority of material life, but that in the name of structural identity no provisional differentiation of these contradictory parts is permitted into the system to keep it moving. But the apparition of structuralism registers a warning also to the most modern forms of Marxism, which risk, in their wholesale repudiation of a dualistic and mechanical materialism, the repudiation of materialism itself.

Language is described by Marx and Engels as the "materialization" of "spirit," as "practical consciousness" which "only arises from the need, the necessity, of intercourse with other men." And a second line of thought facilitated by the close scrutiny of superstructure, once more consistent with this dialectical account of language, proceeds by recognizing the saturation of ideological creativity not only with social existence but also with its transformative powers. From this perspective, metaphors for the relation of consciousness to social being, art to life, which appear self-evident from a more comprehensive vantage point, all at once suggest their negations: not reflection but supersession; not fetishism but defetishization; not conservation but subversion; not *catharsis* but revolution. The *locus classicus* for this reversal, which unlike the structuralist reversal remains dialectical, is Engels's intimation that Balzac's projective vision excels not despite but because of his determinant ideological limitation. Modern developments of this idea have gone in several directions. Depending on whether the term ideology is allowed its broadest or narrowest meaning, the projective power of consciousness, its "utopian" capacity, may be either identified with or distinguished from its ideological nature. But in either case, this utopian capacity has been associated in particular with the concrete and sensuous character of art, because it is precisely art's immediate engagement in materiality that facilitates the dialectical reversal into "detachment" (Lukács) and "distantiation" (Althusser)—in a capitalist age, Marcuse's "language of negation" and Brecht's "alienation-effects"—the liberating position achieved through the negation of the negation.

The concept of the utopian reversal is delicate enough to occasion considerable disagreement in the realm of application. Thus the avant garde utopianism which Brecht and Marcuse advance as an authentic negation appears to Lukás no more than the self-reflective "ideology of modernism": "we are invited to measure one type of distortion against another and arrive, necessarily, at universal distortion (*Realism in Our Time*). What nonetheless unites these theorists is the general conception of ideology (or utopia, or art, or "good" art) as contradictory, as a dynamic slice of the historical dialectic whose complex provisionality is announced in the bristling instability of its form, which simultaneously proclaims its unity and gestures towards greater unities of which it constitutes one part.

So far we have been considering what can be learned about the relation of dialectics and materialism from Marx's hypothesis of an experimental, static cross-section of history in the first part of the "Introduction" to the *Grundrisse*. But of course this vertical slice is a heuristic and provisional act of division, and in the second part Marx reinserts it into its horizontal continuum, into the ongoing dialectical movement of history. Nor is it very surprising that our own discussion of the first part has led us inadvertently into the territory of the second. Now, in any case, the complexity of dialectical interaction becomes three dimensional. For each artificially separated slice, itself a contradictory whole composed of divergent parts, is now transformed in turn into a part whose own subdivisions continue to interact with one another even as they engage (as indeed they always have) with the segments of other, temporally distinct, provisional wholes. How does the determinant force of material production exert itself over time? How are the social and economic formations of different historical periods related to one another, and what is the role of conceptual categories in mediating and facilitating material change?

The subject is enormous, but a few important points may be singled out for our present purposes. We already have seen how every historical moment reveals itself, under scrutiny, as a contradictory conjunction of identity and difference. The analysis of historical change confronts us with this same fundamental phenomenon but now greatly complicated and intensified. Thus from the most abstract and elevated perspectives we obtain a view of historical process that omits the finer movements of retrogression of which progress is composed. Thus "the so-called historical presentation of development is founded, as a rule, on the fact that the latest form regards the previous ones as steps leading up to itself, and . . . it always conceives them onesidedly." On the other hand, "bourgeois society is the most developed and the most complex historic organization of production." But if we therefore can say "that the categories of bourgeois economics possess a truth for all other forms of society" out of whose "nuances" and "ruins" bourgeois society has evolved a "higher development," we also must acknowledge the later social formation to be indiscriminately composed of archaic vestiges which have not been fully incorporated and assimilated, a contradictory agglomeration of the ill-digested remains of precursory forms "whose partly still unconquered remnants are carried along within it." Thus "relations derived from earlier forms will often be found within [later ones] only in an entirely stunted form, or even travestied." And from this perspective, the reality of historical change lies not in what has come into being but in what has ceased to be. Each perspective, of course, is partial except as it is conjoined with its negation. Present categories can contain those of the past "in a developed, or stunted, or caricatured form etc., but always with an essential difference." Thus the deceptive simplicity of the maxim that "the ideas of the ruling class are in every epoch the ruling ideas" masks the contradictory complexity with which a dominant ideology "incorporates," with greater or lesser authority, the "archaic" or "residual" shards of the past and the "emergent" anticipations of the future.

But the dialectical relation between the earlier and the later age as they comprise the instantaneous juncture of historical change can also be illuminated from a slightly different angle. Let us return to the "three moments" of material production, social intercourse, and consciousness to observe, now as a historical process, how they "must come into contradiction with one another." Here too, the account will depend upon the amplification of metaphor. Consciousness registers the fact of change most immediately as a transformation in and of consciousness. Those ideological premises by which an earlier age had lived as though they were "natural" and transparent conditions of life, given for all time, suddenly are perceived by the present as, on the contrary, "accidental" and contingent. Nevertheless the most general determinant of this change, the "decisive" priority, follows from Marx's most basic assumptions: "what appears accidental to the later age as opposed to the earlier . . . is a form of intercourse which corresponded to a definite stage of development of the productive forces." "Thus all collisions in history have their origin . . . in the contradiction between the productive forces and the form of intercourse."

So long as this fundamental contradiction remains latent, forms of intercourse will seem to coexist with their productive forces in a harmonious whole rather than to constrain them, and to consciousness the circumstances of life will appear the natural conditions of existence rather than a narrow and "one-sided" experience in social conditioning. (This is that stable state of affairs in which, to modernize the metaphor, hegemony incorporates all potential negations, and all anomalies seem tautologically to confirm the reigning paradigm.) But when contradiction is manifested to consciousness, the very "conditions of self-activity" all at once appear as "accidental . . . fetters upon it." Now although this "contradiction of consciousness" is one of the subsidiary forms that revolutionary change will assume, "from a narrow point of view one may isolate one of these subsidiary forms and consider it as the basis" or determinant force of revolution. But this "narrow point of view" is identical with that assumed by consciousness itself toward its own powers of determinacy, when it detaches itself from the conditioning "one-sidedness" of the material ground within which it has taken shape, "naturalizing" itself instead as the revolutionary perception of the accidental and hence the origin of the new historical epoch. "From this moment onwards consciousness *can* really flatter itself that it is something other than consciousness of existing practice, that it *really* represents something without representing something real."

By seeking thus to escape its "one-sided" dependence on material conditions, consciousness in fact fulfills the "narrowness" of its perspective, attributing to a relatively narrow slice of dialectical totality not a provisional but an unconditioned and unconditional efficacy. Such a consciousness is "ideological" in the sense intended by Engels when he writes that "ideology is a process accomplished by the so-called thinker consciously, it is true, but with a false consciousness. The real motive forces impelling him remain unknown to him . . . as all action is *mediated* by thought, it appears to him to be ultimately *based* upon thought." When Marx argues that to understand an individual or an age we must supersede its own self-understanding, he is cautioning against what Engels calls false consciousness. But by now it is evident that there is also a self-understanding for Marx that is profoundly "true," and it should come as no surprise that the ideal type of this consciousness—the negation of the negation, ideology's "utopian" projection—is nothing other than dialectical method. For the enabling condition of dialectical method, the self-conscious acknowledgment of its own conditionality, also defines the capacity of consciousness to bracket the "narrow" "one-sidedness" of its viewpoint by embracing it fully. This can be done in a number of ways. To consider one way that is characteristic of literary form let us now return our attention to the ideology of *Marriage à la Mode*.

III

The heroic high plot of Leonidas and Palmyra is based upon a venerable romance convention, that of revealed parentage, whose aristocratic ideology is, of course, clear enough. Simply put, birth confirms worth. Those per-

sonages whom we have come to know as personally noble at last are revealed
always to have possessed aristocratic nobility. By this means the moral
authority of the given social hierarchy is demonstrated. The external arrangements of the social system are vindicated (after much doubt and confusion) as an authentic guide to internal merit. "Nobility" is shown to be an
undivided whole, a mark of outer status that accurately signifies a state of
inner virtue. All readers will acknowledge the way in which Dryden's high
plot conforms to this aristocratic model, and its validation of social ideals
like duty, honor, and the sacredness of oaths only substantiates the reading.
Yet Dryden's management of these aristocratic conventions is rather un-
conventional. For one thing, the entire play (and not just the end of it) is
taken up with Hermogenes' successive and inconsistent revelations of lineage,
each of which is believed or disbelieved by his courtly auditors according
to their own political or amatory interests (see 1.1.342–54, 384–90, and
432–35; 3.1.359–401; 4.1.100–116; and 4.4.1–19). Thus Dryden encourages us to observe the role of subjective bias in the "discovery" of noble
blood. And he thereby encourages the suspicion that noble blood is no more
than a metaphor for what we covet and value, that the signs of "nobility,"
so far from being clearly correlated with birth, are a complex function of
personal emotions and interests.

This tentative but complicating elevation of individual experience over
a priori dogma may be seen as well in the antiaristocratic response of the
heroic Leonidas to his presumptive father's insistence on an arranged
marriage:

> You are a King, Sir; but you are no God;
> Or if you were, you could not force my will.
>   (2.1.314–15)

Leonidas seems to be moved less by the ideals of duty, piety, and the perpetuation of noble lineage than by his right to (as he calls it) "freedom in my choice"
on the marriage question:

> 'Tis hard to have my inclination forc'd.
> I would not marry, Sir; and, when I do,
> I hope you'll give me freedom in my choice.
>   (2.1.285–87)

Now of course it is quite conventional in romance that the claims of love
should struggle against those of duty before succumbing to them—or rather,
before the war of love and duty is finally and wonderfully suspended through
a variety of romance reconciliations. Yet the language of Leonidas is suffi-

ciently evocative to suggest less the stubborn resolve of the heroic ideal than the bourgeois individualism of contemporary republicans, dissenters, and modern young gentlemen who would marry not for the family but for themselves. And in conjunction with the complicating emphasis on subjective standards of judgment, this language seems to stand out as a contradictory fragment of "emergent" ideology that is carved in relief against the aristocratic facade. This in turn may serve to argue that the ideological character of the high plot of *Marriage à la Mode* is, even in its own terms, more contradictory than Dryden's ostentatious separation of styles would seem at first to suggest. But it is time now to pause briefly in our interpretation of Dryden's play in order to look more closely at the particular cross-section of history with which we are concerned and to whose dramatic evocation I have just drawn attention.

The most important socioeconomic developments of the period are the several interrelated features of the capitalist revolution: the rationalization of agrarian production, the transformation of labor relations, and the increase in horizontal and vertical mobility. One effect of these developments is radically to destabilize traditional notions of how personal identity is defined by external, socioeconomic circumstance. Where aristocratic ideology assumes an accord between birth, wealth, rank, and power, the unprecedented social mobility of this period created a crisis of what sociologists would call "status inconsistency," whereby an easy correlation between the several external registers of place was seen no longer to be the rule. To put it most succinctly, people could no longer be dependably "read" simply by noting one or another indicator of their outward status. And it is precisely this problem in reading that is reflected in both the inability of Dryden's characters to know who among them is noble and in the apprehension of his readers that Leonidas speaks like a bourgeois individualist.

The immediate manifestations of this inconsistency—the decayed and impoverished noble lord, the parvenu merchant prince—were evident everywhere in seventeenth-century life. Its political expression also took many forms. For example, the royal sale of aristocratic honors, titles, and genealogies to newly wealthy subjects was, when handled discreetly, a traditional and useful means by which governments might counteract the most apparent cases of status inconsistency. But under the early Stuarts, honors were sold with such impunity as to severely discredit the accepted belief in inherited nobility as an outward sign of inward grace. Again, the central event of the English Revolution—the execution of Charles I—broke the monarchal lineage and replaced the principle of inherited merit by the principle of the career open to the talents, to the industrious valor of the conscientious individual whose merit is demonstrated by his upward mobility. And six years after the first presentation of *Marriage à la Mode*, Shaftesbury, Monmouth, and thousands of their followers sought to alter the royal succession once more by arguing the priority of inner Protestant virtue over the relative insignificance of genealogical bastardy.

These political developments are echoed in the dimension of socioeconomic policy and ideology. Dryden's life spans the crucial slice of an age-long transformation in the aristocratic conception (and then more gradually in the English conception at large) of the nature and function of marriage. At the beginning of this transformation, marriage is conceived primarily as a collective institution useful in the consolidation of maintenance of family status, fortunes, and estates. At its end, marriage has become primarily a psychological and emotional relationship between individuals. I shall return to the subject of marriage because it is also, in some measure, the subject of Dryden's play. But for the moment let me observe a correlative socioeconomic transformation that is equally vast and gradual, the change in the method of literary production and consumption from a system of patronage to one based upon a market economy and the commodification of literary products. In fact Dryden's "Prologue" and dedication themselves help us to locate *Marriage à la Mode* at a contradictory stage in this transformation.

The "Prologue" evinces two opposed attitudes toward the new theater of the Restoration. First Dryden disparages the vulgar sensationalism of the city spectacles, as well as that of the Duke's Company's new playhouse. But he then admits cheerfully that "We'll follow the new Mode which they begin," in order more comprehensively "T'oblige the Town, the City, and the Court" (ll. 34, 37). Thus Dryden's sensitivity to the fluidity and instability of his age shows itself in his sanguine readiness to address the entire, polarized social spectrum of the Restoration audience. His dedication to the Earl of Rochester is similarly, if less explicitly, double. On the one hand, Dryden courts the favor of his aristocratic patron through the artfully conventional suggestion that Rochester's capacity to judge good poetry is inherent in his noble rank (ll. 10–32). Yet we also know that Dryden is dependent for his living on the theatrical returns of the nascent literary marketplace, where "poetic virtue" is rewarded and confirmed by the dizzying ascent up the ladder of merely mass approval.

At the far end of these long revolutions, we know, the crisis of status inconsistency was quelled, not through a revival of aristocratic ideology, but through its permanent replacement by the individualistic standard of inner virtue, whose presence is proved and signified by the external achievements and upward mobility of its possessor. We already have detected the muted influence of this standard in the unexpected individualism of the heroic Leonidas, who, like Monmouth rather than York, receives his political support from "the City" (see 4.4). To what extent does the low plot of *Marriage à la Mode* provide a coherent model of the more individualistic ideology toward which England is slowly moving?

It is easy enough to understand the profane and self-indulgent sensuality of Palamede, Rhodophil, and the rest as exemplary of the new individualism. Palamede is nothing if not mobile—according to Doralice, he is a "travelling Monsieur"; to Melantha, he is "a Gentleman . . . who (in short) has voyag'd" (1.1.34; 2.1.44). And Melantha herself is, of course, the very type of the upwardly mobile "town-lady," mesmerized by all things new, French, or of the Court. But Melantha is also, at least to some important degree, satirized for the impertinence of her aspirations, and hence a vehicle for the invalidation of bourgeois fantasies about the external reward of inward merit. But the contradictions are a good deal more extensive than this. We are tempted to read the cynical questioning of the marriage vow that greets us in the opening song of act 1, scene 1, and that occupies much of the low plot's dialogue thereafter, as a strictly modern and "libertine" assault upon traditional ideals of love, honor, and the pledged troth. Yet the most obvious and ultimate source for this attitude toward marriage is neither Hobbes nor Puritanism, but the traditionalistic, even feudal, set of beliefs associated with the medieval conventions of courtly love. The dalliance of Palamede and Doralice enacts the age old fantasy of male "service" to the coy and imperious lady, the standard aristocratic model of love, one of whose premises is that it be adulterous. This is not so much to deny the libertinism of Rhodophil and Palamede as to argue its status, both historically and within Dryden's play, as a powerfully contradictory and "residual" ideology which recapitulates aristocratic values even as it appears to subvert them.

The apparently modish self-indulgence of Dryden's "gay couples" therefore is complicated by the aristocratic ideology of which it forms one half. The other half—the institution of marriage—both Palamede and Melantha are quite content to regard in the most traditional light imaginable. For Palamede has cut his travels short in order to comply with the marriage arrangements required by his wealthy father. In this respect he is much more the dutiful and self-denying aristocratic hero than Leonidas. As he admits, "I have given my consent, for fear of being disinherited; and yet know not what kind of woman I am to marry" (1.1.107–9). He is ignorant of this crucial detail because what takes priority in the not very modern marriage plans of Palamede and Melantha is not freedom of choice but the perpetuation of the family line and the consolidation of the estate. In the words of Doralice, "to morrow you are to take an Oath in the Church to . . . get heirs for your estate . . . Love and Courtship are to be no more" (5.1.202–5).

But what most directly informs us of the contradictory nature of these postures is the way in which the old opposition between love and marriage is made the self-conscious and problematic subject of much of the low plot's dialogue. Rhodophil states the problem most poignantly when he observes that "there's something of antipathy in the word Marriage to the nature of love; marriage is the meer Ladle of affection, that cools it when 'tis never so fiercely boiling over" (4.1.169–72). He and Palamede—and their creator as well—are caught up in the dialectical flow of a cultural revolution. Bound by the fetters of an aristocratic convention that is almost weak enough now to appear no more than an "accidental" matter of words, they strain for a utopian vision of marriage as an outward institution that will negate the negation, that will express, rather than repel, the primary and internal passions of love. This needfulness may be felt in the fact that the courtly love opposition is worried over to such a degree that it becomes a dynamic contradiction—between mistress and wife—that cries out for resolution.

Thus Palamede and Rhodophil obsessively return to the mysterious fact that each treats the wife of the other as a mistress, that one man's love is another man's duty. Like Dryden, Rhodophil especially knows that the imaginative supersession of cultural convention is not easy to achieve. Early on he confides to his friend: "that about two years ago I lov'd her passionately; but those golden days are gone, *Palamede*: Yet I lov'd her a whole half year, double the natural term of any Mistress, and think in my conscience I could have held out another quarter; but then the World began to laugh at me, and a certain shame of being out of fashion seiz'd me" (1.1.145–51). To his wife Rhodophil complains: "if thou couldst make my enjoying thee but a little less easie, or a little more unlawful, thou shouldst see, what a Termagant Lover I would prove. I have taken such pains to enjoy thee, *Doralice*, that I have fanci'd thee all the fine women in the Town, to help me out. But now there's none left for me to think on, my imagination is quite jaded. Thou art a Wife, and thou wilt be a Wife, and I can make thee another no longer" (3.1.77–84). But the flagging powers of imagination are given a crucial stimulus by the dislocating yet liberating presence of the other as a mirror reflection of the emotions that lie potential within the self. Thus Rhodophil tells his wife: "*Palamede* has wit, and if he loves you, there's something more in ye then I have found: some rich Mine, for ought I know, that I have not yet discover'd." Echoing the pun on the personal pronoun, Palamede also observes: "here's an argument for me to love *Melantha*; for he has lov'd her, and he has wit too, and for ought I know, there may be a Mine; but if there be, I am resolv'd I'll dig for't" (5.1.323–30).

These protracted exchanges in the low plot closely parallel the protracted revelation of noble birth in the high plot. Both provide an opportunity for the characters and audience to ponder the capacity of personal assessments to measure, to sanction, perhaps to constitute, the form of outer institutions, even as externals remain largely confirmed in their autonomous authority. Thus the low plot ends in two marriage contracts that pledge affectional loyalty according to the emergent, voluntaristic terms of modern marriage, but in a language of "articles" and "treaties" that evokes the residual terms of the aristocratic, arranged marriage of duty (5.1.359–68. For the use of the traditional language see 1.1.107 and 2.1.32). So far from amounting to an artificial and unmotivated comic conclusion, these marriage contracts show a contradictory ambivalence that is essential to the movement and meaning of the entire play.

All of this suggests that the ideological attitudes of Dryden's divided plots allusively impersonate each other in a way that one might call "masquerade." And the actual masquerade that occupies act 4 exists only to formalize what happens throughout the course of both plots: the repeated discovery that externals are frequently a treacherous guide to internals. As Rhodophil implies at one point, masquerade is like a magical spell of invisibility drawn from the old romance (4.1.129–30). But in Dryden's play, masquerade directs us equally to the new, capitalist magic of social mobility and self-transformation. Under these conditions, externals lose the unquestioned authority they enjoyed before the world became modish. Social status may fail to signify individual worth, clothing to signify personal identity, words to signify things.

And the duplicity of words is, after all, a major preoccupation of Dryden's play. Of course Melantha is our central example of the distrust of language to keep pace with changing reality, and Dryden employs a complex association of neologism, coinage, the creation of the *nouveaux riches*, and the aridity of exchange value, to invalidate this distrust in its most extreme form (for example, see 1.1.172–99; 3.1.184–94, 220–36). Indeed, Melantha makes part of the complex analogy explicit when, in a parody of aristocratic inheritance, she reminds her woman Philotis that "thou art heir to all my cast words, as thou art to my old Wardrobe" (2.1.15–16). But as we now might predict, Melantha's distrust of words must be taken very seriously as well. For evidence of this we need go no farther than the heroic Leonidas, who establishes another aspect of the analogy between social, physical, and linguistic signification with his terse maxim: "Duty's a Name; and Love's a Real thing" (4.4.46). On the other hand, the authority of words cannot be rejected out of hand, a point that is made in the parallel scenes, both high and low, in which lovers and rivals manifest their faith in the signifying power of words by silencing them before they can be spoken (see 4.4.79–86; 5.1.170–80, 422–25).

What do these observations suggest, then, about the ideology of Dryden's play? Just as Palamede and Rhodophil relativize each other's reified posture by mirroring an alternative to it, so the marriage compromise they achieve mirrors the royal jointure with which the high plot concludes. But it is clear enough by now that ideological terms like "aristocratic" and "individualistic" can have only a relative meaning in *Marriage à la Mode*. The antithetical stereotypes are posited only as part of the larger process by which they are transformed into dialectical unity. For Dryden's decorous separation of the two plots reflects, on the level of dramatic form, the persistent contradiction between love and duty, worth and birth, inner and outer that preoccupies action within each plot. His divided plot therefore is presented to us less as a fact than as an invitation: to discern not only the different but also the identity that draws the two plots into a dramatic whole. Marriage modernized, "marriage à la mode," is both the central literary metaphor and the historically dynamic institution by which this unity is expressed. And the tentativeness of its achievement emphasizes its dialectical character, its optimistic but delicately provisional comprehension of parts that have a powerful tendency also to pull in opposite directions and to deny their consistency. *Marriage à la Mode* therefore is itself a historical cross-section. Through this formal tension it acknowledges, on a level apart from that of conscious intention, the conditionality with which the suspension of movement is achieved, and it does this with an economy that is characteristic of great art—which is to say of great ideology. But to argue the dialectical unity of Dryden's play is in the end only to intimate its hopeful if uncertain participation in that tantalizing and portentous dream of the Enlightenment: the breakdown in the separation both of literary styles and of social stations. In this utopian claim to speak with and for universal humanity, the capitalist projection only recapitulated, as Marx well knew, the precursory claim of the Christian revolution which it decisively superseded.

STEVEN N. ZWICKER

Politics and Religion
in Religio Laici

Four months after the publication of *Absalom and Achitophel*, Dryden issued another anonymous poem; but if anonymity in *Absalom and Achitophel* were part of an effort to deflect and subvert partisan response, such caution was superfluous for *The Medall*. In the "Satyre against Sedition" anonymity was a ruse; Dryden meant to engage, indeed to inflame, the opposition in his prefatory "Epistle to the Whigs." And in the poem itself, there is not the slightest gesture of conciliation. *The Medall* is a harsh and brilliant and momentary lapse into a flagrancy that the poet could not or would not long sustain. In November of the same year, eight months after publication of *The Medall*, came another poem of political argument; this one, however, bore the poet's name and declared itself: *Religio Laici or A Laymans Faith. A Poem.*

But *Religio Laici* does not begin with political definition. It begins in nocturnal calm and spiritual uncertainty. The opening motif is religious pilgrimage; the mode is confessional, the manner epistolary. Yet neither spiritual quest nor generic and stylistic claims goes very far in describing the poem's rhetoric or its structural and argumentative properties. Dryden guides the religious pilgrim on a path to salvation; he narrates a history of philosophical and religious beliefs. Yet at the poem's close we discover that "common quiet" and not salvation is mankind's concern. This is an odd discovery for a confession of faith, though I suspect that for its original audience, men steeped in the language and strategies of political and religious

From *Politics and Language in Dryden's Poetry: The Arts of Disguise.* © 1984 by Princeton University Press.

controversy, such a conclusion was not surprising. An audience familiar with
the poet laureate's controversial and brilliant poems on Exclusion would not
only have understood the logic that drew this poem from confession to
politics; they might have anticipated such a conclusion, and would have been
attentive to the kind of political statement that the poet laureate was making
late in 1682, at the beginning of what we have come to know as the Tory
revenge.

Of course, Dryden's enemies were bound to find politics lurking under
Dryden's cover of religious confession. His collaboration on *The Duke of
Guise* was denounced as partisan hackwork. But it was not an enemy who
thought that the religious poem was fundamentally about politics, an analogue
to *Absalom and Achitophel*. Charles Blount, friend and admirer of Dryden,
read *Religio Laici* in the context of Exclusion, and proposed his own continuation of the poem as public defense now that "the Name of Christ is made
use of to palliate so great Villanies and Treasons under the Pretext of God's
cause, against both king and government." Of course, Anglican monarchists
had long combatted irreligion and civic disorder in such terms; James I's "no
bishop, no king" was only the most obvious and most concise statement of
that conflation. And an understanding of the extent to which the languages
of religion and politics were interconnected, even interchangeable, in the later
seventeenth century ought to dispel some perplexity over Dryden's motives
in choosing religious confession as an occasion for political statement. But
even the general understanding, so ably argued by E. N. Hooker [in his essay
"Dryden and the Atoms of Epicurus"], does not resolve all of the paradoxes
and problems in *Religio Laici*, nor does it very precisely locate either Dryden's
religious or political stance in the poem or, more specifically, the bearing
that the statement of religious charity has on his political argument. Religion
and politics were inextricably bound in this age—and the political meaning
of religious frenzy had once again come fully into view with the Popish Plot
and Exclusion—but Dryden nevertheless choose theology and not politics
as his initial ground in *Religio Laici*.

While it might be clear that "common quiet" is a tenet of Anglican mon-
archism, it is not at all clear why Dryden should repeatedly stress the private
and confessional character of *Religio Laici* in light of that conclusion. But
this is only the most obvious of the poem's paradoxes. Despite Dryden's claim
in *Preface* and poem that Father Simon's *Critical History of the Old Testament* "bred" his charity, the role of that history in the poem is not obvious.
The *History* is an attack on the textual integrity of the Old Testament, and
Dryden dismisses the whole subject of textual criticism as irrelevant to salvation. Recent scholarship suggests that Dryden had, in fact, only a cursory

knowledge of Father Simon's work. *The Critical History* had, however, some slight controversial interest in 1682, the year of its English translation. The same cannot be said for the Athanasian creed. And to that subject Dryden devotes considerable attention in both *Preface* and poem. He combats Athanasius's harshness toward heathens, and uses the Egyptian bishop to stress his own charity in matters of conscience. Yet the meaning of that much-vaunted charity is puzzling in the context of Dryden's splenetic handling of the sectaries. Indeed, the distance between Dryden's charity for the heathens and his harshness toward dissenters is not only puzzling; by the end of the poem it has taken on the appearance of a calculated disturbance.

Such opposition is at once reminiscent of the play between generosity and political harshness in *Absalom and Achitophel* and in Charles II's attitude toward religion and politics by the time of Exclusion. The invocation of religious charity against a backdrop of political uniformity began to emerge as early as the Declaration of Breda, and it is certainly a policy that the king had hoped to adopt in the pursuit of a Tory revenge which would come to political climax in the judicial murders of Russell and Sidney and to religious climax after Charles's death with James's Declaration of Indulgence of 1687. But the Tory revenge was not entirely Charles's to wield; in the religious aspects of the Tory revenge, the king was captive rather than architect of policy.

Religio Laici claims to be a defense of the Anglican confession against enemies of piety, but it is a defense of a specific shade of that confession. The Anglicanism of *Religio Laici* which Dryden claims as personal and private was, in fact, a public conviction of some importance. The poet laureate and historiographer royal was moved to personal confession in 1682 in order to articulate the king's position at a time when the king's own expression of that position would have been difficult, given his reliance on the bishops and Anglican squirearchy in the parliamentary defeat of Exclusion. The High Church party called not only for political revenge, which Charles realized in the remodeling of charters, but also for a harsh repression of dissenting religion, a call that the king had never favored. A confession of conscience by the poet laureate would permit the public reiteration of the king's belief in liberty of tender conscience while insisting on the primacy of political order.

From the time Charles assumed the crown, he favored a measure of public conformity to the Church of England; but he also insisted on a liberty of conscience. However genuine his belief in religious toleration, the king steadily aimed at such toleration, no doubt both to ease the political circumstance of English Catholics and to promote civic quiet among his Protestant citizenry. This is the position of the Declaration of Breda, and it

is the language of the king's Indulgences of 1662 and 1672. In these public
statements, Charles combined resolute support for the Anglican doctrine,
discipline, and governance as the standard for "the general public worship
of God" with an express and contradictory approval of "liberty of tender
conscience." What the king advocated was something like theological indifference and civic order, and such I believe is what Dryden advocates in *Religio
Laici*. But the poem also draws a very marked distinction between spiritual
toleration and the obligations of private reason in matters of state. The narrator's charity allows a wide latitude on matters pertaining to salvation; on
that question the poem seems to admit not only heathens but a number of
other souls, Catholic and Protestant alike, to heaven. Liberty of conscience
was not, however, to be confused with political disorder or with political
weakness. When liberty of conscience is abused as political license, *Religio
Laici* harshly and splenetically condemns that liberty. The theologian in this
poem is willing to tolerate a wide margin of dissent, but the politician is not.
The poem shares a political stance and a technique of argument with *Absalom and Achitophel*, and nowhere is this more obvious than in both poems'
strategic celebration of the middle way.

But it is not only to *Absalom and Achitophel* that the techniques of
Religio Laici point. There are connections to the earlier poetry and
refinements of the position that Dryden adopted in *Absalom and Achitophel*
which reflect the particularly delicate circumstance in which the king found
himself after the defeat of Exclusion. The language and argument of *Religio
Laici* must be understood both as a reflection of the poet's general practices
and in terms of those specific political accommodations. From the title
through the *Preface* to the concluding lines of the poem, Dryden depicts
himself as theological amateur. Perhaps the role of amateur had become
something of a reflex, but there is more to this narration than a familiar
argumentative trope. Of course, there are similarities among all of Dryden's
works in their use of humility and incapacity as argumentative techniques;
and the confessions of humility and incapacity are also part of a stylistic claim
especially important in *Religio Laici*, where humility and honesty are linked
as narrative stance and stylistic definition. But the humility of *Religio Laici*
is not only personality; it is also a technical position in relation to the Anglican
clergy on matters of doctrine and worship. Dryden's position as a layman
is a self-conscious assertion of distance from the Anglican clergy. In part,
Dryden uses this posture in order to range broadly over topics that the professional might not dare assemble; he also argues that the disinterested layman
may be able to penetrate moral and theological problems more deeply than
the cleric. Moreover, the whole treatment of Athanasius depends on the self-

conscious amateurism that Dryden adopts in the *Preface*. The denial of Athansius is at the center of Dryden's claims for charity, claims that this poet might
not have made had he "prudently" followed the advice of his judicious clerical
friend.

But the aim of this poem is not to establish the Anglican confession as
stated by the Anglican clergy. It is to establish a confession of that faith not
in defiance of but in distinction to the repressive position on dissenting
theology that the Anglican clergy now loudly proclaimed after the defeat of
Exclusion and the exposure of the Popish Plot. The position that this artless
theological amateur would like to occupy is that familiar territory midway
between extremes, that honest ground threatened on both sides. By identifying theological charity and political order with the true *via media*, Dryden's
poem implicitly defines the king's religion and politics as those most conform-
able to the true spirit of the Anglican confession.

The device of the innocent narrator is, of course, only part of this strategy
of the middle way. Not only does Dryden self-consciously identify his position as that endangered and embattled midpoint in the *Preface* (146–60),
but the systems of argument in the poem render the same conclusion. The
narrator conducts his search for the middle ground along a chronological
continuum, through a structure of progressively more difficult and strident
refutations, and between spiritual and intellectual extremes. The narrative
moves over time and ascends in argumentative power, and the cumulative
force is the poem's final discovery that common quiet is mankind's most urgent
concern. The rhetorical and dialectical thrust of argument and structure reach
their climax in the penultimate stanza, where the narrator recoils from his
tangle to ask, "What then remains, but, waving each Extreme, / The Tides
of Ignorance, and Pride to stem?" (427–28). Dryden releases a spring that
he has carefully wound for the preceding four hundred lines. The question
suggests a fit of exasperation, but the drama has been prepared from the
opening calm, and to such calm, now purged of doubts and perplexities, the
poem returns. What this poem discovers is that theological precision does
not determine salvation, which is a gift of God and is apparently dispensed
to heathens and Christians alike. What is more difficult to obtain is common quiet and, to that end, even theological convictions must be sacrificed.
Common quiet is the *summum bonum* of theological inquiry.

The central moral principle of *Religio Laici* is charity; this is a motif
steadily adumbrated in the *Preface*, a theme that acts as an argumentative
crux in the poem; it is part of Dryden's posture as layman, it guides the discussion of pre-Christian religions and textual authority in Scripture. Charity links
spirit and intellect; it is at once personality and argumentative technique.

And it is, of course, a stance crucially reminiscent of Charles II's public statements on theological matters. As such, Dryden's treatment and invocation of charity deserve close attention, particularly for the ways in which Dryden articulates that theme, for where he chooses to make his stand is not on the much contested ground of salvational authority in the late seventeenth century, but on questions of spiritual authority in the third century.

What precisely suggested the propriety of the Athanasian controversy as ground for a discussion of charity is difficult to determine; yet that distant ground is where the poet begins. Dryden claims that a judicious and learned friend censured his discussion of the Egyptian bishop; yet he chose, in the face of that criticism, to make Athanasius his stalking horse for charity; and I suspect that Dryden made this choice partly because the problems that Athansius poses are so distant from the religious pressures of the 1680s. In matters of a purely spiritual character, Dryden wants to clear the space between theology and politics as fully as possible. Dryden's suggestion that his clerical friend found his stance on Athanasius troubling and dangerous is part of this strategy, for Dryden wants to insist that *Religio Laici* is personal confession rather than clerical authority. And in his charity, he runs counter to the spirit of the Anglican clergy in 1682. He is willing to call on the stock of historical treatises of the Anglican Church, for the distance that Dryden desired was not from the historical spirit of the Church—not from Hooker—but from the contemporary spirit of that Church, from a stance less charitable than his own in matters of salvation.

And we hear of that charity in both *Preface* and poem. Dryden's errors in the *Preface* are those of charity; the Athanasian Creed on the question of condemnation is "of too hard a digestion" for Dryden's charity; and it is this same charity that confronts the Egyptian bishop in the poem. The subject in both *Preface* and poem is heathen salvation, "It has always been my *thought*, that Heathens, who never did, nor without Miracle cou'd hear of the name of Christ were yet in a possibility of Salvation" (38–40). For all those who lived before the incarnation, Dryden reserves the possibility of salvation in Christ. And for those generations between revealed religion in Israel and the incarnation, the possibility of salvation was first the fading light of revelation, and then the "light of Nature" (63). What remained of revealed religion was the notion of one deity, and that notion itself, without benefit of purer forms of worship, was sufficient for the posterity of Noah. Not only could the progeny of Cham and Japhet claim salvation, but those who lived wholly without the possibility of revelation might also be saved. Nor does Dryden, while criticizing the Deists and those who would "prove Religion by Reason" celebrating reason over revelation (89), at any point deny them the possibility of salvation. He reproves the false application of reason in matters of the spirit, but that reproval is not damnation.

Whatever the extent of Dryden's interest in the question of salvation for heathens—and there is, of course, the evidence of religious debate in *The Indian Emperor* and *Tyrannic Love*, which suggests a longstanding interest in that question—the conclusions that he reaches on such issues as the knowledge necessary for salvation, the role of Scripture, and the function of forms of worship were meant to apply not only to the posterity of Noah but also to Dryden's exact contemporaries: to Anglicans, to sectaries, to Deists, and to Roman Catholics. Dryden nowhere argues directly that the form of worship within or without the Anglican confession is wholly indifferent to salvation, but such a conclusion would be justified by applying the debate over heathen salvation to contemporary religion. The application is most directly invited in Dryden's refutation of the Preface to the Athanasian Creed. To apply that Preface to heathens, Dryden argues, is to ignore its partisan context. Athanasius's Preface was developed not to exclude heathens from salvation, but as "a kind of Test, which whosoever took was look'd on as an Orthodox Believer. 'Tis manifest from hence, that the Heathen part of the Empire was not concerned in it: for its business was not to distinguish betwixt Pagans and Christians, but betwixt Hereticks and true Believers. This, well consider'd, takes off the heavy weight of Censure, which I wou'd willingly avoid. . . . the Anathema, reaches not the Heathens, who had never heard of Christ, and were nothing interested in that dispute" (114–24). The most telling suggestion is Dryden's casual remark that the Preface was drawn up as "a kind of Test" to distinguish one sort of Christian from another. The Preface derives from third-century polemics, but such tests have a contemporary meaning. They might be appropriate among Protestants, but should they be applied to Catholics who are not "interested in that dispute"? On the propriety of the Test the court had been abundantly clear as Charles attempted to brush aside such tests in 1662 and 1672. Moreover, the Test Act had a particular political character: it was prompted "if not invented by the Earl of Shaftesbury who resolved to strike directly at the Duke of York and his friends."

But it was not simply the Test that Dryden raised in this discussion; Dryden attacks Athanasius because the poet would pursue, under cover of patristics, an advocacy of charity, of kindness, of "mollified Interpretation" of Scripture toward all Christians (110). *Religio Laici* was branded by Dryden's contemporaries as atheistical, and it is not difficult to understand why. Dryden criticizes the elevation of reason by the Deists; he is scornful of ancient philosophy, but he damns neither heathen nor Deist. The thrust

of his whole discussion of theology is that what is necessary for salvation
is simple, clear, and accessible, because of God's grace, to heathen and Christian alike, lettered and unlettered. Of course, the knowledge of Scripture made
it easier for the Christian to achieve salvation because Scripture points a broad
path. Yet it was more likely that Socrates and those who followed "*Reasons*
Dictates right; / Liv'd up, and lifted high their *Natural Light*" would find
salvation than a "Thousand *Rubrick-Martyrs*" (208–11). Dryden jokes at
the expense of Roman Catholic ceremony, but he is also making an important theological point: ceremony itself is quite indifferent to salvation. And
of that, the poet is so powerfully convinced that he is willing to confront
Church authority:

> Nor does it baulk my *Charity*, to find
> Th' *Egyptian* Bishop of another mind:
> For, though his *Creed Eternal Truth* contains,
> 'Tis hard for *Man* to doom to *endless pains*
> All who believ'd not all, his Zeal requir'd;
> Unless he first cou'd prove he was inspir'd.
> Then let us either think he meant to say
> *This Faith*, where *publish'd*, was the onely way;
> Or else conclude that, *Arius* to confute,
> The good old Man, too eager in dispute,
> Flew high; and as his *Christian* Fury rose
> Damn'd all for *Hereticks* who durst *oppose*.

> (212–23)

Not only does Dryden assert his own charity against Athanasius, he
argues that such authority is not divine, that Athanasius is guilty of the false
inspiration and zeal that characterizes the piety and fanaticism of dissenting
Protestants. Athanasius emerges from this passage as an enthusiast who
mistook polemic for inspiration, who damned with "*Christian* Fury" all who
opposed him. The attack is softer than the portrait of Corah as Titus Oates;
Athanasius was a fool rather than a villain ("The good old Man, too eager
in dispute, / Flew high"). But the categories of criticism are familiar and
damaging: false prophecy, zeal, and fanaticism. It is exactly these terms that
Dryden uses to strike against the spirit of Calvin in the second half of *Preface*
and poem, and the link is not fortuitous. Athanasius's false zeal is a foil to
the poet's charity, to the charity of the true Anglican spirit; it also links
Catholicism and Calvinism in their advocacy of extremes. Moreover, the play
on "high flying" suggests the similarity of the Egyptian bishop to those

Anglican "high flyers" who would deny salvation to all but those conforming to their tenets and ceremonies. Dryden's Anglican confession offers charity and affirms spiritual and temperamental moderation. That moderation, the midpoint between extremes, is the key to the second half of the poem, which turns from spiritual to civic behavior.

What acts as a structural link between theology and politics is the digression on Father Simon's *Critical History of the Old Testament* (224–51). Phillip Harth has suggested that the digression is the core of this poem—originally, he speculates, a piece of complimentary verse intended to preface Henry Dickinson's translation of the *History*. If this were so, the publisher bought himself a rather strange commendation. The thirty lines that compose the "digression" playfully compliment the translator, but they are also a sarcastic denial of the *History* itself. And how could it have been otherwise? It is a central premise of *Religio Laici* that in things necessary for salvation, the Scriptures are ample, plain, and clear; this premise is used to deny the institutional arrogance of the Roman Catholic Church and the impudence of dissenting "inspiration." In light of the polemical importance of Scripture plain and clear, it would be odd indeed to find Dryden complimenting a book that discovered the textual corruption of Scripture and argued against any certainty of its divine authorship and authority. Dryden found a way of using Father Simon's *History* against Rome, but that is a secondary issue based on the theory of corrupt transmission. Of the central premise of the *History*, Dryden is scornful.

The attack on Father Simon is not a direct refutation of his *History*. Of Father Simon's discoveries, Dryden suggests he is not competent to judge. And the digression on the *History* begins with an assertion of technical incompetence and a linking of charity and laity:

> Thus far my Charity this path has try'd;
> (A much unskilfull, but well meaning guide:)
> Yet what they are, ev'n these crude thoughts were bred
> By reading that, which better thou hast read,
> Thy Matchless Author's work: which thou, my Friend,
> By well translating better dost commend.
>
> (224–29)

Henry Dickinson has read Father Simon "better" than Dryden, and can commend *The Critical History* "better" than the poet because he has translated it. What Dryden can commend in this author is very little indeed; and when he turns from translator to author, the mode changes from innuendo to sarcasm:

> Witness this weighty Book, in which appears
> The crabbed Toil of many thoughtfull years,
> Spent by thy Authour, in the Sifting Care
> Of *Rabbins* old Sophisticated Ware
> From Gold Divine; which he who well can sort
> May afterwards make *Algebra* a Sport.
> A Treasure, which if *Country-Curates* buy,
> They *Junius*, and *Tremellius* may defy:
> Save pains in various readings, and Translations;
> And without *Hebrew* make most learn'd quotations.
> A Work so full with various Learning fraught,
> So nicely pondred, yet so strongly wrought,
> As Natures height and Arts last hand requir'd:
> As much as Man cou'd compass, uninspir'd.
>
> (234–47)

The *History* is a trot for country curates; ponderous, crabbed, and uninspired, it is "fraught" with learning. Of Simon's great discovery, that the text of Scripture is corrupt, Dryden argues that rather than deny the sanctity of the holy writ, it undermines Rome:

> If *written words* from time are no secur'd,
> How can we think have *oral Sounds* endur'd?
> Which *thus* transmitted, if *one* Mouth has fail'd,
> *Immortal Lyes* on *Ages* are intail'd:
> And that some such have been, is prov'd too plain;
> If we consider *Interest, Church,* and *Gain*.
>
> (270–75)

Intended to cast the authority of all Protestantism in doubt, in fact the "secret meaning" (252) of the *History* argues more sharply against Roman Catholicism than Protestantism. Scriptures are "not *every where* Free from Corruption," but they are uncorrupt, sufficient, clear, and entire "In *all* things which our needfull *Faith* require." In affirming this conclusion, the compliment which Dryden pays to Father Simon's *History* at the opening of the digression comes clear: "Yet what they are, ev'n these crude thoughts were bred / By reading that, which better thou hast read, / Thy Matchless Author's work." Dickinson has read Father Simon more carefully than Dryden; this the poet allows. But what Dryden has discovered is that his charity based on a broad reading of Scripture is not only untouched by Roman Catholic apologetics, it is reaffirmed by this confrontation.

And now the poet asserts his convictions with a new boldness:

> Shall I speak plain, and in a Nation free
> Assume an honest *Layman's Liberty?*
> I think (according to my little Skill,
> To my own Mother-Church submitting still:)
> That many have been sav'd, and many may,
> Who never heard this Question brought in play.
> Th' *unletter'd* Christian, who believes in *gross,*
> Plods on to *Heaven*; and ne'er is at a loss:
> For the *Streight-gate* wou'd be made *streighter* yet,
> Were *none* admitted there but men of *Wit.*
> The few, by Nature form'd, with Learning fraught,
> Born to instruct, as others to be taught,
> Must Study well the Sacred Page; and see
> Which Doctrine, this, or that, does best agree
> With the whole Tenour of the Work Divine:
> And plainlyest points to Heaven's reveal'd Design:
> *Which* Exposition flows from *genuine Sense;*
> And which is *forc'd* by *Wit* and *Eloquence.*
>
>   (316–33)

The gate to heaven is not so straight as some would like to make it, and the path that guides the Christian pilgrim to that gate is broad and unlettered. The sophistication of *The Critical History* is irrelevant to salvation. The passage reiterates and links a doctrinal and stylistic issue by conflating plainness and liberty, charity and laity. The style of heaven is limpid, plain, and clear; and the conflation of theology and style points back to the opening assertions of humility and forward to the invocation of Sternhold and Shadwell. Style is the man, and heaven is to be won not by wit but by charity and plainness. But salvation is not the only business of this poem; it is in a way not even its central, and certainly not its most pressing concern.

That business, the politics of public conformity and civic quiet, forms Dryden's subject in the second part of *Preface* and poem, and both pursue the subject through a technique of dialectical analysis. The technique is a staple in Dryden's repertoire; its structure of the middle and the extremes is crucial to Dryden's efforts to assert moderation, allowing the poet the political geography of the middle ground and preparing the portrayal of the opposition through caricature of extremes. In *Absalom and Achitophel*, the middle way enabled Dryden to jeer at Catholic ceremony and to harass the sectaries; and the same is true of *Religio Laici*, where Dryden derides both Roman Catholics and fanatics, though the wit exercised on the Catholics has a noticeably softer edge than that practiced on the sectaries. Both king and poet laureate maintained a show of moderation and balance in their handling of the sectaries, but there is no question that the royal memory of benefits from the civil wars repeatedly sought for ways in which to ease the conditions of English Roman Catholics. And both king and poet laureate linked a general theological charity with the harsh condemnation of Protestant sectarian politics. Such a connection leads the poet from a discussion of Scripture to politics in 1682:

> The Scripture is a Rule; that in all things needfull to Salvation, it is clear, sufficient, and ordain'd by God Almighty for that purpose, . . . But, by asserting the Scripture to be the Canon of our Faith, I have unavoidably created to my self two sorts of Enemies: The Papists indeed, more directly, because they have kept the Scripture from us, what they cou'd; and have reserv'd to themselves a right of Interpreting what they have deliver'd under the pretence of Infalibility: and the Fanaticks more collaterally, because they have assum'd what amounts to an Infalibility, in the private Spirit: and have detorted those Texts of Scripture, which are not necessary to Salvation, to the damnable uses of Sedition, disturbance and destruction of the Civil Government.
>
> (140–54)

The discovery of "two sorts of Enemies" is the crux of political dialectic in the poem. As in *Absalom and Achitophel* and *The Hind and the Panther*, the middle way is neither philosophical conviction nor temperament, but political strategy. Regardless of real political geography, where the king stood was the middle ground. In *Religio Laici*, the charitable layman, whose opinions exactly mirror those of the king, distinguishes himself from the theological rigidity of the Anglican clergy and discovers a middle way between the arrogance of papal infallibility and the "rigid opinions and imperious discipline of *Calvin*" (247).

It was not, of course, difficult to make a case for the Anglican confession as the *via media*. Hooker's great invocation had made this a standard rhetorical trope for Anglicanism, and Dryden invokes the "venerable Hooker" more than once in condemning the Presbyterian discipline. But Dryden's *via media* is not a middle ground in theological terms; it is an attempt to portray and to justify the king's political position in relation to Roman Catholics and dissenters. By linking devotion and politics, Dryden would link spiritual toleration and political exigency, exactly the king's own position after the defeat of Exclusion. In *Religio Laici*, the position is not developed topically, though there is a glancing reference to the Test Act in the *Preface*, a suggestion of Catholic innocence in the Popish Plot, and a memory of loyalty to

Charles; but the cast of Dryden's whole discussion of Catholicism and sec-
tarianism bears the imprint of the political position that the king himself had
developed over the previous twenty years. It reflects as well Dryden's position in *Absalom and Achitophel*, where the criticism of Jebusites is noticeably
more oblique than the handling of the sectaries. Of the spiritual implications
of Roman Catholicism, we hear nothing at all; indeed, the papists are
"*part* / Of that vast Frame, the Church" (360). They falsely arrogate authority in the interpretation of Scripture, but such institutional arrogance is not
as dangerous as the private impudence of dissenting Protestants. What springs
from the reform of Roman Catholic clerical arrogance is private zeal and
political destruction.

And to that subject Dryden turns with a harshness that seems to contradict the spirit of religious charity so often invoked in *Preface* and poem.
But charity is sharply limited to theology. The poem is divided, analytically
and rhetorically, between theology and politics. The humble layman at the
opening of the *Preface* and the anxious pilgrim at the opening of the poem
are both postures, preparations for spiritual inquiry. The politician hardly
needed such humility, and when Dryden turns to politics, he reaches a familiar
stride:

> Thus Sectaries, we may see, were born with teeth, foul-mouth'd
> and scurrilous from their Infancy: and if Spiritual Pride, Venome,
> Violence, Contempt of Superiours and Slander had been the marks
> of Orthodox Belief; the Presbytery and the rest of our
> Schismaticks, which are their Spawn, were always the most visi-
> ble Church in the Christian World.
>
> (275–80)

Here is no trace of the diffident pilgrim, no inquiring spirit, no philosophical
skepticism, but the familiar rhythms and ironies of contempt. The language
is sharp and splenetic, the syntax is broken into short, harsh expletives; this
is the rhetorical culmination of a movement that had begun in suspension
and careful qualification at the opening of the *Preface*. The condemnation
of sectaries forms the explosive climax of both *Preface* and poem, the point
at which Dryden had aimed from the beginning.

The movement from qualification to condemnation in the *Preface* is exactly mirrored in the poem, which begins with a masterful invocation of
rhetorical diffidence. The hushed suspension of the opening lines creates a
delicately unsettled mood. Imagery and language suggest uncertainty; the
rhythms are unsteady; the syntax is inverted; the opening altogether denies
certitude:

> Dim, as the borrow'd beams of Moon and Stars
> To *lonely, weary, wandring* Travellers,
> Is *Reason* to the *Soul*: And as on high,
> Those rowling Fires *discover* but the Sky
> Not light us *here*; So *Reason's* glimmering Ray
> Was lent, not to *assure* our *doubtfull* way,
> But *guide* us upward to a *better Day*.
>
> (1–7)

At the poem's close, Dryden claims to have written in verse fittest for discourse, nearest prose, and yet the effects at the opening are achieved not by conformity to the syntax and rhythms of prose but by a careful departure from those norms. The subject of the first independent clause is suspended until the third line; and in the second and third clauses, negation and compound verbs attenuate the sense. The grammatical and syntactical extensions suspend the movement of argument; the language and syntax suggest hesitation, and the verse rhythms echo that hesitation. The poem begins in unusual metrical inversion, and that rhythmic trepidation is reflected in the carefully deliberated rhythms of the second line. The argument itself is steadily carried past the line endings so that verse and syntax contradict rather than compel assent. The effect of the whole is similar to the claims of spiritual and intellectual diffidence at the beginning of the *Preface*; but while those prose rhythms suggest uncertainty, the verse here orchestrates an even subtler hesitation, hardly the rugged measures of the Sternhold psalter. This is verse aiming not at discourse but at persuasion. The design of the poem as a whole is to begin in uncertainty and to conclude in condemnation. In a gradually ascending line of assurance, the narrator moves through the false steps of ancient philosophy, the errors of Deism and natural religion, toward popery and fanaticism. The climax to this rhythm of rational inquiry comes at line 400, when the disinterested philosopher weighs the consequence of religious reformation:

> 'Tis true, my Friend, (and far be Flattery hence)
> This good had full as bad a Consequence:
> The Book thus put in every vulgar hand,
> Which each presum'd he best cou'd understand,
> The *Common Rule* was made the *common Prey*;
> And at the mercy of the *Rabble* lay.
> The tender Page with horney Fists was gaul'd;
> And he was gifted most that loudest baul'd:
> The *Spirit* gave the *Doctoral Degree*:
> And every member of a *Company*

Was of *his Trade*, and of the *Bible free.*
Plain *Truths* enough for needfull *use* they found;
But men wou'd still be itching to *expound:*

. . . .

While Crouds unlearn'd, with rude Devotion warm,
About the Sacred Viands buz and swarm,
The *Fly-blown Text* creates a *crawling Brood;*
And turns to *Maggots* what was meant for *Food.*
A Thousand daily Sects rise up, and dye;
A Thousand more the perish'd Race supply.
So all we make of Heavens discover'd Will
Is, not to have it, or to use it ill.

(398–424)

Now we are on familiar ground; the hesitation, the slanted rhymes and oblique rhythms of the opening all have disappeared. This is the manner not of spiritual quest but political condemnation, and the evocation of *Absalom and Achitophel* is neither surprising nor accidental. Not only are the epithets familiar, not only is there a similarity of argument and imagery, but the voicing of the argument is strikingly reminiscent of the overt political poem. Here is the lock step of rhythm and rhyme that Dryden had made his own in *Absalom and Achitophel.*

The verse paragraph begins by suggesting balanced inquiry, the guileless search for truth. But the claims of disinterestedness and balance quickly give way to argument by juxtaposition of extremes: the book / the vulgar hand; the common rule / the common prey; the tender page / the horny fist. The dissenting pretense to spiritual inspiration is undercut by images and epithets that turn spiritual yearning into physiology: the hand and voice—oddly disembodied and disjointed figures themselves—become maggots and swarming insects. Sectarian inspiration transforms the sacred text into garbage. Dryden claims that he has chosen the epistolary manner, the style nearest prose; he intends discovery, not persuasion, but discovery is not among the aims of this passage.

While offering wide latitude in matters of the spirit, this poem swiftly and harshly condemns sectarian politics, and the spirit of the condemnation is not disinterested inquiry. Dryden's aim in this poem is to argue the king's case in religion and politics; like the king he is cautiously lenient toward Catholics, and like the king he is willing to tolerate a wide spectrum of religious beliefs. But such toleration, the poem argues, should not be construed as political indifference or political weakness. The king had the task of moving forcefully against political dissent, and he did so in no uncertain terms following the dissolution of the Oxford parliament. But he did not wish, as did members of the High Church party, to condemn religious dissent in spiritual terms. So long as religious dissent remained wholly a spiritual matter, the king's message was toleration; he did not aim to impose a uniformity in these matters. What he had advocated through his reign was religious toleration and political discipline; *Religio Laici* is an attempt to give the authority of verse to a policy now under siege. What the king could no longer advocate, the poet laureate might expound in the freedom of poetry and laity.

JAMES A. WINN

The Promise of Dryden's Elegy
for Hastings

John Dryden's first known poem, "Upon the Death of the Lord Hastings"
(1649), has usually been dismissed as a piece of embarrassing juvenilia,
characterized exclusively by its "Metaphysical" extravagance, especially in
the notorious lines on the smallpox, and by its clumsy versification. But these
faults hardly justify ignoring the only extended poem we have between
Dryden's birth and his much more polished efforts of 1659 and 1660. If much
of the imagery is conceited in the manner of Cowley, and many of the lines
clogged with awkward contractions, the poem still gives tentative indications
of Dryden's future excellence. Although written entirely in couplets and
printed with only one break (setting off the brief closing envoi addressed to
Hastings's *"Virgin-Widow,"* Elizabeth Mayerne, whom he was to have mar-
ried on June 25, 1649, the very day after he died), Dryden's effort shows
more skill in organization than most of the poems in *Lachrymae Musarum*
(1649), the volume of elegies for Hastings in which it first appeared. He is
able to make sections of up to twenty lines cohere as structural units, often
by building towards small rhetorical climaxes or cadences, then altering his
tone and diction to signal an altered rhetorical relation between the speaker
and his implied audience. Uncertain and embryonic in this adolescent poem,
these skills would become the tight verse-paragraphing and deft "modulation" of the mature Dryden. If the schoolboy poet was far too susceptible
to the temptations of cleverness, he had the good sense to organize his poem
around the most universal themes suggested by the particular death of young

From *Modern Language Review* 79, part 1 (January 1984). © 1984 by the Modern
Humanities Research Association.

Hastings, to forge connexions between that death, the public events of the 1640s, and the Renaissance cultural traditions of which his schooling at Westminster under Richard Busby had made him aware.

The strengths and weaknesses of the poem are apparent in its opening lines:

> Must Noble *Hastings* Immaturely die,
> (The Honour of his ancient Family?)
> Beauty and Learning thus together meet,
> To bring a *Winding* for a *Wedding-sheet?*

The ideas introduced here (the untimeliness of Hastings's death, his status as the only heir of an important family, his physical beauty and mental precocity, and the irony of his death on his wedding eve) are in no way unique to Dryden's poem, occurring in most of the others in the volume. But while some of the other poets had concentrated on the bereavement of Hastings's fiancée, Dryden merely glances at that theme here, delaying its development until the envoi. Similarly, the parentheses around line 2 mark it off as a polite but perfunctory nod to Hastings's family; their nobility and grief are not Dryden's subjects. Despite some wanderings, he will essentially address three universal themes: as the word "Immaturely" dominates the first line in length and accent, so the theme it adumbrates, the irony that death should fall upon the young while the old survive, will dominate the poem, receiving particular development towards the end but appearing as well in the sections devoted to Hastings's "Beauty" and "Learning," abstractions that make their first appearance here as personified figures holding a winding-sheet, like statues on a baroque funerary monument.

The theme of learning comes first, with a series of insistent rhetorical questions. By breathlessly questioning the worth of acquiring *"Vertue,"* "Grace," and "Art" through "Merit," "Discipline," "Labour," and "Study," the speaker indirectly credits Hastings with all those attributes. The first-person plurals suggest the identity of the audience; when Dryden asks, "shall Art / Make us more Learned, onely to depart?" (1.7), he surely refers specifically to the scholars of Westminster School, who might well ask such questions after seeing one of their schoolmates graduate into the jaws of death. For adolescents in the process of having Greek grammar flogged into them by Busby, the notion that Hastings's death was a warning *against* study must have been comforting, but Dryden, despite his own adolescence, does not draw that conclusion. What the California editors call "an attempt at passionate utterance" is more like an impersonation of a schoolboy response to a classmate's death, and the wiser speaker of the last couplet in this section, who can speak of "Our *Noble Youth*" as if he were suddenly older, invalidates the boyish questions with a stern *reductio ad absurdum:*

> Our *Noble Youth* now have pretence to be
> Dunces securely, Ign'rant healthfully.
>
> (1.13)

After that cadence the tone shifts to direct praise of Hastings's linguistic skills:

> Rare Linguist! whose Worth speaks it self, whose Praise,
> Though not his Own, all Tongues Besides do raise.
>
> (1.15)

Quiet irony replaces stagy posturing: if these lines were spoken of a living Hastings, the idea that his own tongue did not speak his praise would be a compliment on the modesty of one "whose Worth speaks it self"; but death, not modesty, has permanently stilled that tongue, so that the present-tense verbs later in the same section ("In his mouth Nations speak," 1.19) are sadly incorrect. Already the language seems royal; nations conventionally speak through the mouths of kings, even if kings like Alexander lack Hastings's skill with languages, which makes him a "native" of all countries and leads to the climactic biblical allusion:

> A young Apostle; and (with rev'rence may
> I speak'it) inspir'd with gift of Tongues, as They.
>
> (1.23)

When that gift came upon the Apostles at Pentecost, Peter explained the miracle to those who thought they were drunk by quoting the prophet Joel, who had predicted that "your young men shall see visions, and your old men shall dream dreams" (Acts 2:17; compare Joel 2:28). Perhaps a memory of that passage lies behind the aphoristic couplet with which Dryden concludes this section, a compressed statement of the theme of youth and age:

> Nature gave him, a Childe, what Men in vain
> Oft strive, by Art though further'd, to obtain.
>
> (1.25)

The most successful sections of this poem develop the oppositions between the four chiastically ordered nouns in this couplet, oppositions relevant to both Hastings and Dryden. Hastings, a child, has died as men do, on the eve of taking on the adult role of husband. He cannot father children of his own, though the envoi will find comfort in a more symbolic and artistic kind of fathering, the making of poems. Dryden, a child now taking on the adult

role of poet, is writing a Royalist poem in opposition to the political beliefs
of his natural father, though calculated to please his surrogate artistic father,
Busby. The themes he develops are those which continued to engage his attention throughout his career: the tension between generations, central to
Absalom and Achitophel and virtually all the plays; and the tension between
art and nature, a leading problem of the criticism, richly reflected in such
mature works as the poem to Godfrey Kneller and the elegy for Anne
Killigrew.

   Now comes the theme of physical beauty, abstractedly developed with
imagery from astronomy, an interest that remained with Dryden all his life,
and another instance of the influence of Busby, who taught Aratus to fourth-
formers, and whose library contained works by Theodosius, Ptolemy, Tycho
Brahe, and Kepler. Dryden's concern to display his learning makes lines
27–38, developing a comparison between Hastings's body and the "Sphear"
of Archimedes, coldly intellectual, but in lines 39–46 the tone shifts again:
having made Hastings into a heavenly body, Dryden challenges "learned
Ptolomy," by 1649 a somewhat discredited astronomer, to measure "this
Hero's Altitude." I suspect that this is a bad joke for the boys of Westminster;
line 74 will refer to Hastings as "one so young, so small," and Dryden may
mean to undermine the already lighthearted picture of a Ptolemy unable to
find the altitude of the star Hastings, by reminding his classmates of the ease
with which a real tailor could measure the height of the real Hastings. He
would learn to manage comic moments within a serious poem more deftly
by the time he wrote the Killigrew ode, and there can be little doubt that
such jokes weaken the Hastings elegy, but the habits of mind they reveal,
a restlessness about maintaining decorum and a temptation to undercut his
own seriousness, have been frequently detected by modern critics in Dryden's
adult poems and plays.

   For these lines are not merely playful. Dryden is preparing his climax
by establishing a less refined but more dramatic tone. In the ensuing lines
on the disease, Hastings will be made analogous to Charles I, an identification prepared in part by the phrases here that make him a "Hero" and a "new
star" (l. 46), and especially by the restating of the theme of youth and age
in terms of light: "this Ray, (which shone / More bright i' th' Morn, then
others beam at Noon)" (l. 43). Not only is the opposition between generations here collapsed into a contrast between "Morn" and "Noon," but the
imagery of stars, beams, and rays had long been established as the imagery
of monarchy—not least by the Jacobean and Caroline masques, where that
imagery could become spectacle through lighting and machinery. Charles I,
himself only five feet four inches tall, was magnified at his masques by being

placed in the highest and best seat, and magnified verbally by sun imagery, not only in the poetry of the masques, but in the prose of *Eikon Basilike*, which ran through sixty editions in the year preceding this poem.

To present this climactic section, Dryden returns to the device of the question, but this time he answers his own question:

> Replenish'd then with such rare Gifts as these.
> Where was room left for such a Foul Disease?
> The Nations sin hath drawn that Veil, which shrouds
> Our Day-spring in so sad benighting Clouds.
>
> (l. 47)

Having established the royal sun imagery, Dryden can present "the Nations sin" as the veiling or shrouding of the sun, producing an unwholesome atmosphere in which Hastings's "Foul Disease" can appear. For this negative version of the royal imagery there was also ample precedent, for example in these lines from Thomas Carew's poem, "Upon the Kings sicknesse," probably written during the final illness of James I in 1625:

> That ruddie morning beame of Majestie [that is, Charles],
> Which should the Suns ecclipsed light supply,
> Is overcast with mists and in the liew
> Of cherefull rayes, sends us down drops of dew.
>
> (l. 29)

As Carew had presented Charles clouded over by James's illness, Dryden presents him "shrouded" by "The Nations sin." So badly damaged is the covenant between heaven and earth, itself analogous to the broken covenant between king and people, that

> Heaven would no longer trust its Pledge; but thus
> Recall'd it; rapt its *Ganymede* from us.
>
> (l. 51)

This extravagant turn of wit begins the process by which the poem runs off the rails. The pun on the world "Pledge" (security deposit and toast) deflects our attention from the carefully-prepared sun imagery of the preceding lines, as do the ensuing allusions to Pandora's box, Venus's naevi, jewels and foils, and weeping pimples. Presumably the young poet hoped to produce a climactic effect by crowding in every invention he could manage, offering plenitude as a version of intensity. Or perhaps his uncertainty about how his Puritan family in Titchmarsh might respond to the Royalism of this section led him to obscure matters with these extraneous images. Still, the

copiousness that weakens these lines is very much in the tradition of
Westminster poetry and oratory; when Busby and his predecessors sought
to "*whet* up and *raise* [the] *Phansies*" of their students, they encouraged such
multiplication of metaphors, and a chastened version of such copiousness
remains one of the strengths of Dryden's adult poetry. The damage done to
the poem is undeniable, but perhaps a little limited by the fact that Dryden
punctuates all these attempts at Cowleian wit as questions, thus labelling
them as inadequate explanations for the disease. The real explanation,
presented as statement, is political; it describes the pox.

> Who, Rebel-like, with their own Lord at strife,
> Thus made an Insurrection 'gainst his Life.
>
> (l. 61)

This personification of the pox as rebels is the vehicle for a larger comparison of two deadly phenomena: the disease that ravaged Hastings's body
and the war that ravaged England. Usually explained as a "Metaphysical
conceit," the metaphor owes much to the Royalist propaganda of the Civil
War, which frequently portrayed the Parliamentary forces as infections in
the body politic. The grotesquerie, while fatal to the decorum of the elegy,
is surely intentional. Outrage often provoked this kind of response from
Dryden; the boy who could picture Cromwell and the Roundheads as pimples
became the man who could picture Shaftesbury as a counterfeit coin, a
squeaking bagpipe, and a painful cure for veneral disease:

>   thy Mercury
> Has pass'd through every Sect, or theirs through Thee.
> But what thou giv'st, that Venom still remains;
> And the pox'd Nation feels Thee in their Brains.
>   (*The Medall*, l. 263; see also ll. 8–10, 34–35)

The similarity with this later satire suggests the anger behind Dryden's lines,
and points the problem as well. Funeral elegies of the seventeenth century
have a wider range of tone and diction than those of later eras, but even
in 1649 grief usually sings in softer notes. The noisiness of Dryden's climax,
produced not only by the sheer number of metaphors but by the violence
of some of them, negates the abstraction he had earlier sought. After the
ugly physical picture of the disease here, even astronomical imagery, lofty
and detached in the earlier parts of the poem, comes crashing to earth:

> No Comet need foretel his Change drew on,
> Whose Corps might seem a *Constellation*.
>
> (l. 65)

The next section regains some composure and detachment by distancing us from Hastings's death in time instead of space, making him an avatar of various Roman worthies before restating the theme of youth and age in seasonal imagery:

> But hasty Winter, with one blast, hath brought
> The hopes of Autumn, Summer, Spring to nought.
> Thus fades the Oak i' th' sprig, i' th' blade the Corn;
> ˙Thus, without Young, this *Phoenix* dies, new born.
>
> (l. 77)

Even here there are political overtones: Hastings died on June 24, 1649, and could thus hardly be termed a victim of "hasty Winter," but Charles I stepped on to the scaffold on a cold day in January, and the poem has already connected the two deaths. The disordering of the seasons, the blighting of fertility, and the final death of the phoenix reverse more positive images usually associated with monarchy. In Ben Jonson's masque, *The Vision of Delight*, performed before James I in January 1617, a spring scene elicits these questions from a character named *Wonder:*

> What better change appears?
> Whence is it that the air so sudden clears,
> And all things in a moment turn so mild?
>
> . . . .
>
> How comes it winter is so quite forced hence,
> And locked up under ground?

Another character, *Fant'sy*, doubtless pointing towards James's chair, replies:

> Behold a King
> Whose presence maketh this perpetual spring,
> The glories of which spring grow in that bower,
> And are the marks and beauties of his power.

The appearance of spring in the dead of winter is a royal miracle, made visible by the artifice of Inigo Jones and the magical poetry of Jonson. But in a nation without a king, a winter blast can kill a promising youth in June.

In Dryden's next section, we hear again the shrill questioning voice of the angry youth:

> Must then old three-legg'd gray-beards with their Gout,
> Catarrhs, Rheums, Aches, live three Ages out?
>
> (l. 81)

Again, Dryden is expressing more than one eighteen-year-old's frustration at the death of another. According to Conrad Russell, "the Royalists were, on average, ten years younger than the Parliamentarians," and Royalist propaganda could therefore picture the Civil War as a generational struggle in which grey-haired Puritan generals left gay young blades dead on the battlefield ("Introduction" to *Origins of the English Civil War*). Having been exposed to such propaganda, and having learned from Busby to regret the loss of a court whose rich and varied culture he was just too young to have seen, Dryden questions a world where "none live but such as should die," a category presumably containing old men, regicides, and a grey-haired Parliamentary leadership that included members of his own family. Eleven years later, celebrating the return of Charles II, he would return to the same theme:

> Youth that with Joys had unacquainted been
> Envy'd gray hairs that once good days had seen:
> We thought our Sires, not with their own content,
> Had ere we came to age our Portion spent.
>
> > (*Astraea Redux*, l. 25)

But these later lines, the work of a greatly-improved poet, do not yield to shrillness as does the attack on "Ghostly Fathers" in the Hastings poem, where even Dryden seems to recognize and apologize for his bitter excess:

> Grief makes me rail; Sorrow will force its way;
> And, Show'rs of Tears, Tempestuous Sighs best lay.
> The Tongue may fail; but over-flowing Eyes
> Will weep out lasting streams of *Elegies*.
>
> > (l. 89)

The final image is as flat and conventional as anything in the poem, but two briefer phrases, linked by internal rhyme and including the only first-person singular in the poem, are more revealing. "Grief makes me rail," while evidently an apology for the excesses I have indicated, suggests the similar impulses behind elegy and satire; "The Tongue may fail," undercutting the earlier praise of Hastings's talented tongue, acknowledges not only the inadequacy of words as expressions of grief but the poet's recognition that his control is not yet that of a mature artist.

By adding the envoi, which might have been merely sentimental, Dryden gains one more shift in perspective. Instead of offering Elizabeth religious anodynes, as had other poets, Dryden urges her to consummate her thwarted marriage intellectually:

> With greater then *Platonick* love, O wed
> His Soul, though not his Body, to thy Bed.
>
> > (l. 97)

Hastings's body, in the section of the poem devoted to its beauty, has been transformed from a glassy orb into a blistered corpse, but his soul has gone unmentioned since the lines on Archimedes's sphere, in which "Heavn's Gifts," the sundry talents that "appear / Scatter'd in Others," are described as "fix'd and conglobate in 's Soul." It is this soul, this seminal concentration of virtues, that Dryden urges Elizabeth to take into her bed:

> Let that make thee a Mother; bring thou forth
> Th' *Idea's* of his Vertue, Knowledge, Worth.
>
> > (l. 99)

But bringing forth ideas, however apt the maternal metaphor, is what poets do, and if we suspect that Dryden is speaking to himself as much as to Elizabeth, the next line confirms our suspicions: "Transcribe the Original in new Copies" (1.101). Dryden is asking Elizabeth to do what he has done, to make Hastings into a work of art. Transformed into an idea by Dryden's poem and Elizabeth's memory, Hastings can cast his "Irradiations" in an England darkened by civil war; he can be a "great Grandsire . . . Of an Heroick Divine Progenie" so that Dryden need no longer rail at greybeards.

In the absence of any other primary document from Dryden's Westminster years, we must base our conclusions about his reading, opinions, and poetic development on this interesting but hardly imposing poem. Reading too much into such a conventional and occasional poem is an obvious danger, and the Royalist sentiments overtly expressed here, which are certainly less polemical than those expressed in several of the companion poems, are scarcely an adequate basis for any sweeping conclusions about the political allegiances of the eighteen-year-old Dryden. One might explain the poem's Royalism simply as a consequence of its occasion, the death of the son of the Earl of Huntingdon, whose fiancee was the daughter of Sir Theodore Mayerne, physician to the late king. One might argue that Dryden was simply writing to order, as on numerous later occasions, hoping to please Busby, the Hastings and Mayerne families, and the other Royalist contributors to *Lachrymae Musarum*, and in some sense this is doubtless true. But the Royalism of the poem's *style* suggests that Dryden had been more profoundly affected by Busby, whose interest in classical imagery and theatrical effects was of a piece with his Laudian faith in liturgy and monarchy; some of the poem's more vigorous moments suggest that he had also been affected by reading Royalist satire. Both influences were important for Dryden's future development: the visual and mythological imagery drawn from the masque tradition would reappear, in a chastened form, in his official court poetry; the histrionic raillery and violent imagery that sometimes weaken this poem would find a more appropriate place in the great satires of his maturity.

When Dryden personifies "Beauty and Learning" in the opening lines, presents Hastings as a glass model of the universe, and describes death as a disordering of the seasons, he comes quite close to some of the visual effects and Platonizing tendencies of the Caroline masque. Orgel's and Strong's description of the set for *Albion's Triumph* (1632), a masque presented by Inigo Jones and Aurelian Townshend after Jones's break with Jonson, will suggest Dryden's debt to such "almighty architecture":

> The *meaning* of what the court is witnessing depends on its ability to make certain assumptions about the truth of images. Two symbolic figures, of Theory looking toward heaven, and Practice gazing downward, adorn Jones's proscenium, "showing that by these two all works of architecture and ingining have their perfection." . . . If we recall Ficino's observation that Archimedean models of the spheres reveal the essential divinity of man's mind, we shall see that the architect's aims are quite as serious as the poet's had been. Through "architecture and ingining"— the word retains its implications of wit and understanding—we create the universe, and comprehend and control its workings.
>
> (*Inigo Jones: The Theatre of the Stuart Court*)

Much of what is said here is directly applicable to Dryden's poem, which asks us to share its assumptions about the truth of its images, to participate willingly in the fiction that Hastings is an exemplar of all the art, beauty, learning, and virtue that have perished with the court. His poem also has "two symbolic figures" perched on its proscenium: "Beauty and Learning" with their winding-sheet. He explicitly presents Hastings as an "Archimedean model of the spheres." His Cowleian excesses of fancy and invention are, to use Jones's word, "ingining," effects designed to ravish our understanding by wit and surprise; if they fail, as Jones's machines sometimes failed for those not seated at optimal angles, the contrast with the Puritan emphasis on naked truth, direct language, and the rational ordering of the sermon remains marked.

In their use of mythology, *Albion's Triumph* and the other masques were attempts, however unrealistic, to present Charles as an ideal ruler, a new Roman emperor, a version of Jove, a sacramental hero. They failed as propaganda, since they were restricted to a tiny audience, and since their mythological and hierarchical claims were no answer to the pressing economic problems of the 1630s; moreover, Puritans like Dryden's family regarded the drama, especially drama with actresses, as immoral. But later the execution of the King, the standard imagery of the Caroline masque took on a more tragic and nostalgic force; *Eikon Basilike*, hawked on the streets within hours of the beheading, began this process, and many of the poems in *Lachrymae Musarum*, not least Dryden's, draw on the image-complex of Charles as martyr developed in that tract. Milton, angrily objecting to the popularity of *Eikon Basilike* in his own *Ikonoklastes*, accurately identifies the source of its imagery in the masque tradition: "But quaint emblems and devices begged from the old pageantry of some Twelfthnight's entertainment for Whitehall, will do but ill to make a saint or martyr." However self-evident this objection may have seemed to Milton, in practice the "quaint emblems and devices" of the masque tradition worked *better* as ways to create and perpetuate a cult of Charles as martyr than they had as ways to praise a live Charles on the throne. As Dryden would discover when he attempted to employ some of this imagery for his poems in praise of Charles II, the suspension of disbelief required to accept a living and palpably flawed monarch as a "sacred Majesty," a divinely ordained avatar of Hercules, Christ, and sundry other heroes, is different in kind from that required when the same imagery is used of a dead man; panegyric can be invalidated by the actions of its subject, as elegy cannot. Dead at eighteen, and thus eternally promising, Hastings was an ideal subject on which to lavish the idealization, abstraction, and iconography of the Royalist style; like the unknown sitter for a great portrait, he lives only as a work of art, a virtually self-contained universe created by "architecture and ingining."

Nostalgia and mythopoesis were not the only Royalist responses to defeat and disaster, however. The anger, self-dramatization, and physical shock I have pointed out in Dryden's poem also have Royalist analogues, for example in the bitter satirical verse of Cleveland or the mordant prose of Berkenhead. The similarities extend to matters of form. Cleveland's outrage at the reversal of traditional values by the Parliamentary victors sometimes finds a tight, compressed expression:

> *Faces about*, saies the *Remonstrant* Spirit;
> Allegeance is Malignant, Treason Merit.
> ("To *P. Rupert*")

And some of Dryden's tightest lines in the Hastings poem employ similar techniques to point similar ironies:

If Merit be Disease, if Vertue Death;

. . . .

Our *Noble Youth* now have pretence to be
Dunces securely, Ign'rant healthfully.

Both examples depend heavily on trochaic inversion ("*Faces about*"; "Dunces securely"), zeugma ("Treason Merit"; "Vertue Death"), alliteration ("Malignant . . . Merit"; "Disease . . . Death"), and emphatic caesurae. These devices, which one associates with the satiric couplets of the mature Dryden and Pope, seem out of place in an elegy, but in the Royalist writings on which Dryden was drawing, satiric and elegiac impulses quite naturally occurred together, as they did for the Puritan Milton of *Lycidas*, who used the occasion of the death of Edward King to "foretell the ruin of our corrupted clergy." After the execution of King Charles, Royalist writers often expressed their frustration by assuming the pose of Prince Hamlet, mourning for a simpler and more noble past, but expressing their sorrow with a paradoxical wit, a fondness for images of disease, and a hostility towards the previous generation of which Dryden's attack on "old three-legged gray-beards" is a strong example. As they saw it, the King had been murdered, the rightful heir dispossessed, the throne usurped: something was rotten in England; the time was out of joint. Paul Fussell has made a similar point about Dryden's heirs, the Augustan humanists, who were also fond of Hamlet and for whom "elegiac action is seldom undertaken at any great distance from satiric or mock-heroic manoeuvres, for to regret the past is by implication to condemn the present" (*The Rhetorical World of Augustan Humanism*). Yet powerful as this combination of motives was for Pope or Dr Johnson, it was surely even more sharp and potent for Dryden, who had gained from Busby a lively sense of what he had lost in the collapse of the Caroline court. The anger that spills over in parts of the Hastings poem, in which may be detected the first faint stirrings of the more sustained savagery of *The Medall*, arises from the same impulses as the sorrow.

"Upon the Death of the Lord Hastings" naturally has more in common with the elegies of Dryden's maturity (the Killigrew ode, *Eleonora*, or *Threnodia Augustalis*) than with his mature satires: those later elegies also magnify the dead by invoking the classical and Christian imagery of the Renaissance; they too exhibit an old-fashioned rhetorical structure. Superficially, Dryden's official panegyrics appear to employ the same techniques of amplification but, as I have shown, there is an important difference between elegy and panegyric. Dryden's Restoration panegyrics, concerned as they were to exorcise the Civil Wars and the Interregnum, could not recover the mythological and hierarchical illusions of the masque, which were already unrealistic in their own time. His gestures towards that past world are always hedged in by conscious or unconscious irony, by a profound sense of the fragility of human institutions, successions, and hierarchies. As the chief architect of the chastened Royalist style of the Restoration, Dryden was acknowledging changed literary circumstances as well as partisan necessities by developing, to the immeasurable benefit of his eighteenth-century heirs, the satiric consequences of a literary strategy that measured the present against the classical or biblical past and found it ludicrously wanting. By every standard, including that of propaganda, *Absalom and Achitophel* is a more successful poem than, say, *Britannia Rediviva*. But the energy that fuels the great satires has a common source with the nostalgia apparent in the baroque court panegyrics, a source already detectable in the Hastings elegy: Dryden's sense of having been born too late, his longing for an irrecoverable past. While the panegyrics normally invoke that past by alluding to myth or ancient history, the emotional source for the nostalgia they express lies in the complicated feelings Dryden and his readers had about their own times, particularly the passing of the court of Charles I, where ceremony and the arts had been prized as they would never be again. The elegy for Hastings allows us to examine those feelings at the moment of their origin, and to glimpse in the uncertain technique of its schoolboy author some early instances of the complexity, penetration, and organizational skill of the poet he would become.

PETER M. SACKS

"To the Memory of Mr. Oldham"

Dryden's poem for John Oldham represents a rejection of his earlier exercise in the flamboyantly metaphysical, or "hydrographical," school of Cleveland; and this turn away from his elegy for Hastings exemplifies a general shift of taste toward the Augustan norms which Jonson had heralded at the beginning of the century.

To the Memory of Mr. Oldham

> Farewel, too little and too lately known,
> Whom I began to think and call my own;
> For sure our Souls were near ally'd; and thine
> Cast in the same Poetick mould with mine.
> One common Note on either Lyre did strike,
> And Knaves and Fools we both abhorr'd alike:
> To the same Goal did both our Studies drive,
> The last set out the soonest did arrive.
> Thus *Nisus* fell upon the slippery place,
> While his young Friend perform'd and won the Race.
> O early ripe! to thy abundant store
> What could advancing Age have added more?
> It might (what Nature never gives the young)
> Have taught the numbers of thy native Tongue.
> But Satyr needs not those, and Wit will shine

From *The English Elegy: Studies in the Genre from Spenser to Yeats.* © 1985 by the Johns Hopkins University Press.

Through the harsh cadence of a rugged line.
A noble Error, and but seldom made,
When Poets are by too much force betray'd.
Thy generous fruits, though gather'd ere their prime
Still shew'd a quickness; and maturing time
But mellows what we write to the dull sweets of Rime.
Once more, hail and farewel; farewel thou young,
But ah too short, *Marcellus* of our Tongue;
Thy Brows with Ivy, and with Laurels bound;
But Fate and gloomy Night encompass thee around.

Like Jonson's epigram, Dryden's poem is cast in heroic couplets, and it shares the earlier poem's epitaphic blend of dignity, brevity, and restraint. Its three principle sections (ll. 1–10, 11–20, 21–25) all employ the fiction of address, and this repetition both tightens and underlines the neat ordonnance of the work. The opening lines, beginning with "Farewel" and including the stoical attention to degree ("too little," "too lately") as well as to the precariousness of possession, are especially reminiscent of Jonson. And as the elegy unfolds, we recognize a similarly Neoclassical preoccupation with the issues of poetry itself. In this case, the concerns are explicitly those Augustan topics of craft, decorum, elegance, and the classics.

The following reading of the poem dwells mainly on two subjects: Dryden's treatment and display of poetic technique and his use of allusion.

John Oldham, twenty years Dryden's junior, died in 1683 at the age of thirty-one. He had been a promising satirist with a flair for caustic and headstrong verse. As Dryden's "too lately known" admits, the two men had only become acquainted a relatively short time (two years) before Oldham's death. But Dryden's poem expresses an elevated spirit of comradeship, and much of the elegy's interest lies in his attempt to accommodate a clear-eyed sense of Oldham's poetic immaturity with a gracious and compassionate farewell.

Almost immediately, we note how Dryden emphasizes his attitude toward poetry itself as a source of highest value. In the cases of Oldham and himself, the very shape and definition of the soul is one accorded by the practice of poetry. So, too, any discussion of Oldham's life and death is, according to Dryden's poem, best conducted with reference to his poetry. The entire question of a premature death, and the consideration of the precise loss involved, is therefore weighed in terms of poetic development and in terms of that typically Renaissance and Neoclassical concern, the shape of a career. Furthermore, it is scarcely surprising to find that whatever consolation the elegy may invent will also relate to a principally poetic context.

By conventional elegiac figures of vegetation, very possibly borrowed from Milton, Dryden associates Oldham with the figure of the young fertility god ("O early ripe! . . . Thy generous fruits"). *Generous* retains some of its original meaning, but the procreative power is definitely transferred to that of poetic creativity, and Dryden keeps his attention carefully focused on questions of poetic achievement.

Had he lived longer, Oldham might have attained the kind of finesse and smooth control that Dryden is even now self-consciously exercising. Dryden takes pains to demonstrate these attainments not only in the entire design of the poem but in the deliberate shows of formal mastery that mark certain lines. While seeming to defend Oldham's rough versification ("Wit will shine / Through the harsh cadence of a rugged line"), Dryden writes an enjambed series of rugged, irregular feet, through whose apparent harshness the momentum travels to its fulfilling cadence. So powerfully imitative is the rhythm of the line that it appears to render the cadence itself transparent to the light of wit.

A second example of this kind of self-conscious virtuosity is Dryden's description of poetic maturation: "and maturing time / But mellows what we write to the dull sweets of Rime." Again, he seems to be deferring to Oldham's immature strength. The "But" and the "dull sweets" seem to suggest that Dryden holds these mellowings somewhat cheaply. This is important, for I think that the posture of deference is part of the successful mourner's complex blend of symbolic obeisance and self-approval in relation to the dead. The latter intention is surely there in the amplitude with which Dryden formally embodies the very qualities that he seems to slight. Enjambment, followed by an alexandrine, draws out the utterance into the continuous and lengthy period of maturation. This is precisely the kind of formal solace we crave after the abrupt discontinuity of "O early ripe!"

The play of alliteration and assonance in these lines is more detailed than I can here afford to note, but we should at least register how the consonants of *mellows* are among the most heavily alliterated, so that the lines themselves seem to resolve into one long utterance of the word: "*m*aturing ti*m*e / But *mellows* *w*hat *w*e *w*rite to the du*ll* *sw*eets of Ri*m*e." Within the alliterations are further plays, such as the reversal of "mello*ws*" in "*sw*eets," or, even more telling, the complex alliterative and assonantal modulation from "time" to "write" to "Rime," a progression in which rhyming becomes the resolution of writing and time. Even the harshness of the dental *t* is made to yield and ripen to the soft *m* we heard so often earlier in the line. Finally, rhyme itself has been prolonged and matured in this last word of the only rhymed triplet in the poem. Here, then, is the yield of maturity, the consolations offered by a surviving poet's form, which in itself seems to bring to fruition the early promise of a poet whose works had been abruptly "gather'd ere their prime."

To the consolations of formal virtuosity Dryden adds the consolatory effects of two perfect allusions. Appropriately enough for a poem of and about mellowness and craft, both allusions are from the *Aeneid*. The first is to the footrace in *Aeneid* 5.315ff. The second is to Aeneas's sighting of Marcellus in the underworld in *Aeneid* 6.

The situation of the footrace itself is significant, for it is that of the funeral games for Aeneas's father, Anchises. With this allusion to Classical mourning practices, and in particular to those performed by Aeneas, Dryden thus brings to his poem and to his act of mourning the stature of Virgil's great exemplar of piety and decorum. Furthermore, as we know, contests have an especially important function, not only in their original form of funerary ritual but in the closely related form of singing matches or other scenarios of contest within many elegies. I have discussed [in *The English Elegy*] the elegiac contest in its relation to such issues as the struggle for inheritance, the proof that certain powers survive, the foregrounding of an elegist's skill, and the dynamic of work and its compensatory reward. The richness of the topos should therefore be recollected even as we regard the more specific aspects of Dryden's purpose.

An immediate function of the allusion is to provide a reserved yet elevated statement of Dryden's friendship with Oldham. Earlier in the poem, he had established his affinity with the younger man, and there, too, he had mediated that expression by referring to shared poetic pursuits. Now, he again purifies the relationship of the merely personal, referring to it indirectly by way of Virgil's poetry. In each case, poetry itself provides a zone that lends both dignity and a measure of neutrality to an expression of personal feeling. Interestingly, whereas Dryden comes upon the allusion as though principally to clarify the nature of his "race" against Oldham, he is honoring the actual relationship by comparing it to that of the two men whom Virgil himself had chosen as the very exemplars of friendship. In fact it is Nisus, the Dryden figure, whom Virgil singles out for fame in this regard: "Nisus, for friendship to the youth renowned." And it is Nisus who goes on to demonstrate the virtue of his friendship and to win a significant *consolation* prize.

The details of the race are familiar, but their complex contribution to Dryden's poem have never been entirely registered. Readers have certainly noted the dominant parallels: Nisus (Dryden) started ahead of Euryalus (Oldham) in the race (of life). Although closer to the goal (death), Nisus slipped, and Euryalus went on to win. Thus the allusion neatly captures the paradoxical reversal of expectation and consolingly converts Oldham's seeming defeat into a victory. But if we explore the event further, we recall that Euryalus won because the fallen Nisus had intervened on his behalf (Nisus deliberately tripped Salius, who had been running between him and Euryalus). While illustrating Nisus's selfless assistance to his friend, the detail invites us to recognize that it is, after all, the intervention of the elegist, with his fiction of the race, that allows the dead Oldham any such thing as a victory. The allusion thus reflects what Dryden is even now performing for his friend.

While we are on this point, we should remember that Nisus slipped in the blood of the oxen that had been sacrificed in the rites for Anchises. Virgil describes him as "besmeared with filth and holy gore," a description surely befitting a mourner if we think either of the primitive rites or of an elegist's related conjunction of self-abasement and self-consecration.

Finally, Virgil concluded the footrace episode with an elaborate scenario of judgment and reward, motifs that we recognize as crucial to the concern of almost every elegist. Again, the details are minutely appropriate, for Virgil concentrates especially on the ability of a fair judge, Aeneas, to remedy the blunders of Fortune (" 'But . . . Fortune's errors give me leave to mend, / At least to pity my deserving friend' "). The lines are astonishingly apt, and it is intriguing that it is Nisus, the Dryden figure, who formulates most clearly the concept of the consolation prize. He pleads on his own behalf, but the wider relevance to Dryden's purpose is obvious:

> "If such rewards to vanquished men are due"
> (He said), "and falling is to rise by you,
> What prize may Nisus from your bounty claim,
> Who merited the first rewards and fame?"

When we see Nisus-Dryden the elegist rewarded with "an ample shield, / Of wondrous art," this bestowal upon him of an aesthetically wrought instrument of defense seems, as does every other detail that the allusion has evoked, to be almost uncannily appropriate.

This brings us to Dryden's concluding allusion:

> Once more, hail and farewel; farewel thou young,
> But ah too short, *Marcellus* of our Tongue;
> Thy Brows with Ivy, and Laurels bound;
> But Fate and gloomy Night encompass thee around.

The first line is wonderfully poised, a renewed address with its own internal echo repeating, almost answering, "Farewel" across the caesural pause. "Once more, hail and farewel" seems to blend the conventional pastoral elegiac "yet once more" with the Roman *ave atque vale* of Catullus and others. The result combines reluctant, repetitional lingering with formal dignity.

Like the allusion to Euryalus, the allusion to Marcellus associates Oldham once again with a figure (in this case, two figures) in the *Aeneid* (6.1180–1247). And once again, Dryden has chosen a context associated with Aeneas's devotion to his dead father. Here we are actually in the underworld, where Anchises adumbrates the future of Rome. Dryden's allusion to Marcellus is complex, as it points both to the victorious general Marcus Claudius Marcellus and to the promising but short-lived nephew of Augustus. In Virgil, although these men are seen together, walking side by side, it is the very unfulfillment of the association that is mourned. In Dryden's poem, on the other hand, the final description of Oldham is carefully designed to integrate the figures of both the victor and the vanquished. This is done in two principal ways, as Arthur Hoffman has shown. "*Marcellus* of our Tongue" suggests a conquering warrior in the field of language (a suitable metaphor for a pugnacious satirist who warred against knaves and fools). Admittedly, Dryden could also be thinking of Oldham as the young Marcellus cut off from a promised career of poetic exploits. But the reference to the crowning ivy and laurels maintains the victor's triumph and deliberately complicates Virgil's univocally dark description of the young man (*Sed nox atra caput tristi circumvolat umbra*). As has been noted, Dryden's final line is a near-literal translation of Virgil's verse.

Dryden's closing lines have a grandeur that itself is somewhat consoling, and the image of a laureled brow encompassed by the gloom is heroic. But perhaps the deepest consolation stems from the fact that Oldham has once again, as in the Euryalus allusion, been elevated to the status of a noble figure in the *Aeneid*. Just as an explicitly Christian elegy, such as Dryden's own poem for Anne Killigrew, would have elevated the elegized to a Christian heaven, so in this consummately Augustan poem the figure of the dead is elevated to the domain of the classics.

But the allusion demands still closer scrutiny. Surely much of its force is missed if one forgets that Virgil follows the *Sed nox atra* line with Anchises' powerfully expressive lament for Marcellus. The lament includes high praise, profound regret, and a ceremonious, elegiac sweetness ("Full canisters of fragrant lilies bring, / Mixed with the purple roses of the spring. / Let me with funeral flowers his body strew"). Consequently, if we read with anything approaching Dryden's comprehensive sense of his allusion, this entire display of grief will be brought to bear on the figure of Oldham, even as Dryden excludes its burden from his actual text. It is an astounding feat of tact and indirection. The expression of grief is there, but only by allusion.

Also, we miss much of Dryden's triumph if we do not note that just as the Oldham-Euryalus allusion had the attendant effect of likening Dryden himself to a figure in the *Aeneid*, so, again, the final allusion has a similar but even greater associative effect on the elegist. Oldham becomes Marcellus and is described, in Dryden's last line, by words originally spoken by Aeneas. For this moment, therefore, Dryden speaks with the voice of the Trojan hero: the elegist is lifted to the plane of the immortalized father of Rome.

But beyond even this, Dryden is speaking with the voice of Virgil, creator of Aeneas's speech. Or perhaps we should say that Dryden has contrived to have Virgil speak again through him. And as we listen to Dryden-Aeneas-Virgil addressing and describing his Oldham-Marcellus friend, we hear what is no less than a timeless farewell. Once again, as in Jonson's epigram, we witness an Augustan elegist's uncanny strategy of impersonation, a brilliant compound of self-glorification and self-effacement, of inheritance and submission. The elegist seems to merge with the mask of the revived dead: Virgil, Catullus, and, by extension, that all-inclusive ancestral mask, the inherited language of literature.

Chronology

1631   John Dryden is born on August 19 at Aldwinckle All Saints in Northamptonshire. His parents, Erasmus Dryden and Mary Pickering Dryden, are landed gentry with strong Puritan leanings.

1646   Enters Westminster School in London with the prestigious honor of King's Scholar.

1649   Publishes his first poem, "Upon the Death of the Lord Hastings," in the year Charles I is executed.

1650   Dryden is admitted to Trinity College, Cambridge.

1654   Receives his B.A. from Cambridge in March. His father dies in June.

1655   It is possible that Dryden is now in the employment of Cromwell's Protectorate.

1659   Dryden writes *Heroique Stanzas* in memory of Oliver Cromwell.

1660   Restoration of Charles II to throne of England. Dryden expresses his new loyalty to the Royalist party with his panegyric on the Restoration, *Astraea Redux*.

1663   Dryden's first play, *The Wild Gallant*, is produced. He marries Lady Elizabeth Howard, daughter of the loyalist noble Thomas Howard, Earl of Berkshire.

1666   In this year of the Great Fire of London, Dryden writes *Of Dramatick Poesie* (published in 1668), and his son Charles is born.

1667   Dryden writes the political poem *Annus Mirabilis* and the plays *Secret-Love* and *Sir Martin Mar-All*, and, with the assistance of Davenant, adapts Shakespeare's *The Tempest*. He dedicates his play

217

The Indian Emperor to the Duke of Monmouth, the illegitimate
son of Charles II.

1668   Son John born. Dryden succeeds Davenant as England's Poet
        Laureate.

1669   Son Erasmus-Henry born and Dryden appointed the Histori-
        ographer Royal.

1670   Dryden writes part 1 of *The Conquest of Granada* (part 2 comes
        out the next year).

1672   Dryden writes the plays *Marriage à la Mode* and *The Assignation*.

1675   Dryden writes his heroic play *Aureng-Zebe*.

1677   Dryden writes *The Author's Apology for Heroic Poetry and Poetic
        License* and attaches it to *The State of Innocence*, his operatic ver-
        sion of *Paradise Lost*. He rewrites Shakespeare's *Antony and
        Cleopatra* in his *All for Love*.

1678   The scandalous Popish Plot begins, and Dryden composes most
        of *Mac Flecknoe*.

1681   During the Exclusion Crisis Charles II dissolves Parliament. Dryden
        publishes *Absalom and Achitophel*.

1682   Dryden writes *The Medall* and *Religio Laici* and completes *Mac
        Flecknoe*.

1684   Dryden writes "To the Earl of Roscomon" and "To the Memory
        of Mr. Oldham" and publishes *Miscellany Poems*.

1685   Dryden's translations of Lucretius and Horace are published in
        Sylvae, and he writes the libretto for the opera *Albion and Albanius*,
        as well as *Threnodia Augustalis*, a poem on the death of Charles
        II. Charles's Catholic brother, James II, ascends the throne, and
        Dryden converts to Catholicism.

1686   Dryden writes "To the Memory of Anne Killigrew" for the introduc-
        tion to a book of her poems.

1687   Dryden writes *The Hind and the Panther* and the "Song for St.
        Cecilia's Day."

1688   The revolution that dethrones James II deprives Dryden of his posts
        as Poet Laureate and Historiographer Royal, as Catholics cannot
        hold office under William and Mary. In need of income, Dryden

spends the next six years writing several plays, poems, essays, and translations.

1694   Writes *To My Dear Friend Mr. Congreve*, "To Sir Godfrey Kneller," and his last play, *Love Triumphant*.

1697   Dryden writes "Alexander's Feast" and publishes *The Works of Virgil*, which includes his translations of the Pastorals, Georgics, and the *Aeneid*.

1700   Dryden writes "To my Honour'd Kinsman" and *The Secular Masque* and publishes his translations of Ovid, Chaucer, and Boccaccio in his *Fables Ancient and Modern*. He dies on May 1 and is buried in Westminster Abbey.

Contributors

HAROLD BLOOM, Sterling Professor of the Humanities at Yale University, is the author of *The Anxiety of Influence*, *Poetry and Repression*, and many other volumes of literary criticism. His forthcoming study, *Freud: Transference and Authority*, attempts a full-scale reading of all of Freud's major writings. A MacArthur Prize Fellow, he is general editor of five series of literary criticism published by Chelsea House. During 1987–88, he was appointed Charles Eliot Norton Professor of Poetry at Harvard University.

JOHN HOLLANDER is A. Bartlett Giamatti Professor of English at Yale University. He is the author of *The Untuning of the Sky: Ideas of Music in English Poetry 1500–1700*, *Vision and Resonance*, *The Figure of Echo: Modes of Allusion in Milton and After*, and *Rhyme's Reason*. He has also written several volumes of poetry, including *Spectral Emanations*, *Reflections on Espionage*, *Tales Told of the Fathers*, *The Night Mirror*, *Blue Wine*, and *Powers of Thirteen*.

EUGENE M. WAITH, Professor Emeritus of English at Yale University, is the author of *The Herculean Hero*, *Patterns of Tragicomedy in Beaumont and Fletcher*, and *Ideas of Greatness: Heroic Drama in England*.

RUTH NEVO is Professor of English at Hebrew University in Jerusalem. She is the author of *The Dial of Virtue: A Study of Poems on Affairs of State in the Seventeenth Century*, *Comic Transformations in Shakespeare*, and *Tragic Form in Shakespeare*. She has also translated into English the *Selected Poems* of Chaim Nachman Bialik.

MARTIN PRICE, Sterling Professor of English at Yale University, is the author of *To the Palace of Wisdom: Studies in Order and Energy from Dryden to Blake*, *Swift's Rhetorical Art: A Study in Structure and Meaning*, and *Forms of Life: Character and Moral Imagination in the Novel*.

GEORGE DEF. LORD is Professor of English at Yale University. He is the author of *Heroic Mockery: Variations on Epic Themes from Homer to Joyce*, *Homeric Renaissance: The* Odyssey *of George Chapman*, and *Trials of the Self: Heroic Ordeals in the Epic Tradition*.

EARL MINER, Professor of English at Princeton University, is the author of several books on English and Japanese literature, including *The Metaphysical Mode from Donne to Cowley*, *The Cavalier Mode from Jonson to Cotton*, and *The Restoration Mode from Milton to Dryden*, *John Dryden*, and *The Japanese Tradition in British and American Literature*.

LAURA BROWN teaches English at Cornell University and is the author of *Alexander Pope* and *English Dramatic Form, 1660–1760: An Essay in Generic History*.

PAUL H. FRY is Professor of English at Yale University. He is the author of *The Poet's Calling in the English Ode* and *The Reach of Criticism*.

MICHAEL McKEON is Associate Professor of English at Boston University and the author of *Politics and Poetry in Restoration England: The Case of Dryden's* Annus Mirabilis.

STEVEN N. ZWICKER is Professor of English Literature at Washington University in St. Louis. He is the author of *Dryden's Political Poetry* and *Politics and Language in Dryden's Poetry*.

JAMES A. WINN is Professor of English at the University of Michigan. He is the author of *A Window in the Bosom: The Letters of Alexander Pope* and *Unsuspected Eloquence: A History of the Relations between Poetry and Music*.

PETER M. SACKS teaches English at the Johns Hopkins University. He is the author of *The English Elegy* and several articles on English and American poetry. A volume of his poetry, *In These Mountains*, is forthcoming.

Bibliography

Barbeau, Anne T. "The Disembodied Rebels: Psychic Origins of Rebellion in *Absalom and Achitophel.*" *Studies in Eighteenth-Century Culture* 9 (1979): 489–502.

Bell, Robert H. "Dryden's 'Aeneid' as English Augustan Epic." *Criticism* 19 (1977): 34–50.

Blair, Joel. "Dryden's Ceremonial Hero." *Studies in English Literature 1500–1900* 9 (1969): 379–93.

Bredvold, Louis I. *The Intellectual Milieu of John Dryden.* Ann Arbor: University of Michigan Press, 1934.

Brower, Reuben. "An Allusion to Europe—Dryden and Tradition." *ELH* 19 (1952): 38–48.

———. *The Fields of Light: An Experiment in Critical Reading.* 1951. Reprint. Westport, Conn.: Greenwood, 1980.

Budick, Sanford. *Dryden and the Abyss of Light: A Reading of* Religio-Laici *and* The Hind and the Panther. New Haven: Yale University Press, 1970.

Clark, John R. " 'To the Memory of Mr. Oldham': Dryden's Disquieting Lines." *Concerning Poetry* 3 (1970): 43–49.

Cousins, A. D. "Heroic Satire: Dryden and the Defence of Later Stuart Kingship." *Southern Review* (Australia) 13 (1980): 170–87.

Cullum, Graham. "Dryden: Public Order in Private Places." *The Critical Review* 20 (1978): 72–87.

Donnelly, Jerome. "Fathers and Sons: The Normative Basis of Dryden's *Absalom and Achitophel.*" *Papers on Language and Literature* 17 (1981): 363–80.

Ehrenpreis, Irvin. "Continuity and Coruscation: Dryden's Poetic Instincts." In *John Dryden II,* by Irvin Ehrenpreis and James M. Osborn. Los Angeles: William Andrews Clark Memorial Library, 1978.

Eliot, T. S. *John Dryden.* New York: Terence & Elsa Holliday, 1932. Reprint. New York: Haskell House, 1966.

Empson, William. "Dryden's Apparent Scepticism." *Essays in Criticism* 20 (1970): 172–78.

———. *Using Biography.* London: Chatto & Windus, Hogarth Press, 1984.

Ferry, Anne Davidson. *Milton and the Miltonic Dryden.* Cambridge: Harvard University Press, 1968.

Frost, William. "Dryden's Versions of Ovid." In *Expression, Communication and Experience in Literature and Language,* edited by Ronald G. Popperwell. London: Modern Humanities Research Association, 1972.

223

——. "Dryden's Virgil." *Comparative Literature* 36 (1984): 193–208.

Fry, Paul H. " 'Alexander's Feast' and the Tyranny of Music." In *The Poet's Calling in the English Ode.* New Haven: Yale University Press, 1980.

Frye, B. J. *John Dryden:* Mac Flecknoe. Columbus, Ohio: Merrill, 1970.

Fujimura, Thomas H. "Dryden's *Religio Laici* and Roman Catholic Apologetics." *PMLA* 80 (1965): 190–98.

Garrison, James D. *Dryden and the Tradition of Panegyric.* Berkeley: University of California Press, 1975.

Gransden, K. W. "What Kind of Poem Is *Religio Laici?" Studies in English Literature 1500–1900* 17 (1977): 397–406.

Griffin, Dustin. "Dryden's 'Oldham' and the Perils of Writing." *Modern Language Quarterly* 37 (1976): 133–50.

Hagstrum, Jean H. *The Sister Arts.* Chicago: University of Chicago Press, 1958.

Haney-Peritz, Janice. "Dryden's Ethical Experiment: A Reading of 'Horace. Ode 29. Book 3.'" *Journal of English and Germanic Philology* 83 (1984): 21–45.

Harth, Phillip. *Contexts of Dryden's Thought.* Chicago: University of Chicago Press, 1968.

Harth, Phillip, Alan Fisher, and Ralph Cohen. *New Homage to John Dryden: Papers Read at a Clark Library Conference, February 13–14, 1981.* Los Angeles: William Andrews Clark Memorial Library, 1983.

Hinnant, Charles H. *"All for Love* and the Heroic Ideal." *Genre* 16 (1983): 57–74.

Hooker, E. N. "Dryden and the Atoms of Epicurus." *ELH* 24 (1957): 177–90.

Hope, A. D. *"All for Love,* or Comedy as Tragedy." In *The Cave and the Spring: Essays on Poetry.* Chicago: University of Chicago Press, 1965.

——. "Anne Killigrew, or the Art of Modulating." In *The Cave and the Spring: Essays on Poetry.* Chicago: University of Chicago Press, 1965.

Hughes, Derek. "The Unity of Dryden's *Marriage à la Mode." Philological Quarterly* 61 (1982): 125–42.

Hume, Robert D. *Dryden's Criticism.* Ithaca, N.Y.: Cornell University Press, 1970.

Huntley, Frank L. "Dryden's Discovery of Boileau." *Modern Poetry* 45 (1947–48): 112–17.

Jack, Ian. *Augustan Satire: Intention and Idiom in English Poetry 1660–1750.* London: Clarendon, 1978.

Jefferson, D. W. "The Poetry of *The Hind and the Panther." The Modern Language Review* 79 (1984): 33–44.

Jones, R. F. "The Originality of *Absalom and Achitophel." MLN* 46 (1931): 211–18.

King, Bruce, ed. *Dryden's Mind and Art.* Edinburgh: Oliver & Boyd, 1969.

——. *Twentieth Century Interpretations of* All for Love: *A Collection of Critical Essays.* Englewood Cliffs, N.J.: Prentice-Hall, 1968.

Kinsley, James, and Helen Kinsley, eds. *Dryden: The Critical Heritage.* London: Routledge & Kegan Paul, 1971.

Latt, David J., and Samuel Holt Monk. *John Dryden: A Survey and Bibligraphy of Critical Studies, 1895–1974.* Minneapolis: University of Minnesota Press, 1976.

Law, Richard. "The Heroic Ethos in John Dryden's Heroic Plays." *Studies in English Literature 1500–1900* 23 (1983): 389–98.

Love, Harold. "Dryden's Rationale of Paradox." *ELH* 51 (1984): 297–313.

——. "Dryden's 'Unideal Vacancy.'" *Eighteenth-Century Studies* 12 (1978): 74–89.

McFadden, George. *Dryden: The Public Writer, 1660–1685.* Princeton, N.J.: Princeton University Press, 1978.

McHenry, Robert, and David G. Lougee, eds. *Critics on Dryden.* Readings in Literary Criticism 15. London: Allen & Unwin, 1973.

McKeon, Michael. *Politics and Poetry in Restoration England: The Case of Dryden's Annus Mirabilis.* Cambridge: Harvard University Press, 1975.

Mason, H. A. "Living in the Present: Is Dryden's 'Horat. Ode 29. Book 3' an Example of 'Creative Translation'?" *Cambridge Quarterly* 10 (1981): 91–129.

Maus, Katharine Eisaman. "Arcadia Lost: Politics and Revision in the Restoration *Tempest.*" *Renaissance Drama.* New Series 13. Edited by Leonard Barkan. Evanston, Ill.: Northwestern University Press, 1982.

Miner, Earl. *Dryden's Poetry.* Bloomington: Indiana University Press, 1967.

———. "The Poetics of the Critical Act: Dryden's Dealings with Rivals and Predecessors." In *Evidence in Literary Scholarship: Essays in Memory of James Marshall Osborn,* edited by René Wellek and Alvaro Ribeiro. Oxford: Clarendon, 1979.

———, ed. *Writers and Their Background: John Dryden.* Athens: Ohio University Press, 1972.

Nevo, Ruth. *The Dial of Virtue: A Study of Poems on Affairs of State in the Seventeenth Century.* Princeton, N.J.: Princeton University Press, 1963.

Nicoll, Allardyce. *Dryden as an Adapter of Shakespeare.* The Shakespeare Association. London: Humphrey Milford, Oxford University Press, 1922.

Paulson, Ronald. "The Fictions of Tory Satire." In *The Fictions of Satire,* 120–28. Baltimore: Johns Hopkins University Press, 1967.

Price, Martin. *To the Palace of Wisdom: Studies in Order and Energy from Dryden to Blake.* Carbondale: Southern Illinois University Press, 1964.

Reverand, Cedric D. "Dryden's 'Essay on Dramatick Poesie': The Poet and the World of Affairs." *Studies in English Literature 1500–1900* 22 (1982): 375–93.

Ricks, Christopher. "Allusion: The Poet as Heir." In *Studies in the Eighteenth Century III: Papers Presented at the Third David Nichol Smith Memorial Seminar, Canberra 1973,* edited by R. F. Brissenden and J. C. Eade, 209–40. Canberra: Australian National University Press, 1976.

Roper, Alan. "Characteristics of Dryden's Prose." *ELH* 41 (1974): 668–92.

Schilling, Bernard N. *Dryden and the Conservative Myth: A Reading of* Absalom and Achitophel. New Haven: Yale University Press, 1961.

———, ed. *Dryden: A Collection of Critical Essays.* Englewood Cliffs, N.J.: Prentice-Hall, 1963.

Seidel, Michael. "A House Divided: Marvell's *Last Instructions* and Dryden's *Absalom and Achitophel.* In *Satiric Inheritance, Rabelais to Sterne,* 135–68. Princeton, N.J.: Princeton University Press, 1979.

Swedenberg, H. T., ed. *Essential Articles for the Study of John Dryden.* Hamden, Conn.: Archon, 1966.

Towers, Tom H. "The Lineage of Shadwell: An Approach to *Mac Flecknoe.*" *Essays in Criticism* 19 (1969): 355–70.

Vieth, David M. "The Art of the Prologue and Epilogue: A New Approach Based on Dryden's Practice." *Genre* 5, no. 3 (1972): 271–92.

Waith, Eugene M. *The Herculean Hero in Marlowe, Chapman, Shakespeare and*

Dryden. New York: Columbia University Press, 1962.

——. *Ideas of Greatness: Heroic Drama in England*. London: Routledge & Kegan Paul, 1971.

Wallace, John M. "Dryden and History: A Problem in Allegorical Reading." *ELH* 36 (1969): 265–90.

Ward, Charles E. *The Life of John Dryden*. Chapel Hill: University of North Carolina Press, 1961.

Wasserman, Earl R. *The Subtler Language: Critical Readings of Neoclassic and Romantic Poems*. Baltimore: Johns Hopkins University Press, 1959.

Wendorf, Richard. "Dryden, Charles II, and the Interpretation of Historical Character." *Philological Quarterly* 56 (1977): 82–103.

Wilding, Michael. "Allusion and Innuendo in *Mac Flecknoe*." *Essays in Criticism* 19 (1969): 355–70.

Williamson, George. "The Occasion of *An Essay of Dramatic Poesy*." In *Seventeenth-Century Contexts*. London: Faber & Faber, 1960.

Zwicker, Steven N. *Dryden's Political Poetry: The Typology of King and Nation*. Providence: Brown University Press, 1972.

——. *Politics and Language in Dryden's Poetry: The Arts of Disguise*. Princeton, N.J.: Princeton University Press, 1984.

Acknowledgments

"The Sky Untuned: The Trivialization of Universal Harmony in the Odes" (original-ly entitled "The Sky Untuned: The Trivialization of Universal Harmony") by John Hollander from *The Untuning of the Sky: Ideas of Music in English Poetry 1500–1700* by John Hollander, © 1961 by Princeton University Press, © 1970 by W. W. Norton & Co., Inc., © 1986 by John Hollander. Reprinted by permission.

"The Herculean Hero in *All for Love*" (originally entitled "Dryden") by Eugene M. Waith from *The Herculean Hero in Marlowe, Chapman, Shakespeare and Dryden* by Eugene M. Waith, © 1962 by Eugene M. Waith. Reprinted by permission of the author and Columbia University Press.

"*Absalom and Achitophel*" (originally entitled "That Kingly Power, thus ebbing out, might be drawn to the dregs of Democracy") by Ruth Nevo from *The Dial of Virtue: A Study of Poems on Affairs of State in the Seventeenth Century* by Ruth Nevo, © 1963 by Princeton University Press. Reprinted by permission of Princeton University Press.

"Dryden and Dialectic: The Heroic Plays" (originally entitled "Dryden and Dialec-tic") by Martin Price from *To the Palace of Wisdom: Studies in Order and Energy from Dryden to Blake* by Martin Price, © 1964 by Martin Price. Reprinted by permission.

"The Restoration Myth from *Astraea Redux* to *Absalom and Achitophel*" (original-ly entitled "*Absalom and Achitophel* and Dryden's Political Cosmos") by George deF. Lord from *Writers and Their Background: John Dryden*, edited by Earl Miner, © 1972 by G. Bell & Sons Ltd. Reprinted by permission of Ohio Univer-sity Press and G. Bell & Sons Ltd.

"The Heroic Idea in *Mac Flecknoe*" (originally entitled "Dryden's Heroic Idea") by Earl Miner from *The Restoration Mode from Milton to Dryden* by Earl Miner, © 1974 by Princeton University Press. Reprinted by permission of Princeton University Press.

"The Ideology of Restoration Poetic Form: John Dryden" by Laura Brown from *PMLA* 97, no. 3 (May 1982), © 1982 by the Modern Language Association of America. Reprinted by permission of the Modern Language Association of America.

"The Other Harmony of Dryden's 'Preface to *Fables*' " by Paul H. Fry from *The Reach of Criticism: Method and Perception in Literary Theory* by Paul H. Fry, © 1983 by Yale University. Reprinted by permission of Yale University Press.

"Marxist Criticism and *Marriage à la Mode*" by Michael McKeon from *The Eighteenth Century: Theory and Interpretation* 24, no. 2 (Spring 1983), © 1983 by Michael McKeon. Reprinted by permission.

"Politics and Religion in *Religio Laici*" (originally entitled "Politics and Religion: The 'Middle Way' ") by Steven N. Zwicker from *Politics and Language in Dryden's Poetry: The Arts of Disguise* by Steven N. Zwicker, © 1984 by Princeton University Press. Reprinted by permission of Princeton University Press.

"The Promise of Dryden's Elegy for Hastings" by James A. Winn from *Modern Language Review* 79, part 1 (January 1984), © 1984 by the Modern Humanities Research Association. Reprinted by permission.

" 'To the Memory of Mr. Oldham' " (originally entitled "Jonson, Dryden, and Gray") by Peter M. Sacks from *The English Elegy: Studies in the Genre from Spenser to Yeats* by Peter M. Sacks, © 1985 by the Johns Hopkins University Press, Baltimore/London. Reprinted by permission of the Johns Hopkins University Press.

Index